Contents

Series Editor's Preface

Aesthetics does not only involve a range of philosophical concepts connected to the understanding of art, but also art itself. The subject matter enters into the vocabulary, and without knowing a good deal about the cultural context in which art is created and appreciated, it is difficult to understand the nature of what is being discussed. Many of the controversies in art themselves have a philosophical form, and many of the discussions in how to assess art involve an understanding of the art itself. Yet it is of course not necessary to grasp the whole of art history in order to understand the form of arguments about how to assess art and what concepts exist in that process. On the other hand, it is much easier to know what is going on in aesthetics if one knows something about the wider context within which the aesthetic concepts operate. Although aesthetics is a technical philosophical area of its own, like metaphysics, epistemology and so on, it does start with the process of someone wondering how to assess an art object, and what is involved in such an activity. Guter has done a thorough job in linking the various ideas and issues to each other, giving readers a perspicuous grasp of how to navigate through the topic. There is a particularly well developed series of entries on many of the major thinkers in the field, and by following the links that the author makes between different issues, their cultural contexts and the individuals who wrote about them, a good overall view of the topic can be realized. The detailed bibliography will also be very helpful to those orientating themselves in the subject. Of course, the brief descriptions here can only whet the appetite, as is the case for all the books in this series, but we very much hope that it will encourage readers to move onto some of the original texts and thinkers who are here clearly and concisely introduced.

Oliver Leaman
March 2010

Introduction

Aesthetics is one of the most intellectually stimulating and enriching fields of philosophical inquiry. This statement may sound a bit strange to anyone who is easily impressed by the longevity of ancient metaphysical problems or by the cutting-edge verve of recent empirically informed debates in the theory of consciousness, or by the applicative promise and popular demand of business ethics, and so tends to dismiss aesthetics as peripheral to philosophy. Yet, as Frank Sibley, one of the important early analytic aestheticians of the twentieth century, has observed, aestheticians encounter ranges of concepts wider than and inevitably inclusive of those studied by most other branches of philosophy. That is to say, over and above a certain set of distinct philosophical problems – pertaining not only to the nature of the aesthetic, but also to such perennial notions as beauty, pictorial representation, expression and so forth – which have traditionally preoccupied aestheticians, we find a broad spectrum of criss-crossing concerns with other philosophical fields, ancient and new alike, from epistemology, ontology, ethics, and even logic, to the philosophy of language and mind, the philosophy of education, and even the philosophy of information and computation. Aesthetic problems tend also to be interdisciplinary, informed not only by theories and practices of the various arts, but also by theoretical concerns and empirical data originating from the natural and the social sciences. And insofar as the subject matter of aesthetic inquiry is art – its essence as well as its practice – aesthetics is also historically informed, steeped in the marvel of this great intellectual, creative achievement that is art.

This book is meant to be a modest guide for the perplexed to this richly diverse, intellectually rewarding field of philosophic inquiry. To use this book efficiently, it would help to know what to expect of it. The book is designed to enable newcomers to aesthetics to open relevant portals into the intricate concerns and conceptions in the field as practiced today in the English-speaking countries, while offering useful reminders and pointers to those who are more versed in its riches. This book does not claim to be exhaustive, although I hope to have made it comprehensive enough to address issues that are really essential to current debates in Western aesthetics, and thus to sustain the reader's interest in problems and viewpoints indigenous to aesthetic theory, while prompting further inquiry into their intersection with other fields of knowledge, conceptual problems, and human concerns broadly construed. This is an invitation to aesthetics. The book is organized in strict alphabetical order, like a dictionary, but its cross-referenced entries suggest, and give rise to thematic clusters, historical narratives, and argumentative formations, when followed with closer attention. The reader is invited to zoom in and out; that is, to use the book alternately as a quick reference for names, positions, key arguments and the like, using my suggestions for further reading to probe deeper into the subject at hand, but also as a roadmap or a bird's-eye view of the field.

It should be noted that, compared to other fields of philosophy, such as ethics and epistemology, aesthetics is characterized by a unique complexity. For one, it seems quite obvious that, in both ordinary and academic discourse, aesthetic concepts are properly used also on occasions which do not involve bona fide instances of art–natural and man-made settings, the way people look and act, games of all sorts, and even mathematical proofs and scientific discoveries. It seems that our philosophical subject matter here is patently disjunctive (albeit in the inclusive sense): we either look into philosophical problems involving works of art in some way, or else look into philosophical problems specifically concerning the notion of the aesthetic. As a focus of philosophic inquiry, we may refer to art in terms of practice, activity or object. Hence we may probe theoretically into the various practices of art, the activities involved in creating works of art or in appreciating them, and of course the actual objects, ontologically varied as they may be, that are works of art. This mode of thinking need not necessarily evoke the notion of the aesthetic, which may pertain equally to experiencing subject and to the things experienced. On the other hand, our reference to artworks may be steeped in the aesthetic, couched in terms of the perceptual properties, features or aspects of the objects under theoretical scrutiny, or else in terms of our attitude, states of mind and experiences pertaining to these objects. And this mode of thinking may equally concern the creative, the receptive, and the evaluative dimensions of art.

Aesthetics and the philosophy of art may be treated as two distinct domains of thought: they are congruent yet not synonymous. Contemporary aesthetics, at least in the analytic tradition, is to a large extent the philosophy of art, although the former is clearly the broader term, extending also over natural phenomena as well as over man-made things that are otherwise not works of art in any proper sense. Indeed, in the continental tradition, aesthetics is commonly broader than any philosophy of a particular art in its overarching systematic embrace. It would be fair to say that the field of aesthetics, broadly construed, is not unified. It is not neatly organized around a set of foundational or constitutive questions in the manner in which, for example, ethics gravitates around such perennial questions as 'how to live?' or metaphysics does around 'what is there?' or epistemology does around 'what is knowledge?' It has been suggested that the identity of aesthetics as a philosophic field is rather fixed by marking the boundaries of the field; that is, by marking both the range of relevant phenomena and the scope of our disciplinary concern in these phenomena. Still these boundaries keep changing, shape-shifting and expanding insofar as new forms of art emerge or as mutual concerns with other philosophic fields or with other disciplines present themselves. In this sense, the ideational topography of aesthetics resembles that of the philosophy of science, another relatively 'young' philosophic field, whose subject matter is spread across the various sciences, intimately related to their theoretical structuring, to the growth of scientific knowledge, and to their theoretical responses to their respective phenomena. Still, contrary to the philosophy of science, we have no clear, pre-philosophical identification of the class of judgments, the range of phenomena and concepts that together might indicate a universally shared domain of aesthetic thought. The vocabulary of aesthetics is distinctly open-textured.

For these reasons I opt in this book for the inclusive stance. That is, I mean to portray the field of aesthetics by drawing its intra-philosophical range as well as its interdisciplinary compatibility. I also opt for the inclusive stance with regards to the distinction between analytic (broadly construed as Anglo-American) aesthetics and continental aesthetics. Undoubtedly, there are real differences in style, scope, and content between analytic and continental aesthetics, which ultimately boil down to the question what philosophy is. Luckily, we do not have to take up this thorny issue here. However, I find it misfortunate that, more often than not, beginners' guides to aesthetics tend to take sides in this divide, or at least conveniently ignore the other side. I tried to remedy this by including in this book not only key concepts and figures from both philosophic traditions, but also by addressing some issues and problems of mutual concern to both traditions, and by highlighting points of agreement and disagreement whenever relevant. Some entries (for example, authenticity, culture, interpretation, language and text) are specifically comparative, comprising the core of this particular narrative in this book.

Aesthetics A–Z is not a mere concatenation of entries. Its internal structure, which subsists in its extensive cross-referencing, enables the interested reader to overview the ideational terrain, heterogeneous as it may be, hence to appreciate the possibilities of further inquiry. The book consists of various types of entries. I should stress that the length of the entry is not a straightforward indicator of its importance. Certain issues or positions are easier to encapsulate than others, so the relevant entry may be shorter regardless of its specific weight. The length of the entry is also a function of the layout of related, cross-referenced entries. Some topics had to be broken down into distinct, specialized entries, while others were easier to present in the form of a single self-contained entry. Either way, the entries are intended to be mutually reinforcing through extensive cross-referencing. This enables one to pursue matters to different levels of detail and scope, and to make connections between different dimensions of theorizing about art and the aesthetic. The relative importance of any given subject or topic has to be appreciated against these gravitational fields. Some entries directly explain the main positions, theories, and debates that shape or have shaped the field of aesthetics. Where relevant, cross-references can be followed in order to underscore the historical origins or background of contemporary positions or theories. For example, the entry on formalism explains what formalism is and summarizes the problems and issues raised by formalist approaches to art. The reader can proceed to more specific entries that pertain to formalism (for example, significant form, definition of art, and so on), to entries that situate the position in its historical context (for example,

Kant, Hanslick, Bell), and to entries that put the position in broader philosophical context (for example, expression, aesthetic attitude). Another type of entry deals exclusively with key figures, historical and contemporary. In the former case, such entries focus on the philosophical legacy of the figures discussed and on persisting issues and debates. In the latter case, they point to the historical background or origins of their positions or arguments. For instance, the entry on Plato underscores inter alia the persisting theme of art and knowledge, and the entry on anti-essentialism points out the influence of Wittgenstein's concept of family-resemblance. Other entries open up intra-philosophical and interdisciplinary issues and perspectives. These include shared philosophical concerns with other branches of philosophy, with the various arts, and with the empirical and social sciences. Here also the reader may utilize the cross-references in order to explore further the conceptual terrain.

Within each entry in *Aesthetics A–Z*, terms or names in bold print indicate that those topics are also individually explained in the book. In addition, at the end of most entries, other relevant entries are indicated by 'See'. These two methods of reference complement one another; they do not overlap. If a term is in bold print in the body of an entry, then it is not also listed in 'See'. In some cases, grammar demands that the term in bold print in the body of an entry is not exactly the same as the term in the corresponding entry. For example, the appropriate cross-reference for the word 'mimetic' in bold print is 'mimesis', the appropriate cross-reference for 'ontological' is 'ontology', and the appropriate cross-reference for 'aesthetic attitude' is 'attitude, aesthetic'. However, I have tried to avoid this as much as possible. On some occasions, I have opted for a certain terminology, usually for the sake of conceptual unity and economy, being aware that there are other terms, which are also being used in the literature to denote roughly the same thing, or else that they are covered by my term of choice. In such cases, I have added a forwarding reference in the body of the text. For example, the now commonly used term 'visually-indistinguishable-pairs argument' refers to the alternative, actually original term '*is* of artistic identification', and the specific term '*trompe l'oeil*' refers to the inclusive term 'illusion', where it is discussed, albeit briefly. The last part of each entry is 'Further reading'. The recommended texts may include primary sources authored by the person discussed or that are otherwise constitutive in relation to the ideas discussed, or important secondary sources. Choosing secondary sources is a tricky thing; all in all I have tried to balance current scholarship with stalwart classics.

Finally, I should say that while taking a broad view of its subject matter, *Aesthetics A–Z* is not meant to be mainly a survey of recent and contemporary literature. The bibliography is tailored to fit the book alone; it is neither comprehensive nor exhaustive enough to be a bibliography for the entire field of aesthetics. Aesthetics is one of the fastest growing fields of philosophic inquiry nowadays. I have had to make a few rough choices, trying my best to be as accurate and fair as possible; still some readers may take exception to my decisions about what to include and how the philosophical issues have been handled. Surely, many of the topics discussed in this book are themselves a matter of ongoing philosophical debate. We can never assume that we are given a neat and unproblematic set of facts, concepts and definitions that somehow do the work for us. Such is the philosophical predicament. That is why *Aesthetics A–Z*, like any decent travel guide, is meant mainly to suggest routes of interest through a fascinating landscape of ideas. The actual walking in this landscape is cheerfully left for the reader.

Eran Guter

Acknowledgments

I would like to express my gratitude to Oliver Leaman, editor of the *Philosophy A–Z* series, first for inviting me to write this book and also for being very supportive along the way. Many thanks go to Carol Macdonald, the commissioning editor for Edinburgh University Press, for caring and prompting. As always, I am deeply indebted to my wife, Inbal Alexandron-Guter, not only for her sound advice on both professional and practical matters, but also for providing me with the quality time that I needed for writing. I am also grateful to my two daughters, Eden and Alma, for brightening up my day. This book is lovingly dedicated to the memory of my father Moshe Guter and to the memory of my mother Julia Guter (née Sternberg). My father gave me the gift of writing and his old Olympia typewriter was my first magic portal into a world of thought; my mother initiated me at an early age into the beatitudes of aesthetic experience. Tragically, they both passed away too young. This modest offering embraces things that were very close to their heart. *Yehi Zikhram Barukh.*

AESTHETICS A–Z

A

absolute music: Commonly used to distinguish instrumental **music** as such from any kind of program music (including vocal and dramatic, or other **narrative** settings), this term also entails a radical form of **medium** purism when taken in the light of its **romantic** philosophical framing. Music may be said to be absolute in this strict sense only if its **meaning** and our **understanding** of it are not subordinate to any extra-musical reference including linguistic meaning, representational and even emotional content. Such restrictions on the medium go well beyond **abstraction** in the visual arts since they ideally leave music wholly autonomous as a quasi-syntactic structure, without meaning, or reference, or **representational** features, bearing only accidental relations to the world and to our **emotional** life. Hence a severe problem arises regarding absolute music: why and how such pure sonic structures are important for us, given that they lack those very things – namely, extra-musical content – that seem to play so prominent a role in our **appreciation**, and that seem so vital to the **value** that music holds for us. The problem of absolute music is particularly thorny for advocates of musical **formalism**, who are hard pressed to give an adequate account of musical understanding in terms that are formally objective and wholly internal to the music itself. In particular, the inexorability of the problem of value in the case of absolute music seems time and again to force formalists, when they are rigorous enough, to assert the mystical, ineffable character of the formal, empty as it were, **pleasures** of absolute music.

See **autonomy, aesthetic; expression; Gesamtkunstwerk; Hanslick; language; mimesis; modern system of the arts; persona theory; ut pictura poesis; Wagner**

Further reading: Dahlhaus 1991; Hanslick 1986; Kivy 1990

abstraction: The absence of representational or figurative elements in the plastic arts. When applied to **music**, abstraction commonly means the absence of semantic content in pure instrumental music. In the visual arts, abstraction is achieved either by gradual reduction and elimination of elements, which resemble things in the external world, by excessive use of **ornamentation**, or by using **chance** operations. Music is often said to be abstract on account of its problematic relation to extra-musical reality, although it has been intermittently regarded as a **mimetic** art throughout history. Abstraction characterizes many of the great works of art of the twentieth century. The rise of abstraction in the twentieth century prompted a critical revaluation of the idea that art is an imitation or idealization of the world, hence that it might be representational by definition. Consequently, **formalism** emerged for a while as a much more promising theory of art.

See **Bell; Greenberg; Hanslick; innocent eye; modernism; realism; representation; resemblance**

Further reading: Bell 1958; Walton 1986

Adorno, Theodor Wiesengrund (1903–69): German philosopher, musicologist and composer, a prominent figure in the circle of philosophers, social scientists, and cultural critics known as the **Frankfurt School**. A prolific writer on various issues in aesthetics and in the philosophy of **music**, much of Adorno's aesthetic thinking centered on the problem of modernity as reflected in the dialectic engagement of the individual subject with social reality. For Adorno, the meaning of art is social, manifesting a fundamental divergence between art and social life. He argues that the art of bourgeois culture – in particular music – is becoming increasingly autonomous, emancipated from reference to the social world, by elaborating its own formal nature. Yet this striving toward autonomy constitutes the social meaning of art, insofar as art represents the bourgeois striving toward freedom from the repression of society. Autonomous art is at once a critique of a society steeped in the domination of nature for profit, and itself a progressive mastery of nature. Like **Hegel** before him, Adorno believed that aesthetic theory is needed for the fleshing out of **truth** in art. He believed that when modern art succumbs to the easy pleasures of primitivism or to the culture industry – Adorno bundled the music of Igor Stravinsky together with popular music – it is regressive, since it manifests the repression of subjectivity by the industrial society. For that reason, Adorno also rejected politicized, recruited art.

See **authenticity; autonomy, aesthetic; Marxism; modernism; politics; sociology**

Further reading: Adorno 1973, 1986 and 2002

aestheticism: Often dubbed 'art for art's sake', aestheticism underlines the self-sufficiency of art. Its main tenet is the conviction that aesthetic **value** lies in the intrinsic **properties** of the artwork, such as its **beauty** and expressiveness. This is a rejection of **functionalism**: art is valued for its own sake, not for any external purpose – moral, religious, materialist or other. Such sentiment has been typified, and somewhat vulgarized, by Oscar Wilde's contention that all art is quite useless. Aestheticism is often related to **formalism**, and likewise it is restrictive in respect of the actual scope of our engagement with works of art, and to alternative standpoints regarding the nature and purpose of art. Furthermore, aestheticism often entails **autonomism** regarding the moral status of the work of art, namely, the tendency to dissociate aesthetic value from any reference to ethical flaws or merits. The eventual undermining of both formalism and autonomism in the twentieth century, both in aesthetic theory and in artistic practice, has made aestheticism a theoretically unsound option, and also, arguably, politically incorrect due to its flagrant embrace of amorality.

See **attitude, aesthetic; autonomy, aesthetic; Bell; Bloomsbury Group; disinterestedness; ethics; expression**

Further reading: Bradley 1909; Forster 1972; Wilde 1969

affective fallacy: A term introduced by **Beardsley** pertaining to the **romantic** tendency to render the affective responses of the reader or the critic as informative of the literary work. The counterclaim is that the **interpretation** and evaluation of works of art are independent of the critic's **emotions**. **Wittgenstein** anticipated this idea in his rejection of causal accounts of aesthetic **value**, in particular the construal of aesthetic value in terms of a tendency to cause **pleasure** or displeasure. The affective fallacy can be generalized to all the arts; however, pure instrumental **music** seems particularly susceptible to this fallacy due to its **abstract** nature.

See **Hanslick; literature; New Criticism; psychology**
Further reading: Beardsley and Wimsatt 1949

aleatoric art see chance

allographic art see autographic art/allographic art distinction

analog/digital distinction: The analog/digital distinction is applicable to both **representations** and media. The term 'analog' refers to processes in which one set of physical properties – for example, sound – is stored in, transcribed onto or forged into another, analogous physical form, for example, grooves in vinyl. The resulting analog representation hinges upon technological apparatus and cultural forms that allow the original properties to be recovered by the audience. The analog process materializes in an analog **medium**, which is most commonly a fixed, continuous physical object – canvas, film, magnetic tape, clay, and so on – primed for imprint. By contrast, a digital representation has a discrete, often numerical form, whether it has originated as such (for example, computer-generated images) or else it has been converted from various forms of analog media. In the latter case, the process of digitization consists of two stages: sampling the continuous data at regular intervals, and quantification, that is, assigning each discrete unit a numerical value drawn from a definite range. Digital representations may exist in analog form, spliced onto hard copies (for example, photographs, printouts, audio discs) yet insofar as they remain also in discrete digital form, they are (1) accessible randomly rather than sequentially; (2) mutable, that is, each data sample can be replaced by any other sample; and (3) they can be stored in a computer's memory, retrieved and reproduced endlessly without any further loss of information. Still, contrary to analog representations, a digitally encoded representation contains a fixed amount of information. Such differences yield significant **ontological** differences between analog and digital representations. For instance, in digital media there is no ontological difference between original and copy.

See **authenticity; communication; new media; notation; photographic transparency; photography; representation; resemblance**

Further reading: Lopes 2009; Manovich 2000

animal art: Some animals manifest certain types of behavior, engage in certain activities, or may even produce certain objects, which bear **resemblance** to human artifacts. Some such natural phenomena have been successfully incorporated into works of art. For example, birdsong has been regularly imitated in **music,** from the occasional cuckoo call in the symphonies of Beethoven and Mahler to the elaborate reworking of carefully recorded birdcalls in Messiaen's celebrated *Catalogue d'Oiseaux*. On other occasions, certain objects, which were produced by animals, such as abstract chimpanzee **paintings,** were said to have passed as genuine art on occasion. The idea that artistic creativity is biologically hard-wired, evolutionary grounded, and so may be observed across the animal kingdom, and the corresponding suggestion that the domain of aesthetics is actually trans-human, have been clearly voiced already by Charles Darwin. Darwin theorized that human beings share with other animals a **taste** for **beauty** (construed in **subjectivist** terms as the **pleasure** given by certain colors, forms, and sounds), which plays a role in natural selection. Be that as it may, the very idea of animal art, provided that we do not presuppose that it is self-contradictory, cuts to the core of the **definition of art** as well as the definition of aesthetics. The innovations of twentieth-century art, with its persistent drive toward **abstraction,** and in particular, the advent of ready-made art and the social impact of

conceptual art in general with its deliberate undermining of the notion of **artifactuality**, have all blurred our intuitive distinction between human-made and animal-made objects as legitimate candidates for the status of artwork. This has the unhappy corollary of rendering the notion of artistic **medium** ambiguous. To address this counterintuitive conflation, the **institutional theory of art**, for example, rejects the possibility of animal art on the basis of the inability of animals, even humanoid animals like chimpanzees, to become fully integrated members of the **artworld**. The challenge posed by animal art to the definition of aesthetics reflects the key issues in **environmental aesthetics**, such as the **aesthetic appreciation** of nature, in particular the application of the concept of beauty to natural phenomena.

See **anthropology**

Further reading: Scharfstein 1988

anthropology: Anthropology studies human development and material **culture** from prehistoric times up to the present, whether in the relative seclusion of non-industrial societies of indigenous people or in the shared backyard of the most industrially advanced societies. Thus the specific anthropological study of art falls squarely in the standard domain of studying artifacts in their cultural context. Anthropology usually embraces the various physical, biological, social, cultural, and linguistic aspects pertaining to its subject matter, which may variably lend themselves to the methods of empirical **science** as well as to the humanistic skills required for the **interpretation** of **texts**. For that reason, the fundamental questions in anthropology concern the very possibility of **understanding** cultures different from one's own, and transmitting that knowledge to others. Such questions challenge the very nature of the discipline. Empirical findings in anthropology are of secondary importance to aesthetics, although one could argue that a proper understanding of the great diversity concerning the **definition of art** and its related practices across cultures and periods had some positive influence on the advent of **anti-essentialism** in the second half of the twentieth century. Another example would be the influence of the comparative study of cultures on theories in the **psychology** and history of art, for example, **Gombrich**. Yet it is in the overlapping of some general meta-theoretical concerns that one could see contemporary aesthetics as being anthropologically inflected. The preoccupation of continental aesthetics, most notably within the milieu of **postmodernism**, with relativism, context, symbolic systems, power relationships and social oppression has aligned it with the main tenets of contemporary anthropology.

See **animal art; artifactuality; contextualism; gendered aesthetics; hermeneutics; language; performance art; sociology; structuralism**

Further reading: Scharfstein 2009

anti-essentialism: A position that emerged forcefully around the mid-twentieth century as a reaction against the prevalent essentialist assumption that there is some common nature or quality present in all art. Anti-essentialists were profoundly influenced by **Wittgenstein's** notion of **family-resemblance** and were quick to apply this idea to the concept of art, arguing that art is an 'open concept' for which there cannot be necessary and sufficient conditions. A closed **definition of art** would undermine the natural expansion of art hence it would make artistic creativity impossible. Thus anti-essentialists wish to replace what they perceive as a futile search for the essence of all art with an analysis of the complex logic of the concept of art. Replies to anti-essentialism may involve – for example, in **Dickie** – a critique of the viability of the family-resemblance method for distinguishing between art and non-art or the claim that it does not exclude such a distinction on the basis of non-exhibited properties (intentional or relational) of the objects. Other replies – for example, **Danto's** – may invoke historicism in order to reinstate **essentialism**. Another brand of anti-essentialism became prominent during the second half of the twentieth century in continental aesthetics. **Poststructuralist** rejection of the assumption that underlying all artistic artifacts or **texts** are immutable, essential structures, as well as the **postmodern** emphasis on the indeterminacy of **meaning**, and its overall suspicion of 'grand **narratives**' leave no room for an attempt to define art in terms of necessary and sufficient conditions.

See **Barthes; Derrida; Ziff**

Further reading: Kennick 1958; Weitz 1956; Ziff 1953

Apollonian/Dionysian distinction: A distinction introduced by **Nietzsche** in his essay *The Birth Tragedy* (1872) between two opposite primordial forces at play in the world. Nietzsche's treatment of the polarization between the Apollonian and the Dionysian is layered and it can be understood concurrently as being **ontological** (appearance and reality), **psychological** (dream and intoxication), artistic (visual arts and **music**), and **cultural** (the Greek and the barbaric people). Nietzsche used these distinctions in order to revisit the **classicist** ideal of Greek art and to explain the tragic effect as the dialectic moment when Dionysus speaks the **language** of Apollo in order to enable Apollo to speak the language of Dionysus. For Nietzsche, **Wagner's** *Tristan and Isolde* is the only contemporary achievement of such artistic and cultural magnitude. The Apollonian/Dionysian dynamic was later echoed by **Freud** in his idea of the conflict between the superego and the id.

See **psychoanalysis; tragedy; Wagner**

Further reading: Nietzsche 1967

appreciation, aesthetic: A feat of the competent judge of **aesthetic properties**. Aesthetic appreciation presupposes such notions as **aesthetic experience** and **aesthetic attitude**. It is from the vantage point of this unique state of mind that the **perception**, identification, description and evaluation of aesthetic properties are made possible. Aesthetic appreciation is construed primarily in terms of a reflective, evaluative species of perception, which picks out what is aesthetically worthwhile in a given object. As such it has historical kinship with classical **taste theories**. However, it is noteworthy that **conceptual art** challenges precisely this connection between appreciation and perception. Arguably, in certain forms of conceptual art, what calls out to be appreciated may be sharply divorced from the appearance of the relevant object. Similarly, some cases of **forgery** seem to stress the significance for aesthetic appreciation of other features of works of art, which are not readily perceptible. Either way, the competent judge, having mastered certain fine-shaded **language-games**, has the power to engage the full array of her intellect, **imagination** and **emotions** in order to make fine discriminations concerning the given object, to reason about them, and to offer an **aesthetic judgment**. Beyond matters of natural proclivity, these abilities are nourished, indeed greatly enhanced by **education** and by becoming steeped in art history and theory. In this sense, aesthetic appreciation is a mark of enculturation. Thus aesthetic appreciation is conceptually related not only to perception, but also to **understanding**, if we concede that to understand a work of art is in effect to experience it with a certain kind of appreciative attention. It is important to observe that the notion of aesthetic appreciation is at the crux of the common disjunction between aesthetics and the philosophy of art. Aesthetic appreciation may be understood in two somewhat overlapping senses: (1) as appreciating something from an aesthetic point of view; or (2) as appreciating something as a work of art. Granting primacy to the first sense lends aesthetics *tout court* its broader range in comparison to the philosophy of art: the latter is construed as merely a special case of the former. An emphasis on the second sense yields an essentialist **definition of art** – namely, the idea that an object can be a work of art only if it is susceptible to aesthetic appreciation. This seems to conflict with the possibility of an aesthetic appreciation of nature, or at least it requires the bold assertion that to consider nature aesthetically is to consider it as if it were a work of art.

See **disinterestedness; emotions; environmental aesthetics; essentialism; Kant; pleasure**

Further reading: Danto 1986; Scruton 1974

architecture: Architecture has not taken center stage in modern aesthetics until relatively recently. **Kant** referred merely to its function, and **Schopenhauer** famously demoted architecture to the lower end of his taxonomy of the **representational** arts for being the most deficient as far as objectifying the will is concerned. **Hegel** was the outstanding exception when he praised architecture as supreme in symbolic art, although he referred primarily to the monumental, temple-like stature of architecture. Clearly, the inclusion of architecture among the fine arts, and the prospects of delineating a specialized aesthetics of architecture are troubled precisely by what makes works of architecture philosophically unique and interesting: the tension, inherent in most works of architecture, between the vernacular and the aesthetically autonomous. Works of architecture may stand out aesthetically – representing, **expressing** and symbolizing a broad range of things – but, as opposed to other arts, they are typically inhabited with denizens of ordinary life, not with **fictional** entities. They shelter real people and embody **aesthetic properties** at the same time, so their function is never completely irrelevant to their aesthetic **value**. At one time, at least, the aesthetic value of architecture has even been deliberately reduced to the idea of function, for example by members of the Bauhaus movement, early in the twentieth century. **Ontologically** speaking, works of architecture are allographic, crafted according to a blueprint, but more often than not they are also singular: they are site-specific, always part of a specific environment, occupying a unique location, wherein they become interwoven into the fabric of life. This is related also to the fact that works of architecture are often heterogeneous in the sense of incorporating other self-standing works of arts, for example **sculptures**. Similarly, the relation of architecture to the decorative arts is also uniquely complex: if one does not give in to **aestheticism**, one could acknowledge that architectural **ornamentation** also enhances the architectural work's cultural function. Thus the philosophic study of architecture is bound to run the gamut from cultural studies to **environmental aesthetics**, having its focal point where conceptual probing and **anthropological** sensitivity converge. It is not surprising, then, that aesthetics has shown increasing interest in architecture amid the transition from **modernism** to **postmodernism**, as the intellectual opportunity, as well as the theoretical temptation to construe architectural designs as **texts**, became increasingly manifest. In this context, it is noteworthy that the growing reliance of architectural design on **new** media – indeed the intriguing continuity between the two realms – promises new and exciting terrain for aesthetic theory.

See **autographic/allographic distinction; autonomy, aesthetic; culture; functionalism; modern system of the arts; notation; singular/multiple distinction**

Further reading: Harries 1997; Scruton 1979; Venturi 1998

Aristotle (384–322 BC): Ancient Greek philosopher of enduring influence, a student of **Plato**, and also his great critic, whose broad-ranging corpus of writings permeated Western culture shaping the course of both **science** and philosophy. Aristotle's approach to the arts, reacting against Plato's view, followed directly from his ideas in metaphysics and on human nature. Contrary to Plato, Aristotle believed that intelligible forms are inherent in the perceptible things themselves, and that genuine knowledge always begins in **perceptual** experience. He also held a much broader conception of **mimesis**, including not only the **representation** of how things were or are, but also what they appear or are said to be, and also what they should be. Aristotle shifted the focus from regarding mimesis strictly in terms of the products of mimesis (for example, pictures and poems) to the idea of mimesis as a process, in which we actualize and amplify what is essentially truthful in the given object. This means that, for Aristotle, improving, generalizing, and beautifying something is also mimetic. In Aristotle's kinder view of human nature, our inclination to imitate is not a deviation, but a mark of human rationality. We learn and recognize by imitating, and so it is naturally pleasant. Thus, well-made art does not fall short of science as an epitome of humankind's quest for universal **truth**. This view is spectacularly argued for the art of **tragedy** in Aristotle's *Poetics*, where his explanation of the startling moment of **catharsis** brings together the ideas of mimesis, **pleasure** and moral truth. Aristotle's work remains important not only as a literary and philosophical theory of tragedy, but also as a viable model for the relation of art to the **emotions** and to morality, and as a bold suggestion concerning the varieties of knowledge that art may impart and the prospects of **aesthetic cognitivism**.

See **beauty; epistemology; ethics; metaphor; paradox of tragedy**

Further reading: Aristotle 1995

Arnheim, Rudolf (1904–2007): Contemporary American (German-born) psychologist of art, a proponent of **Gestalt theory**, and a notable philosopher of **film**. Most of Arnheim's work focused on **perception** in its relation to visual art. He argued that perception and cognition are intimately connected, asserting that visual perception is visual thinking. The perception of shape consists in the application of 'visual concepts' – a key term in Arnheim's theory – through which we conceive of an object as three-dimensional, as having a constant shape, and as independent of any particular projective aspect. Thus the main problem of **representation** is always the same: how to translate the three-dimensionality of the visual concept into the two-dimensionality of the picture plane. Any actual solution to this problem depends on the visual attitude and the conventions of **style** adopted by the artist. Arnheim believed that pictorial **realism** is relative to such attitudes and conventions, namely, to a particular emphasis on the structural patterns underlying perception. In this Arnheim seems to be in agreement with **Gombrich**, who also believed that what we see is fundamentally mediated by conceptual schemes, although Gombrich clearly does not yield to the peculiar **phenomenological** fusion of seeing and knowing advocated by Gestalt theorists.

See **innocent eye; ornamentation; psychology**

Further reading: Arnheim 1964, 1969 and 1974

arousalism: The position that the **expression** of **emotions** in art involves, or results in, the actual arousal of appropriate emotions in the audience. Arousalism is an **expression theory of art**. Simple arousalism entails direct causal relation between the artifact and the emotional response elicited, wherein lies the **definition of art** as the generator of emotional response as well as its measure for success and **value**. Simply put, if a work fails to elicit an appropriate emotional response, then it is an artistic failure or even not art at all. As a form of **essentialism**, arousalism is open to the following objections: (1) not all art is expressive; (2) artistic success and value is compatible with alternative emotional responses; (3) recognizing emotional expression in an artwork is compatible with not being moved by it. Arousalism is particularly ill-equipped for accounting for cases, such as the **paradox of tragedy,** in which the emotions elicited in the audience by the work are different from the emotions it expresses.

See **pornography; Tolstoy**

Further reading: Matravers 1998

art for art's sake see **aestheticism**

artifactuality: In the plainest sense, an artifact is anything man-made; a product of human art or craftsmanship. Artifactuality – the property of an object, which has been thus produced – is presupposed, in one way or another, by all traditional definitions of art. An artifact need not be a physical object – poems, musical performances and dance are also man-made – and the mere assumption of artifactuality leaves open the question regarding the nature of an artifact and its particular role in the given theory. Artifactuality may also be related instrumentally to artistic **value**: one might argue that the value of art lies in the benefit it provides to human beings. Since works of art are artifacts, they patently serve human purposes or functions; hence their chief value is found in fulfilling these purposes or functions. The rise of **conceptual art** in the twentieth century problematized the theoretical tendency to connect the **definition of art** with the notion of artifactuality. If natural or found objects – unmediated by human effecting – can also be art, then art qua human endeavor needs to be redefined. This problem has prompted important reconsiderations of the notion of artifactuality in contemporary aesthetic theory, most notably the **institutional theory of art**, which attempted to explain how the status of artifactuality – taken as a non-exhibited characteristic of art – is achieved within the **artworld**.

See **aesthetic properties; Dickie; Marxism; ontology**
Further reading: Dickie 1974 and 1984

artworld: As first coined by **Danto**, the term denotes the context of artistic theory and history of art required for identifying an ordinary object as a work of art. Such an object may enjoy 'dual citizenship' in the artworld and in the real world, its two modes of identification separated and united by what Danto calls the *is* **of artistic identification**. Following Danto's lead (while not endorsing Danto's emphasis on historically related works, **styles** and theories), **Dickie** elaborated the social nature of the artworld in his **institutional theory of art**. According to Dickie's later version of this theory, the artworld is the totality of all artworld systems, whereas an artworld system is a framework for the presentation of a work of art by an artist to an artworld public. The artworld is a semi-formal, social structure consisting of a myriad of coordinated activities (painting, sculpting, performing **music**, presenting at an exhibition, and so on), shared understandings (conventions, theories, and so on), and a hierarchy of institutions (**museums**, galleries, concert halls, critics, academic institutions, professional journals, and so forth), which partake in the production and reception of what the artworld designates as works of art.

See **conceptual art; law; sociology**

Further reading: Becker 1982; Danto 1964; Dickie 1974 and 1984

aspect-perception: A term associated with **Wittgenstein's** later philosophical period. It denotes a broad range of interrelated perceptual phenomena, visual and aural, in which a certain object can be perceived under more than one aspect. Wittgenstein spoke of experiencing the dawning of an aspect. Wittgenstein's discussion of aspect-perception is meant in part to undermine certain psychological approaches, in particular **Gestalt theory**, which tend to reify aspects, turning them into private mental objects. The popularity of the duck-rabbit example and Wittgenstein's recurrent reference to other ambiguous figures and schematic drawings often overshadow his far more important emphasis on other, subtler cases of aspect-perception, in particular facial **resemblance**, musical **expression** and the physiognomy of words. For Wittgenstein, aspect-perception denotes not a **phenomenologically** exotic species of **perception**, but rather a shift in the **language-game** played, wherein an utterance used to express an **interpretation** of a perceptual experience is opted for as a direct, internally related expression of that experience. Furthermore, far from arguing that all perception is actually aspect-perception, Wittgenstein's point seems to be that the very possibility of aspect-perception is constitutive of ordinary perception. This idea is an important part of Wittgenstein's later approach to aesthetics and to the crucial link he observes between aesthetic and conceptual matters. Still it was the moot reading of aspect-perception as a species of perception, underscoring the interpenetration of perception and **imagination**, which prompted certain interesting accounts of pictorial **representation**, for example in **Wollheim**.

See **aspectualism; seeing-as/seeing-in distinction; twofoldness**

Further reading: Wittgenstein 2001

aspectualism: An anti-realist position, which relates **aesthetic properties** and aesthetic **understanding** to the representational properties of our experience. Our descriptions of aesthetic properties do not literally apply to the objects described. Rather, in **aesthetic experience** we perceive aspects of things: we hear sound as movement, we see a color as sad. Aspectualism entails that aesthetic properties are mind-dependent, akin to things that we imagine or pretend, and that we apply them only **metaphorically**. This brand of anti-realism may be open to the counterclaim that it fails to account for the normativity of **aesthetic judgments**.

See **aspect-perception; imagination; Kant; perception; seeing-as/seeing-in distinction**

Further reading: Scruton 1974

attitude, aesthetic: The idea that **aesthetic experience** requires or even consists in adopting a peculiar, voluntary state of mind toward a certain object or event – artificial or natural – when we take aesthetic interest in it, and appreciate it aesthetically. This idea originated in early modern **empiricist taste theories** as well as in **Kant's** aesthetics, and proved immensely fruitful for the grounding of the idea of **aesthetic autonomy**. It has allowed metaphysical leeway for **Schopenhauer, Hegel** and **Heidegger** to argue that our engagement with works of art is revelatory of reality in a unique way. It also propelled the **epistemological** realism of **Bell** regarding **significant form**. Arguably, a non-aesthetic attitude toward something – for example, a flower vase – involves reference to its utility or function in daily life. Conversely, we may choose to adopt an attitude, which involves no such reference, whereupon the object is attended to solely for its own sake. Two main difficulties beset theories of aesthetic attitude: (1) to provide a positive characterization of the aesthetic attitude, specified in non-aesthetic terms, hence non-circularly; (2) to establish that the aesthetic attitude comprises a single, pure phenomenon, which is logically prior to, and constitutive of, aesthetic experience. Meeting the second challenge is particularly relevant to the problem of the **definition of art,** for one might be theoretically tempted to define art in terms of an attitude appropriate to all art. Kant tried to meet both challenges by construing the aesthetic attitude in terms of **disinterestedness**. In one version or another, this idea remained hitherto the characterization of choice among proponents of aesthetic attitude. However, it has been argued, most notably by **Dickie**, that under the guise of disinterestedness the notion of aesthetic attitude fails to meet the two aforementioned challenges. Specified in non-aesthetic terms, disinterestedness is merely freedom from mundane distractions, which may indeed be required for aesthetic appreciation, but not exclusively, and certainly not in a way which comprises or constitutes an ontologically unique attitude toward things. So there is no special aesthetic attitude in the first place, but perhaps motley dispositions toward a particular object, which may be bound together by the notion of the aesthetic, and hence cannot be used to define a particular aesthetic attitude without the risk of circularity.

See **appreciation, aesthetic; Beardsley; concepts, aesthetic; objects, aesthetic; properties, aesthetic**

Further reading: Dickie 1964; Fenner 1996; Kant 1952

auteur theory: More a tendency than a fully fledged theory, this approach to the analysis of **style** in **film** is premised on the contention that the director is the sole gravitational center in the creation of the cinematographic work, overseeing all the various creative aspects of filmmaking, which determine the work's **meaning** and **value**. Such analysis can be reasonably and instructively undertaken only when the director has already produced a substantial oeuvre and owns a distinct differentiating style. Thus the applicability of this theory is relatively limited, and it is flawed insofar as it tends to elevate the director's role over other essential aspects of filmmaking (for example, acting) and their crucial contribution to artistic success. The auteur theory, or 'auteurism', is related to the writing and critical practice of French film critic André Bazin (1918–58) and American critic Andrew Sarris (1928–), who advanced the scholarly practice of studying the entire oeuvre of a filmmaker. It can be adapted to apply also to certain other **hybrid art forms**, which involve the collaboration of different skills and expertise. The auteur theory is loosely related to the debates concerning authorship in **semiotics**, which hinge upon **Barthes'** thesis of the death of the author.

See **intentionalism**

Further reading: Caughie 2001

authenticity: There are three principal senses for this term, which are common in aesthetic theory: (1) authenticity as a relation between performance and its score or script; (2) authenticity as the mark of an original work as opposed to a fake; and (3) authenticity as an **aesthetic property** of an artwork or as an artistic embodiment. On the whole, authenticity is related to **ontological** considerations, albeit equivocally. The first two senses are prevalent mostly in analytic aesthetics and pertain to the **autographic art/allographic art distinction**. A performance of an allographic work is authentic if it is in accord with the relevant **notation** and performance instructions as have been conceived by its author. Performance authenticity can also pertain to **styles** and genres. Philosophical problems arise from the fact that in most cases the script or score does not fully determine the performance, but allows, and often even demands, a range of possibilities for its execution and **interpretation**. On occasion, as in early **music** but also in jazz, the authentic performance must have recourse to the conventions of the relevant performance practice. Hence perfect authenticity is virtually untenable, not only for sheer practical reasons, but also, from the perspective of **hermeneutics**, owing to the nature of the **aesthetic object** as being culturally mediated. Considerations of authenticity of an autographic work pertain to its **artifactuality** – when, where, how and by whom the object has been made – in an attempt to ensure its proper classification as an original, a copy, or perhaps **forgery**. Such classification may be relevant to its aesthetic **value** and may even have an effect on its **aesthetic properties**. The third sense of authenticity is indigenous to continental aesthetics. Following **Heidegger**, authenticity has been understood as being true to oneself, a way of living that does not collapse into self-deception. This notion found its way to the writing of other **existentialist** thinkers and also, albeit with some reluctance, to **Adorno's** philosophy of music. According to Adorno, authentic works are those which follow closely the objective requirements of internal consistency, hence their structure amounts to a full realization of their dominating idea. For Adorno, authentic art works function as critical reflection on both society and musical material: the unresolved antagonisms of reality appear in art in the guise of immanent problems of artistic form. Schoenberg's music is a prime example of authentic **modernism** in this sense.

See **improvisation; type/token distinction**

Further reading: Kivy 1997; Paddison 2004

autographic art/allographic art distinction: An **ontological** division proposed by **Goodman** in order to explain the difference between works of art that are **notational** and those that are not. A work of art is autographic if even its most exact duplication does not count as genuine. For example, Da Vinci's **painting** *Mona Lisa* is paradigmatic of autographic art, because even its most successful reproduction would still count as a fake. By contrast, a work of art is allographic if any reproduction of its original sequence would qualify as an instance of that work. For example, a Beethoven symphony is paradigmatic of allographic art, since even its worst performance would still count as a genuine instance of that work (as long as the score is played in full). Despite its apparent usefulness, Goodman's distinction fails for two main reasons. First, it is not exhaustive. Some notational works of art – for example, music or performance based on **chance** operations – are not properly allographic; other technologically advanced non-notational arts – for example digital **photography** – are not properly autographic. Second, **contextualism** undermines the claim that the identity of a work of art can depend solely on its word, image or note sequence, disregarding its art-historical context of creation.

See **authenticity; forgery**

Further reading: Goodman 1976

automatism: Originally denoting a physiological/psychiatric condition, which is the result of dissociation between behavior and consciousness, the term 'automatism' was appropriated early in the twentieth century by the Surrealists, and used later by the Dadaists to mean a type of creative practice, which is designed to dissociate the artwork from the conscious, logical control of the artist in order to unlock **expressive** qualities of the unconscious or primordial mind. More broadly, automatism denotes various uses of **chance** operations, **improvisation**, spontaneous action, and free association in the creative process of an artwork. Automatism in art can arise quite deliberately from manual techniques (such as *frottage*, *grattage* and *decalcomania* in the visual arts, algorithmic or statistical procedures in musical composition, or random verbal collages in poetry) or accidentally from altered states of consciousness (for example, intoxication, hallucination, trance and ecstasy). Artistically, automatism can be a means to another end (for example, access to unconscious experience) or an end in itself. In **new media** art, the notion of automatism begets its literal sense in cases like self-assembling poetry or other such self-generating artifacts.

See **conceptual art; intentionalism; psychoanalysis**

Further reading: Danto 1999

autonomism: The view that art is an autonomous domain of **value**, and that aesthetic reasoning is independent of other types of reasoning, such as moral, religious, scientific or instrumental reasoning. Thus, autonomism coincides with **aestheticism**; it is squarely opposed to **moralism**, and serves as a standard objection to any form of **censorship** of art. Autonomism has been propelled by the notion of **disinterestedness** as the hallmark of the aesthetic, as well as by the advent of **formalism** in twentieth century aesthetics. These foundations have been compromised by the advent of **contextualism**, which gave rise to various arguments aimed respectively at the notion of **aesthetic attitude** on the one hand and **essentialism** on the other. Full-blooded autonomism is at odds with works of art which deliberately engage the moral sentiments of the audience. It is also at odds with any morally laden discourse about the arts. A moderate version of autonomism would hold that we can evaluate works of art morally, but that ethical flaws or merits are not aesthetic flaws or merits, respectively. That is, a work of art, such as Leni Riefenstahl's notorious propaganda film *Triumph of the Will*, can be at the same time morally despicable for glorifying the Nazi regime, yet arguably a great work of cinematic art. However, even such moderate autonomism is still committed to the strong claim that the aesthetic dimension of a work of art is autonomous. This claim unfoundedly excludes the possibility that, in some artistic contexts, an aesthetic defect may indeed lie in an ethical flaw. In such cases our negative moral evaluation of the work will result also in a negative aesthetic evaluation.

See **autonomy, aesthetic; Bell; ethics; experimentalism**
Further reading: Bell 1958; Devereaux 1993

autonomy, aesthetic: The view that **aesthetic experience** and **aesthetic judgment,** in particular in the context of the proper attitude toward the creation, practice and experience of art, including their analysis and **understanding,**

are sui generis independent of and irreducible to other objects of analysis, other types of reasoning, or data pertaining to other disciplines. Furthermore, aesthetic autonomy may also imply aesthetic **value**. This puts the idea of aesthetic autonomy in sharp contrast to **functionalism**. The theoretical emphasis on the idea of aesthetic autonomy was a natural outcome of the emergence of the **modern system of the arts** and the establishment of aesthetics as an independent field within philosophy in the writings of **Baumgarten** in the eighteenth century. It received its first systematic treatment by **Kant,** who maintained that the judgment of **beauty** is autonomous. Central to Kant's argument is the characterization of the **aesthetic attitude** in terms of **disinterestedness**. Post-Kantian and **romantic** philosophers vigorously utilized this notion of aesthetic autonomy to argue for the primacy of the aesthetic dimension in human development (for example, **Schiller**), or to argue for the metaphysical transcendence of art, in particular **music** (for example, **Schopenhauer**). Later developments of the idea of aesthetic autonomy at the brink of the twentieth century and beyond gave rise to **formalism** and to **aestheticism**. The idea of aesthetic autonomy has met with criticism in various contexts; for example, as propagating **essentialism,** formalism, or an amoral stance regarding the arts (**autonomism**). Still, the most direct criticism of aesthetic autonomy involves the counter-claim that the value of art is extrinsic, pertaining to some function or otherwise involving reference to extra-aesthetic ends. Such criticism could be presented from either an instrumentalist or a pragmatist perspective. Furthermore, it might also be argued that proponents of aesthetic autonomy unreasonably insulate art and the aesthetic from its all-too-human, social context. Such **contextualist** criticism has been voiced by **Marxist** philosophers, for example, who pointed out that the idea of aesthetic autonomy necessarily entails a **political** dimension.

See **Adorno; Beardsley; Bell; Collingwood; Croce; end of art thesis; Frankfurt School; genius; Greenberg; Hanslick; Hegel; Kant; Langer; Marxism; New Criticism; sociology**

Further reading: Bell 1958; Haskins 2000; Kant 1952; Stecker 1984

avant-garde: Taken from French, this term literally means 'the foremost part of an army' or vanguard, and it is commonly used to refer, either descriptively or as a matter of **value** judgment, to artists, artifacts or events at the cutting-edge of contemporary art, which are regarded as subversive in some sense. What exactly counts, or should count as avant-garde, and what might be the proper use of the term, seems to remain a moot, epochal-relative and theory-laden issue. In the most general terms, avant-garde is taken to be oppositional, dissenting and transgressing. It is often used to refer to art which deliberately obliterates categorical distinctions, for example, between forms of art, between art and non-art, between high art and popular **culture**, between the inner and the outer of art space, or even between art and life altogether. For that reason, avant-garde has been often related to the convoluted principle of **aesthetic autonomy**. Yet even such preliminary characterization is far from being theoretically neutral, since it presupposes the existence of rigid boundaries, capable of being violated, which in turn presupposes a certain cultural theory, or a cultural stance, or even a political agenda. Thus, theorizing about contemporary avant-garde necessarily involves the fundamental question whether current historical-cultural conditions are conducive or detrimental to its very possibility, and the answer, whatever it turns out to be, is supposed to be indicative of the current epoch.

See **autonomy, aesthetic; conceptual art; Danto; definition of art; end of art thesis; kitsch; modernism; performance art; postmodernism**

Further reading: Bürger 1984

B

Barthes, Roland (1915–80): French theorist and essayist whose work in **semiotics** was instrumental in propelling the transition from **structuralism** to **poststructuralism**. Barthes work is exemplary in its well informed probing into a very broad range of artifacts of contemporary **culture**, from imagery in art and **photography** to pasta advertising, fashion, and car designs in an attempt to show how the mundane, or the natural, is in fact constructed in accordance with certain ideological **values**, and fulfills an ideological function. According to Barthes, myth is manifest when connotation is naturalized to the extent of being represented as denotation. Barthes' poststructuralist bent is evident in his celebration of the polysemous nature of **texts**, namely, of the inherently indefinite or multiple **meaning** of texts, hence of the transition of the reader from being a mere consumer of the text to becoming an artificer of the meaningful structures of the text. According to Barthes, the difference between 'readerly' and 'writerly' texts is precisely the susceptibility of the latter to the active creation of multiple meaning owing to its dense **narrative** codes. Such textual density exempts the reader from conventions, which normally enable and promote passive textual consumption. Thus, for Barthes, **realism** (literary or visual) in art hinges upon some sort of stylistic effacement and a corresponding conventional restriction on the reader's response, which is the mark of 'readerly' texts. One of Barthes' most influential theses is 'the death of the author'. In his 1968 paper, bearing this title, he argued that the notion of an author – an epitome of **modernism** in Barthes' view – is obsolete insofar as what is written in a text – in the aforementioned expanded sense, which includes the reader's role – cannot be reduced to the authority of its author. For Barthes this is eminently clear in the writing of James Joyce, for instance. In such cases signification is unrestricted by the traces by which the written text is constituted. Hence it is the role of the reader to unify the text, holding all those traces together in active collaboration. With this stance came patent rejection of the **expression theory of art** as well as an overall, somewhat self-deflating rethinking of the role of the critic. In this regard, Barthes' own critical practice is telling, especially his late writings on photography, – for example, *Camera Lucida* – in which he delved in a deeply personal, partly autobiographic inquiry concerning the varieties and conditions of photographic knowledge, ultimately leaving irresolute the vital difficulty whether or not to indulge in this format of creative musing.

See **communication; intentionalism; interpretation; medium; New Criticism; politics; representation; Saussure; sociology; style; truth**

Further reading: Barthes 1972, 1977 and 1981

Baumgarten, Alexander Gottlieb (1714–62): German rationalist philosopher who famously coined the term 'aesthetics' from the Greek *aisthanomai* (meaning: **perception** by means of the senses), and entered the annals of aesthetics as the first academic philosopher ever to lecture on the topic. Baumgarten defined aesthetics as the science of sensual cognition, which was supposed to complement the science of rational cognition, or logic, but also as the theory of art. Owing to its obscure nature, sensual or aesthetic cognition is inferior and can be regarded only as analogous to rational cognition. But Baumgarten importantly delineated it as an independent faculty of the mind, whose unique modes, intrinsically related to **emotion** and **imagination**, not only require specialized philosophic investigation, but also can be fruitfully contrasted with rationality. Furthermore, Baumgarten argued that aesthetic cognition has its own truth claim, a kind of unstructured and rich **truth**, which is inaccessible by logical means. Although Baumgarten's own incomplete project of aesthetics fell into obscurity, his ideas opened up a new conceptual framework, which stimulated some of the crucial historical developments in modern aesthetics, mostly through his direct influence on **Kant** and early **romanticism**.

See **cognitivism, aesthetic; epistemology; objectivism; perception**

Further reading: Baumgarten 1954

Beardsley, Monroe C. (1915–85): American philosopher, one of the founders of the Anglo-American analytic tradition in aesthetics, who was closely associated with the literary circle known as the **New Criticism**. Beardsley's magnum opus, *Aesthetics: Problems in the Philosophy of Criticism* (1958), is considered to be the most sustained and comprehensive philosophical defense of the New Criticism and one of the truly great achievements of Anglo-American aesthetics in the twentieth century, incorporating pragmatist and **phenomenological** elements into the analytic idiom. Beardsley's mode of philosophizing was meta-critical in the sense that it involved a systematic examination of the nature and justification of critical statements made about works of art. In his early work,

Beardsley already established one of the major themes of his philosophy of art – the autonomy of the work of art – arguing against what he dubbed the **intentional fallacy**, on the one hand, and against the **affective fallacy**, on the other. Beardsley believed that the **interpretation** of a work of art and its aesthetic **value** are independent of the intentions of the artist and the emotional reaction of the critic. This comes across, for instance, in his theory of **metaphor**, which explains metaphorical **meaning** as interplay and opposition between two levels of meaning in the term being taken metaphorically – to wit, (1) the lexical designation of the word; and (2) those properties that the word suggests or connotes. Another major theme in Beardsley's work was the nature and characteristics of **aesthetic experience**, whose conceptual primacy ultimately informed his **functionalist definition of art**. According to Beardsley, a work of art is an arrangement of conditions intended to be capable of affording an experience with a marked aesthetic character. Thus he clearly set himself apart from **formalist** views, such as **Bell's**. Following **Dewey**, Beardsley contended that aesthetic experience, wherein we fix our attention upon heterogeneous yet interrelated **perceptual** components, is unified in virtue of its qualities of coherence and completeness. Aesthetic experience is set apart from all other types of perceptual experience by virtue of its unity, complexity and intensity. Consequently, Beardsley defined aesthetic value in functionalist terms as the capacity to produce aesthetic experience of fairly great magnitude. Beardsley's idea that the unity of aesthetic experience consists not only the unity of the artwork in itself but also the artwork as it is unified in the experience of the perceiver informed also his **ontology**. For Beardsley, **aesthetic objects** are perceptual objects, and, as such, they can have presentations, which he defines as the object as experienced by a particular perceiver on a particular occasion. However, a presentation is not identical with its corresponding aesthetic object, which might be a physical object. Like other **aesthetic attitude** theories, Beardsley's theory is open to **anti-essentialist** criticism and to the contention that any phenomenalist characterization of the aesthetic experience is necessarily either underdetermined or circular.

See **autonomy, aesthetic**

Further reading: Beardsley 1981 and 1982; Beardsley and Wimsatt 1946 and 1949

beauty: While there has been very little agreement about the nature of beauty, or even about its very existence, beauty is often considered to be an aesthetic property, and also something which is inherently good and pleasurable, hence an aesthetic **value**. As such, it has been contrasted with the **sublime**. Throughout the history of aesthetics, beauty was commonly understood in one of the following general senses: (1) as a property, or a set of properties of an object, for example, symmetry and proportion, which causes **pleasure** in us; (2) as something 'in the eye of the beholder', not a property of anything, which produces pleasure in us; (3) as a simple indefinable property, apprehended by intuition, that cannot be defined in terms of any other properties. In twentieth-century analytic aesthetics, the interest in the concept of beauty was replaced with an interest in the concept of the aesthetic. Still, contemporary attempts have been made to resurrect the idea of beauty in terms of the pleasure we take in perceiving **aesthetic properties**.

See **classicism; disinterestedness; emotivism; environmental aesthetics; formalism; Hanslick; Hume; Hutcheson; Kant; Lessing; Marxism; Moore; naturalistic fallacy; Nietzsche; objectivism; profundity; subjectivism; sublime; taste theories; Tolstoy; Wittgenstein**

Further reading: Mothersill 1984

Bell, Clive (1881–1964): British critic and theorist of art, a leading member of the **Bloomsbury Group**, and an important proponent of **formalism** in early analytic aesthetics. Like his Bloomsbury peers, Bell was highly influenced by the philosophy of **Moore**. His theory of art, formulated in his early, now classic book, *Art* (1914), is to a significant extent an emulation and an implementation of Moore's ideas – then already a decade old – on **epistemology**, metaphysics and value theory in the field of aesthetics and art criticism. Bell maintained that art (primarily visual art) evokes in us a unique experience, which he confusingly dubbed 'aesthetic emotion', by virtue of the forms and the relations of forms, the arrangements, relations and combinations of lines and colors, which impinge directly on our mind. Aesthetic emotion is Bell's name for the experience of **significant form** – a key term in Bell's theory – which is not a vehicle of any information on the world or the minds of others, but rather the **phenomenological** hallmark of art per se. Bell offered a theory of art, which is formalist by virtue of couching its **definition of art** in terms of the experience of form, and **essentialist** by virtue of deriving significant form (the object of that experience) as a self-subsisting entity from the experience itself, namely, from the aesthetic emotion. Moore's influence is eminently clear in the basic principles of Bell's theory: adherence to immediate experience and the unanalyzability and indefinability of significant form, which is akin to Moore's definition of **beauty**.

See **aestheticism; attitude, aesthetic; autonomy, aesthetic; Kant; open question argument**

Further reading: Bell 1958

Benjamin, Walter (1892–1940): German philosopher and cultural critic, a member of the circle of philosophers, social scientists and cultural critics known as the **Frankfurt School**. While his various texts do not coalesce into a consistent theoretical approach, Benjamin's unique body of work has had an important effect on contemporary literary theory owing to its commitment to immanent criticism, namely, the idea that any methodological or theoretical principles which are to be applied on a given subject matter must emerge from that subject matter. Like his Frankfurt School peers, Benjamin held an overall **Marxist** view of the arts. In his best known work in aesthetics, *The Work of Art in the Age of Mechanical Reproduction* (1935), Benjamin was concerned with the relation between technology and **aesthetic experience**. Contrary to traditional artistic media, he argued, mass media give rise to artistic objects, which do not command awed contemplation. Techniques of mechanical reproduction, such as lithography, **photography** and **film**, dissipate the 'aura' of their respective artistic object, that is, its **ontological** uniqueness, and transform our mode of reception of such objects, thereby enabling us to see the world as revealed by these techniques.

See **culture; end of art thesis; modernism; sociology**
Further reading: Benjamin 1968

Bloomsbury Group: A group of British intellectuals, artists, critics, and writers, named after the London neighborhood where they lived and worked during the first few decades of the twentieth century. The leading figures in this group included art critics and theorists **Clive Bell** and Roger Fry, painters Vanessa Bell and Duncan Grant, novelists Virginia Woolf and E. M. Forster, economist John Maynard Keynes, and others. The group initially formed at Cambridge University, where most of its members studied, and shared great reverence toward Cambridge philosopher and teacher **G. E. Moore**.

Moore's ideas on **epistemology** and on value theory shaped the main features of the Bloomsbury aesthetics. Bloomsbury's advocacy of **formalism** and **aestheticism**, as seen in particular in the influential work of Bell, was kindled by Moore's quest for objects of immediate experience. Arguably, Bell's notion of significant form is the Bloomsbury equivalent of Moore's notion of sense-data. Furthermore, Moore's construal of **beauty** as an experience of an objective entity, which is good in itself, paved the way for Bloomsbury's typical conflation of aesthetics and the **ethics**. This latter idea was also inspired by **Tolstoy**, who was admired by Woolf and Fry. Beside formalism, the contribution of the Bloomsbury group to twentieth-century aesthetics includes also the early advocacy of feminist aesthetics, in particular in the writings of Virginia Woolf, who voiced the lives of women by means of **modernist** stream of consciousness techniques.

See **gendered aesthetics**

Further reading: Bell 1968; Hintikka 1995; Rosenbaum 1998

Burke, Edmund (1729–97): British philosopher and statesman. In his early essay *A Philosophical Enquiry into the Origin of our Ideas of the Sublime and the Beautiful* (1757), Burke followed John Locke's **empiricist** program in developing an account of the workings of the **imagination**. He traced the sources of our responses to the **sublime** and the **beautiful** to experiences of pain and **pleasure** respectively. His original account of the sublime in terms of an intense emotional overriding of reason due to reason's inability to comprehend had an important influence on **Kant's** idea of the sublime and anticipated similar **romanticist** sentiments.

See **emotions; taste theories; ut pictura poesis**

Further reading: Burke 1998

C

catharsis: Derived from the Greek root word *katharos*, which means 'clean' or 'unsoiled', the term denotes the unique **psychological** effect that certain works of art have on their spectators. Originally, as **Aristotle** had used the term in his *Poetics*, catharsis referred to the transmogrifying moment of catastrophe in Attic **tragedy** as the experience of horror purges and purifies the soul of the spectator in an act of communal reaffirmation. In this sense, catharsis also had important medical and **political** connotations. In the nineteenth and twentieth centuries, catharsis, as a psychological term, had an important place in late **romantic** aesthetics, most notably serving as the philosophical crux of the difference between the views of **Schopenhauer** and the early **Nietzsche** on **tragedy**, and it gained broad acceptance, largely due to **Freud**, who pursued the idea that art can be purging and therapeutic.

See **paradox of tragedy; psychoanalysis**

Further reading: Aristotle 1995; Lear 1988

censorship: The suppression or regulation, by government or any other powerful institutions of society, of information, ideas, images or means of **expression**, because they are considered dangerous, disruptive, immoral, or otherwise objectionable. The censorship of artistic expression is founded on the acknowledgment of the power of art to challenge the established order. This idea goes back to **Plato's** distrust of the **mimetic** arts and his consequent suggestion to banish the poets from the ideal state. Censorship may apply to the practice and exhibition of art, depriving in effect the artist of access to his audience or the public access to the work of art, at least as it was originally created. Censorship of art should be distinguished from art criticism, which in practice may mask discrimination and effectively deprive an artist of access to his audience, but still does not enjoy the public claim of legitimacy required for real control over artistic expression. Censorship of art is not necessarily related to aesthetics. When it is, then it serves as the practical counterpart of **moralism**. In this respect, censorship is susceptible to the standard arguments against moralism. However, more often than not censorship of art is propelled by **political** principles (for example, a racist theory, as in the case of the Nazi censorship of art) or religious beliefs, which clearly transgress the moralist framework, as they conflate political power with knowledge. In any case, censorship presupposes that morally suspect works of art really corrupt their audiences. This causal connection is required in order to establish the need for preventing such purported harm. However, the empirical truth of such a causal connection remains hitherto unfounded. Furthermore, since censorship is patently in conflict with the right to freedom of speech, it is commonly replaced by mere classification of contents or distribution zoning in societies which promote freedom of speech and interpret this right as to include artistic expression also.

See **autonomy, aesthetic; ethics; experimentalism; pornography; sociology; value**

Further reading: Devereaux 1993; Schusterman 1984; Williams 1981

chance: Twentieth-century Western art has witnessed a decisive introduction of elements of indeterminacy or randomness into the creative process of the artwork, or in its presentation or performance. The use of chance or aleatoric (from Latin, *alea*, a dice game) operations in art can be divided into three main types, which may coexist in a given artwork: (1) using random processes in order to generate a fixed artwork; (2) allowing the performer to choose from a variety of formal options stipulated by the author of the artwork; (3) underdetermining the performance or presentation of the artwork by means of special **notation**. The visual arts and the literary arts are normally restricted to the first type of chance operations, whereas the resulting work refers or deflects the viewers back to the actual activity or process which yielded it. Such is, for instance, Jackson Pollock's action **painting** from the 1950s. The performing arts and various multimedia events naturally leave ample room for chance operations of all three types. The introduction of chance into a work of art undermines the notion that artistic creation requires, at each moment and at every level, a definite, conscious choice on the part of the artist. It also implies that to some extent the identity of an aleatoric work is underdetermined by its actual form. Hence the introduction of chance openly challenges the main tenets of both **formalism** and **intentionalism** as it undercuts the notion of **artifactuality**. Within the realm of the performing arts, it also challenges the notion of **interpretation**, insofar as interpretation is understood in relation to the purported identity of the work performed.

See **automatism; conceptual art; new media; ontology**
Further reading: Boulez 1972; Cage 1961; Meyer 1960

classicism: A wide-ranging term which generally indicates admiration of, and ideational adherence to, the intellectual, literary and artistic canons of the ancient Greeks and Romans. In artistic practice, as well as in art history, classicism involves harking back to such ancient models in order to imitate them in the service of an ideal vision of human experience – specifically an ideal vision of beauty – which combines grandeur, nobility, repose, and rationality. When contrasted with **romanticism,** the reference to classicism is commonly meant to underscore its rationally bounded, universalist character, as opposed to the latter's emphasis on the freedom of individual **expression.**

See **culture; style**

Further reading: Eliot 1945

cognitivism, aesthetic: The view that works of art may teach us about the world, that the knowledge that they afford is non-trivial, and that this capacity to afford this kind of knowledge determines to some extent their aesthetic **value.** Aesthetic cognitivism is the foundation for an **epistemology** of art, a theory of what we know about the world through art. Aesthetic cognitivism faces the objection, which is standard since **Plato** that, at its best, most creative as a product of the **imagination,** art generally fails to meet the standard adequate to propositional knowledge – affording true, warranted beliefs – and that at any rate knowledge claims are not distinctive of, or adequate to, art and altogether insignificant for the consideration of aesthetic value. The various cognitivist responses given throughout the history of ideas – first and foremost by **Aristotle,** but also by **Hegel** and **Schopenhauer** – have all hinged on idiosyncratic metaphysical considerations, which allow the construal of art as a unique mode of conceptual inquiry into reality and **truth.** In contemporary analytic aesthetics attempts have been made to argue that while works of art (at least purely **fictional** works) may be lacking in terms of propositional knowledge, they may still afford non-propositional kinds of knowledge, such as **emotional** skills, moral values, recognition of possibilities, phenomenal knowledge and so on, whose ultimate test is in their permeation into our ordinary experience and the way they engage our affective responses and our **imagination**. Such lines of argument are calculated to dissolve the issue of warrant and also to show how knowing the world through art is aesthetically relevant to the value of the given work as art. Nonetheless contemporary anti-cognitivists still maintain that the appeal to a variety of non-propositional knowledge relies on a very loose conception of truth, and that by insisting that art is primarily a form of truth-telling they generally dilute what is distinctive about it.

See **education, aesthetic; ethics; Goodman; objectivism; Ricoeur**

Further reading: Kieran and Lopes 2006; Lamarque and Olsen 1996

Collingwood, Robin George (1889–1943): British philosopher and historian. In his book *The Principles of Art* (1938), Collingwood presented an idealist **expression theory of art** akin to the one offered by **Croce**. Collingwood believed that 'art proper' – that is, art as an end in itself (as opposed to craft) – is **expression**, and he construed expression as an imaginary activity in which the artist clarifies, and becomes conscious of, his **emotions**. Artistic creation begins in the burden of inchoate emotion, the nature of which is yet unknown to the artist. The work is complete when the emotion has been clarified, and so creative thought in art is related to self-knowledge. Collingwood importantly identified art with **language**: it is the speaking that clarifies thought, expression is speaking. Collingwood believed that a work of art is not an artifact, but an experience, a mental activity, which may in principle exist complete in the artist's mind unless externalized and communicated to the audience. In art (he thought) **communication** is incidental to expression, but when this occurs (necessarily employing some craft), **understanding** the artwork involves recreating it in the minds of the audience. That is, we know that the artist is expressing his emotions by the fact that he is enabling us to express ours. Collingwood's theory was criticized on account of the many absurdities that ensue from its mentalist **ontology**, the restricting definition of 'art proper', and the incoherence of his criterion of understanding in art.

See **artifactuality; Dewey; essentialism; imagination; medium; ontology**

Further reading: Collingwood 1964

communication: While we colloquially speak of art as communication, acknowledging the inescapably social nature of all art, it is much harder to pin down a comprehensive definition of art as communication. This difficulty is traditionally rooted in the ancient quarrel between philosophy (logic) and poetry (rhetoric), as presented most famously by **Plato**, wherein art is conceived as being **epistemically** deceptive. Other complications are related to the presupposition that we may conceive art as **language** in some sense, and to the general difficulties involved in **essentialism**. In sum, the **definition of art** as communication is too restrictive in terms of the scope of artistic phenomena and it presupposes too much with regard to the ways we actually experience and use artifacts. The term 'communication' lends itself to a standard tripartite analysis: (1) action, that is, the transference, instillation or exchange of ideas, facts, points of view, and so on, by means of a system of signs; (2) content, that is, ideas, facts, points of view, and so on, which may be transferred from an originator to a recipient in the activity of communication; (3) **medium**, that is, a system of signs – speech, writing, visual signs, and so on – including their mechanical or electronic elaborations, which facilitate the transference of content in the activity of communication. While some artistic media are typically also means of communication (for example, writing or **photography**), and while some works of art are certainly informative (for example, documentary films or historical novels), works of art are not ordinarily used merely to report facts, and certain artistic media are typically quite inadequate for this purpose (for example, **music** or **dance**). Still it may be possible *mutatis mutandis* to refer to artworks in terms of communicative action, content or medium. In fact, this idea has propelled the study of artworks in such fields as **interpretation, semiotics** and **hermeneutics**. The idea of art as communication influenced in particular proponents of the **expression theory of art** – for example, **Tolstoy, Croce, Dewey, Collingwood** and **Langer** – who sought to explain expressiveness or even morality in art in terms of a certain **emotional** isomorphism between the artist and his audience.

See **Barthes; culture; expression; new media; sociology**
Further reading: Barthes 1977

concepts, aesthetic: The shareable constituents of aesthetic thought, most commonly pertaining to the description, evaluation and judgment of **aesthetic objects** and **aesthetic experience**. There has been much controversy regarding the **ontological** status of concepts in general – whether they are mental particulars, such as mental representations (ideas), mental states or components of a language of thought, or certain cognitive abilities, which enable us to classify things, or perhaps entirely abstract objects, which mediate between language and thought. From antiquity to the present day, aesthetic theories were necessarily embroiled, even if inadvertently, in

each of these general **epistemological**, logical and metaphysical concerns about the nature, origins, structure
and scope of concepts. For instance, **Plato's** discussion
of **beauty** is informed by his theory of forms; thus, this
concept is taken to be innate, mimetic, objective, and
semantically rigid. Consequently, it can be criticized
in all these aspects. Another example is **Hume**, whose
concept of beauty is informed by **empiricism**, taken to
be a mental representation, which might be condition-
governed insofar as we can establish universal empirical laws of human **psychology**. **Kant** tried to establish
that while aesthetic concepts are **taste** concepts they are
still pure and so universally applicable. In the twentieth
century, **Sibley** reintroduced the debate concerning aesthetic concepts in an attempt to delineate the domain of
the aesthetic in ordinary language. In his view, aesthetic
concepts have their origin in **perception,** their application
is not condition-governed, but they are still objective.

See **judgment, aesthetic; properties, aesthetic**
Further reading: Sibley 2006

conceptual art: The term can be loosely applied to any work
of art, which engages primarily with ideas rather than
exemplifying a perceptual encounter with a unique
object. The term is also used to refer to a contemporary
artistic movement – made famous by the works and theoretical writings of artists like Sol LeWitt, Joseph Kosuth
and the Art & Language group – that emerged in the
mid-1960s simultaneously on both sides of the Atlantic
Ocean. The main tenets of conceptual art were already
laid out by the Dadaists during the first two decades of
the twentieth century, particularly in Marcel Duchamp's
notion of the ready-made: the intellectual ascribing of a
new use to old objects, such as urinals and bottle racks.
In general, conceptual art downplays or even eliminates

artifactuality as it regards the actual execution of the artifact as perfunctory. Nothing in the perceptible properties of the conceptual art work identifies it as art; its impact is intellectual. It challenges the **ontological**, or otherwise traditionally sanctified connection between the artist and a particular artifact, underscores the historical, theoretical and institutional framing of art, and questions the role of artistic intention vis-à-vis the **meanings** attributed to the resulting artifact.

See **avant-garde; end of art thesis; institutional theory of art; medium; postmodernism**

Further reading: Goldie and Schellekens 2007

contextualism: A relatively recent development in contemporary analytic aesthetics, this is the view that works of art and aesthetic practices can be fully assessed only with reference to their respective historical, social, or cultural contexts. Thus contextualism is diametrically opposed to **autonomism**. It is specifically diametrically opposed to **formalism** insofar as it consists in the claim that one cannot account for the identity of the work of art and its **aesthetic properties** without also considering the context of its actual creation, and broadly speaking, its multifarious relations to the **artworld**.

See **appreciation, aesthetic; culture; Danto; Dickie; institutional theory of art; Margolis; sociology; understanding**

Further reading: Danto 1981; Margolis 1999

conventionalism: The doctrine that (1) a given phenomenon arises from or is determined by convention; (2) for any given phenomenon there exist a number of alternative conventions of equal standing; (3) the choice between alternative conventions is free, undetermined by human perception and cognition, by rational deliberation or by the nature of things in the world. One can be a conventionalist about many things: **truth**, morality and justice, mathematical analysis, and so on. In aesthetics, conventionalism most commonly arises with regards to pictorial **representation**, often in reference to the work of **Gombrich** and **Goodman**. A conventionalist about pictorial representation would reject the idea that a picture of an apple **resembles** an apple, or in general, that there is any natural connection between a representation having a particular form and what it represents, maintaining that pictures are actually artificial symbolic systems, which behave like languages. On this view, both the status of a representation as such, and its contents, are ultimately determined by common agreement, which is susceptible to historical change and development. While this position is largely counter-intuitive, it has the advantage of capturing the ability of pictures to denote objects, like words, and to be grouped into larger, meaningful units. It also captures the fact that certain forms of representation – for example, perspective – need to be acquired or require enculturation, and that there is diversity in systems of pictorial representation through history and across cultures. However, the empirical fact that such systems are not extremely varied after all (which might suggest that picture-object connections are not arbitrary, but rather determined to some degree by certain universal features of human physiology, **perception,** or cognition) flies in the face of strong conventionalism, such as Goodman's, which contends that anything can depict anything.

See **innocent eye; realism**

Further reading: Gombrich 1986; Goodman 1976

Croce, Benedetto (1866–1952): Italian philosopher of **Hegelian** conviction, literary critic and statesman, whose

expression theory of art is often bundled together with **Collingwood's**. Croce was an idealist. He believed that art consists entirely in a kind of pre-conceptual activity of the mind, which he called 'intuition'. While we cannot describe intuitions, Croce maintained, we can **communicate** them by expressing their uniqueness in artistic form. To give a concrete example: what Van Gogh did when he painted his delirious *Starry Night* was to give articulate **expression** to the amorphous stimulus imparted on him by the scenery. The painting is an intuition of the scenery; for Croce, intuition and expression are one and the same. This implies that the **meaning** of an artwork is internally, and in an important sense also ineffably, related to the work itself; it cannot be captured in any other way, hence the work is an end in itself, a unique individual.

See **emotions; medium; ontology; understanding**
Further reading: Croce 1995

culture: The term designates a totality comprising of every socially transmitted aspect of our lives by virtue of which we endow our activities with **meaning** and **value**. Of course, this includes both art and our philosophizing about it. The notion of culture lends itself to some duality between a particularist view, which sees culture as organic, self-contained, and self-identifying, hence that which diversifies people, and a universalist view, which sees culture as a hallmark of the universal progress of humankind, hence that which unites people. However, this distinction should be confused with another distinction between common, or popular culture, which some condescendingly dub 'low culture', and 'high culture', which is associated with art in its highest sense. Surely, not all instances of common culture pertain to cultural particularism. **Kitsch** is an example for popular culture claiming universal appeal, but so is ethnic **music**. If there is a difference between the two, it must be between acquired and inherited common culture, and the universalism claimed in both cases must be qualified in itself. Furthermore, not all instances of high culture pertain to cultural universalism. Art in the twentieth century has been notorious in cutting itself off from its roots in common culture, producing artifacts of utmost **abstraction**, and eventually ghettoizing itself. In the last analysis, conflating high culture with cultural universalism is ideological, amounting to the envisioning of art as a **religion** of sorts. On the other hand, collapsing high culture into common culture and conflating this with cultural particularism is also ideological. Rendering any artificial, commercial identity-shaping activity or product as cultural per se has been propelled by the ideology of unruly cultural relativism, which is indigenous to certain strains of **postmodernism** and has been institutionally recognized in the form of the newly formed academic discipline of cultural studies. In general, contemporary aesthetics, on both sides of the alleged analytic/continental divide, has been exceptionally and increasingly open-minded, albeit critical at times, with regards to artifacts and practices which are indigenous to common or popular culture. In fact, aesthetic theory requires both distinctions in order to thrive. It may turn into a critique of culture when it reflects on the purported relation between art (observed across the high culture/common culture divide) and culture (understood in the particularist sense). This is best seen in continental aesthetics, especially in the writings of the **Frankfurt School**. Alternatively, aesthetic theory may pose fundamental questions concerning the very **definition of art**, which patently cut across both distinctions. For that reason, arguably, cultural studies and aesthetics seem to be mutually exclusive intellectual endeavors at present.

See **Adorno; anthropology; Barthes; Benjamin; communication; ethics; Frankfurt School; gendered aesthetics; hermeneutics; language; law; Marcuse; Margolis; modernism; Nietzsche; performance art; politics; poststructuralism; profundity; romanticism; sociology; Wittgenstein**

Further reading: Scruton 1998

D

dance: Dance is one of the most primordial forms of human **expression,** and it has existed as a distinct form of art since antiquity. As such it has certainly fascinated both **anthropologists** and historians. Yet as a subject matter of philosophic inquiry, dance attracted relatively limited attention in comparison to the other performing arts. Dance may be regarded in an inclusive sense – in relation to elements, which are indigenous to other arts, such as soundtrack and costumes – or else exclusively. In the former sense it can be regarded as a **hybrid art form** in itself, and in the latter sense it is commonly regarded in relation to another hybrid art form. This collaborative character of dance has been traditionally acknowledged since **Aristotle's** discussion of **tragedy,** through **Wagner's** idea of **Gesamtkunstwerk,** to contemporary **performance art.** Arguably, this is related to the most unique characteristic of dance: its inherence in sheer human physiognomy at its most visceral. Set in concrete human form, hence capable of sustaining dramatic **narrative,** dance nonetheless lends itself to **abstraction.** Aesthetic approaches to dance to tend either to stress the relation of dance the dancer's body, or else to construe dance in terms of symbolic gestures. The former approach has become increasingly pronounced in **gendered aesthetics;**

the latter is exemplified in the writings of **Langer**, for instance. Dance shares some general philosophical difficulties, regarding both **ontology** and **aesthetic appreciation**, with other performing arts, which yield multiple works, in particular **music** and **theater**. For example, the existence of the work and its relation to its relevant performances, **notational** under-determination, the problem of admissible **interpretation**, and so on.

See **autographic art/allographic art distinction; mimesis; singular/multiple distinction; type/token distinction**
Further reading: McFee 1992; Sparshott 1988

Danto, Arthur (1924–): Contemporary American philosopher of art and art critic, a proponent and interpreter of **avant-garde** art. Much of Danto's work is concerned with the **essentialist** need to produce a **definition of art**, which he identifies not only as the main thrust of aesthetic theories from the eighteenth century onwards, but also as the goal explicitly taken upon itself by art in the twentieth century. His most striking contention is the **Hegelian** thesis that contemporary art had already attained this goal – namely, a philosophical knowledge of its own essence – in 1964 upon the exhibition of Andy Warhol's *Brillo Box*: an exact replica of an ordinary Brillo box, perceptually indiscernible from its real counterpart. Danto famously concluded that herewith a main **narrative** in art history had been brought to an end. In his early work, Danto's argued that the artistic identification of an object as a work of art cannot be premised upon any of its perceptible properties, but rather on the existence of an environment of art history and theory: to wit, an **artworld**. Danto developed this theme further in his important book, *The Transfiguration of the Commonplace* (1981), where he argued that contrary to ordinary objects, works of art are about the world, thereby conveying the artist's **interpretation** and **understanding,** hence that works of art are patently **representational** and theory-laden. Danto's essentialist definition of art is propelled by his historicism. He maintains that a work of art gains its essential property of 'aboutness' by means of some sort of rhetorical ellipsis. This ellipsis requires audience participation: filling in the interpretation. Yet both the work and the interpretation require an art-historical context. In his later work, Danto spelled out the overarching implication of his position, the **end of art thesis.**

See **attitude, aesthetic; conceptual art; Dickie;** *is* **of artistic identification**

Further reading: Danto 1964, 1981, 1986 and 1997

death of the author see **Barthes**

deconstruction: A method, or rather strategy for textual and conceptual analysis (as well as a name for a distinct intellectual movement in literary criticism), which is chiefly associated with **Derrida** and **poststructuralism.** Deconstructing a **text** involves an inventive close-reading in which creative license is given to the reader to implode the purported **meaning** of the text, thereby opening it up to a multitude of contrasting and conflicted meanings. This is to be achieved primarily by means of searching the text for unanticipated significations in turns of phrase, **metaphors,** and peculiar binary oppositions, which the author had used, in effect showing through such play of words how the author's forthright assertion is undermined when underplayed terms inadvertently assert themselves. Deconstruction fully embodies the fundamental poststructuralist conviction that a text is, as **Barthes** put it, a methodological field for a 'writerly' response on part of the reader, which not only thwarts the author's purported intentions, but also dislodges some of our ordinary beliefs about **language** itself, in particular in its relation to **truth**. The result is a radically anti-realist interpretative mode – a successful deconstruction renders the text staggeringly ambiguous – which yields a particularly caustic effect on texts that assert themselves as truthful, transparent accounts of the world (for example, analytic philosophy as well as natural science). Deconstruction has been powerfully applied to the interpretation of literary texts, as well as to the history of art, occasionally producing unusual insights. However, owing to its inevitable connection to the identity and stature of the particular reader, a tendency to accept a particular deconstructive reading, especially when the reading is blatantly uninhibited, may appear awkward or spurious at times – an instance of falling prey to an appeal to authority, that is, a mere rhetorical feat on the part of a celebrity reader qua creator. Sadly, while practitioners of deconstruction are patently immune to such positivist criticism, when deconstruction eventually infiltrated the citadel of natural science, this instigated the so-called 'Science Wars' in the late 1990s.

See **New Criticism; Nietzsche; postmodernism; structuralism**

Further reading: Brunette and Wills 1994; Culler 1982

decorative art see **ornamentation**

definition of art: In general, a definition is a statement which explicates the meaning of an expression or a concept. Traditionally, following **Aristotle**, a definition is supposed to capture the essential nature of the thing defined. Thus, the notion of a real definition is connected to the metaphysical doctrine of **essentialism**. From antiquity until to the first half of the twentieth century, definitions of art were invariably essentialist, attempting to specify the property or the set of properties which would be common to all works of art, and hence would yield the necessary condition for something to be a work of art. Among such early attempts we may count, first and foremost, the definition of art in terms of **mimesis**, that is, art's purported ability to mirror or imitate nature, as exemplified in the works of **Plato** and **Aristotle** in ancient Greece or in the theories of art of the Enlightenment. The adherence to mimesis is generally at odds with works of art in which **representation** is de-emphasized or altogether absent, such as **abstract** art and pure instrumental **music**. Another early definition of art refers to **expression**, commonly the expression of the artist's personal **emotions**, as the essence of all art. Such an approach is exemplified in **Tolstoy's** theory of emotional transmission, in **Croce's** notion of art as intuitive expression, or in **Collingwood's** suggestion to define art as an activity of clarifying an emotion. The adherence to expression is generally too restrictive in three senses: (1) it patently excludes forms of art which tend to be non-expressive or even suppress expression altogether, for example, decorative arts or electro-acoustic music; (2) it may unreasonably restrict the range of genuine artistic emotions (as in the case of Tolstoy); (3) it may unreasonably restrict the range of processes by which a work of art may come into being (as in the case of Collingwood). A third type of essentialist definition of art, exemplified in **Bell's** theory of **significant form**, adheres to **formalism**. Since, trivially, every object has form in some sense, this approach faces the challenge of identifying the sense of form appropriate to works of art. Still it is doubtful whether this can be achieved in a non-circular fashion. Furthermore, this kind of formalist definition tends to conflate the classificatory task of deciding what is a work of art with the evaluative task of deciding what is a good work of art: the answer to the former implies the answer to the latter.

While those early attempts to define art ran into trouble, the rise of **anti-essentialism** around the mid-twentieth century led some philosophers to doubt whether art could be defined at all. If definitions apply only to fixed concepts, and if the concept of art is open-ended, then the quest for a real definition of art is fundamentally misconstrued. However, rather than putting an end to this pursuit, anti-essentialism has proven to be a catalyst for new attempts to define art on different terms. Definitions of art in the second half of the twentieth century may belong to one or more of the following main types: (1) **functional**: typically emphasizing the function of art to promote aesthetic experience; (2) historical: emphasizing the appropriate relation of a given work of art to its art historical context; (3) institutional: emphasizing the social dynamics by which an artifact achieves the status of a work of art. While such definitions of art fare better than any of their predecessors, they still leave much to be desired theoretically. Insofar as a functional definition of art hinges upon the notion of aesthetic experience – for example, **Beardsley's** – it faces the theoretically daunting task of specifying an experience common to all works of art. Historical definitions, such as **Danto's**, are patently locked in relativity: something can be regarded as 'art' only within and relative to its appropriate art historical narrative. Arguably, the **institutional theory of art,** championed by **Dickie,** provides the only type of definition which successfully evades the anti-essentialist critique. Still it remains patently classificatory, unable to identify aesthetic **value**, and it is also unapologetically circular.

See **expression theory of art; modern system of the arts; representation theory of art; Ziff**
Further reading: Davies 1991; Stecker 1997

depiction see **representation**

Derrida, Jacques (1930–2004): Algerian-born French philosopher. His iconoclastic probing into Western philosophical tradition, and in particular, his method of **deconstruction**, which he had invoked in order to facilitate such probing, were crucial to the formation of **poststructuralism** and **postmodernism** with their far-reaching influence on literary theory and criticism, and on the practice and theory of the various arts. Derrida's philosophy is preoccupied with an interrogation of Western metaphysical **language** in a manner which is patently hostile to the Cartesian foundationalist idea that thought precedes language, or in Derrida's sense, the idea that thought signals its self-presence to itself through language, and that this self-presence is the paradigm of **truth**. Derrida's attack on what he dubbed the 'logocentric' core of such metaphysics of presence, which have persisted, he maintained, from antiquity throughout the entire history of Western philosophy, is coupled with his denial that speech (considered as the proper language of thought, as it were) is privileged over writing, and that the traditional attempt to draw a sharp distinction between speech and writing is tenable at all. Thus within Derrida's framework it becomes imperative to set writing free from its logocentric binding to self-present truth in order to open up the possibility for subversive thinking: to wit, thinking on terms other than metaphysical. Derrida's important idea in this regard is that of the textual mark as *différance* (in a sense, 'archi-writing'), that is, as meaning infinitely deferred:

the textual mark calls attention to its own resistance to intelligibility. In conjunction, Derrida experimented for a while with various radical writing techniques. In the opinion of some of his hostile, analytically inclined critics, such writing brought him and his way of philosophizing into disrepute. Other more sympathetic critics also argued against what appears to be some sort of performative contradiction which is patently involved in philosophizing critically while leveling the distinction between philosophy and **literature** at the same time. Nonetheless, it is noteworthy that these deconstructive writing experiments – for example, his work *Glas* – actually had a significant impact on the practice of postmodern **architecture** in recent decades, most notably on the deconstructivist designs of the American architect Peter Eisenman.

See **culture; metaphor; Nietzsche; text**

Further reading: Brunette and Wills 1994; Norris 1987

Dewey, John (1859–1952): American philosopher, who was a leading figure in American Pragmatism. Dewey distinguished himself from traditional aesthetic theories by decisively rejecting the compartmentalization of art and the aesthetic into a special realm set apart from ordinary life. His aesthetic theory is unique in its bold attempt to go against the grain of such standard distinctions in aesthetics as between form and content, intrinsic and extrinsic **value,** fine art and **ornamentation,** and so forth. At the core of Dewey's philosophy we find the concept of experience. For Dewey, experience is a developmental process; it emerges out of interaction between a whole person and his environment, taken a means to some other end, or as an end in itself, sometimes even both at the same time. Dewey thought that some experiences exhibit a consummative quality: they reach a phase of felt unity, wherein the interaction between the individual and his environment culminates in a meaningful, organic closure. In such moments of heightened unified awareness, both the experience and its object become aesthetic. In his seminal work in aesthetics, *Art and Experience* (1934), Dewey expounded art as the pre-eminent (albeit not exclusive) locus for such meaningful experiences. For Dewey, art is experience: rather than being located in a product, such as a **painting** or poem, the work of art takes place when a human being (the artist or the spectator) interacts with a product so that the outcome is an experience. He presented an **expression theory of art** in which artistic creation involves the meaningful embodiment of an **emotion** in a physical **medium**. His theory resembles that of **Collingwood** in the idea that expression is a process of clarification, hence of self-knowledge, and also in the idea that **understanding** art is an ongoing process of **communication** between the artwork and its audience, as the audience engages in recreating the artist's experience. But Dewey differs in underscoring the physical recalcitrance of the medium as an essential part of the process of expression.

See **education, aesthetic; experience, aesthetic; Beardsley**

Further reading: Dewey 1959

Dickie, George (1926–): Contemporary American philosopher of art working mainly in analytic aesthetics and history of aesthetics. Dickie is highly critical of traditional aesthetic theories that wish to allocate a distinct aesthetic realm, whether in **experience, perception,** mental faculties or attitudes. He argued against the notion of **disinterestedness** on the grounds that it fails to specify a mode of attention, and hence cannot play the central role destined for it by so many aesthetic theories. He is also highly critical of the employment of **Wittgenstein's** notion of **family resemblance** on the grounds of its being an inoperable method for identifying art, since everything resembles everything else in some respect. Dickie's controversial answer to both these concerns is his **institutional theory of art,** which has become one of the most important contributions to the contemporary debate concerning the **definition of art.** While the institutional theory of art is purely classificatory, Dickie also holds an instrumentalist view of art evaluation, arguing that a work of art is valuable when it is an instrumental source of a valuable experience.

See **anti-essentialism; artworld; attitude, aesthetic; value**

Further reading: Dickie 1974, 1984 and 1988

Dionysus see **Apollonian/Dionysian distinction**

disinterestedness: A term often used to characterize the **aesthetic attitude** and distinguish it sharply from our ordinary affective and cognitive attitudes toward things in our environment. A disinterested subject has no interest in the contemplated object, other than the contemplation itself. While the idea of disinterestedness originated in the early eighteenth century in the works of British **taste theories,** it was brought into lasting theoretical prominence by **Kant.** According to Kant, an object is beautiful if we take **pleasure** in it while being free from any kind of desire, aim, purpose, or any social, moral or intellectual consideration, even free from any concern regarding the very existence of the object. Kant maintained that disinterested contemplation of the object is based only on the free play between **imagination** and **understanding** and on the a priori principle of purposiveness. Thus, for Kant, disinterestedness is the hallmark of **aesthetic autonomy.** It is a subjective criterion for the judgment of **beauty**, but it is also objective in the sense that it is a logically necessary, universally applicable condition for making a judgment of taste. **Schopenhauer** carried the idea of disinterestedness to a metaphysically extravagant extreme by construing it as refuge – albeit transitory – from the worldly manifestations of the metaphysical will. Contemporary treatments of disinterestedness retain the idea that the **aesthetic experience** is characterized by a **psychological** distance from the object perceived. We are interested in the object for its own sake. However, this stance has been criticized, most notably by **Dickie**, for overemphasizing a triviality: aesthetic experience requires attention to be paid, hence disinterestedness is tantamount merely to the psychological state of focused attention without distraction; it is not a distinctly different, *sui generis* state of mind, which is somehow uniquely aesthetic.

See **aestheticism; museum**

Further reading: Dickie 1964; Fenner 1996; Guyer 1996; Kant 1952; Stolniz 1961

E

education, aesthetic: The term can be used to refer particularly to **Schiller's** contribution to the history of aesthetics. In a more general sense, aesthetic education can be related to the part that philosophy in general has traditionally played in the education of humankind. In this sense, aesthetic education is the cultivation of certain desired human sensibilities, intellectual capacities, and morally constitutive experiences, to a large extent through creating and appreciating works of art, but also through the **aesthetic appreciation** of nature. Aesthetic education as this sort of philosophical tending of the soul or human character has a long and venerable history in Western culture, which predates the modern conception of the aesthetic. It began with **Plato** and **Aristotle,** who attached great importance to the impact of the arts on the soul and its use in **political** life, and culminated in the twentieth century in the influential work of **Dewey,** who argued for the extraordinary significance of art and **aesthetic experience** as an articulation of the development of human life.

See **emotions; environmental aesthetics; ethics; romanticism; truth**

Further reading: Dewey 1959; Eaton 1989; Read 1958

emotions: It is customary to distinguish between **emotions** and other affective states, such as feelings, moods, and desires. The definition of the former includes also cognitive components, such as beliefs, while the latter are defined solely in terms of their experiential aspect. Emotions also involve distinct physiognomy, embodied often in very subtle ways in bodily response, tone of voice, choice of words, and so on. Emotions are ubiquitous in our experience of art. When a certain emotion is conceptually related to the artwork itself (it may also be related by proxy to the artist), ascribed to the work as an **aesthetic property,** then the issue at hand is **expression.** When the emotion is conceptually related to the audience, then the issue at hand is the emotional response to art. Often the latter issue is also a subject matter for empirical studies in the **psychology** of art. Emotions are also indispensable for any complete account of the performing artist, in particular when emotional identification is suggested. In the philosophy of **theater** this is particularly related to the **paradox of acting.** Three other paradoxes that involve the emotions are the **paradox of fiction,** the **paradox of suspense,** and the **paradox of**

tragedy. The first concerns feeling some emotion toward a fictional character while knowing that it does not exist; the second concerns a conflict between suspense and certainty; the third concerns the conflict between experiencing **pleasure** in response to suffering or pain. Since emotions are intentional states of mind, pure instrumental **music**, devoid of any poetic or dramatic **narrative**, raises a particularly thorny difficulty with regards to emotional response. This is due to its **abstract** nature: how can music elicit emotion and what is its proper object of such emotional response? This remains one of the most controversial topics in contemporary analytic philosophy of music.

See **arousalism; catharsis; expression theory of art; fiction; imagination; Langer; make-believe theory; persona theory; sublime**

Further reading: Ben-Ze'ev 2001; Hjort and Laver 1997; Robinson 2005

emotivism: In aesthetics this is the anti-realist view (also known as 'expressivism') that **aesthetic judgments** and evaluations express and arose **emotions** or attitudes, not beliefs. They do not assert something **true** or false. To appreciate **beauty** or other **aesthetic properties** is merely to respond emotionally, and so aesthetic emotivism is diametrically opposed to **aesthetic cognitivism**. At the core of this position there is the contention, which goes back to **Hume**, that there is an essentially **subjective** element in the evaluation of artworks. However, there is an initial implausibility in emotivism insofar as we wish to maintain that evaluations of art must involve some reference to an object and its properties, hence that it necessarily goes beyond mere **expression** of personal feeling. For a while, aesthetic emotivism was heralded in the twentieth century by the Logical Positivists. For instance, their theory **metaphor** hinged upon the idea that word combinations which are metaphoric gain emotive meaning while losing their cognitive, descriptive meaning.

See **empiricism; value**

Further reading: Kivy 1992

empirical aesthetics see **psychology**

empiricism: As a general doctrine in **epistemology**, empiricism maintains that all knowledge is ultimately based on experience. Modes of experience may be purely sensory, or else extended to include **aesthetic experience** among other things. Empiricist theories may differ substantially with regards to the structure of experience – generally construed in terms of something which seems to be presented to the mind – or even to the kinds of phenomena brought together under that concept, although at least some appeal to sense experience remains common. This is most evident in the way classical empiricism informed **taste theories** in the eighteenth century. The distinctly empiricist origins of analytic philosophy in general may account for the fact that analytic aesthetic has retained a considerable interest, albeit critical, in the concept of aesthetic experience and its cognates even in spite of such powerful wholesale rejections as the **institutional theory of art,** for example. Indeed contemporary analytic aesthetics preserves the term 'aesthetic empiricism' for theories which explicitly relate the aesthetic **value** of a work of art exclusively to its intrinsic **properties;** that is, the aesthetic value of a work of art depends on the value of the experience, which it affords, when we perceive it correctly. Still this reductive conception of art seems to be at odds with much late modern art. Thus at the center of the current debate we typically find ready-mades and

other instances of **conceptual art,** which patently undercut the attempt to construe them in experiential terms,
and, for the same reason, cases of fakes and **forgeries.**

See **cognitivism, aesthetic; judgment, aesthetic; perception**

Further reading: Budd 1995; Sharpe 2000

end of art thesis: The idea that the essence of art consists in a historical progress towards philosophical
self-understanding. The attainment of such a form of
self-understanding means that a certain art historical **narrative** has been brought to an end. The thesis originated
in the work of **Hegel,** who announced the end of art as a
significant vehicle of the Spirit. Hegel defined art as the
purely sensuous appearance of the Spirit to itself, and he
argued that upon the transition from the **classical** to the
romantic epoch, the task of promoting the Spirit's self-
consciousness, which had been fully realized by Greek
art, has been effectively overtaken by the philosophy
of art. Hence art ends, by definition, upon its absorp-
tion into philosophy. While Hegel's position may seem
empirically dubious in light of later artistic achievements
in European culture, it may still prove more difficult to
dismiss the idea that art may have become dispensable,
either as a mere entertainment or else as a second-hand
vehicle of serious ideas, which are better expressed by
philosophy or religion. The end of art thesis was carried
over into twentieth-century continental philosophy in
direct response to Hegel's aesthetics, most notably by
Heidegger, who linked, on **ontological** grounds, the rise
of aesthetics – namely, the abstract study of the objects
of sensuous apprehension – to the dying of art, and
also by **Marcuse,** whose **Marxist** bend led him to envi-
sion the end of art in terms of a utopist fulfillment of
the role of art as social reality. This theme appears also

in the work of **Benjamin**, who argued that mechanical reproduction has transformed our mode of reception of artistic objects in a way that renders it impossible for us to conceive artworks traditionally – as bearers of an 'aura' of ontological uniqueness. In analytic aesthetics, **Danto** picked up Hegel's lead, arguing that twentieth-century art – in particular, certain works of pop art and various other forms of **conceptual art** – has witnessed a completion of a particular art historical narrative: the attainment of philosophical knowledge of its own essence. According to Danto, a work of art is embedded in a particular context of history and theory, and can be identified and appreciated as such only through their proper location within this theoretical context. Thus, the history of art is a history of conceptual self-reflection and self-realization, whose apex is an 'irradiation' of the work of art by theoretical consciousness. In contemporary, 'post-historical' art, the essence of art – that is, its quest for self-comprehension – has been exposed, theory overpowers **artifactuality** and anything can become art; henceforth there is no meaning to historical progress in art. Contrary to Hegel, Danto's approach is empirical as he believes that the end of art was vividly manifested by Andy Warhol's *Brillo Box* in 1962.

See **autonomy, aesthetic; avant-garde**

Further reading: Danto 1986; Hegel 1975

environmental aesthetics: A recently established specialized sub-field of aesthetics, partly propelled by the growing public concern for the environment. Environmental aesthetics is typically interdisciplinary, incorporating input from **psychology, anthropology, architecture**, and **science** (ecology) among other fields of knowledge. Environmental aesthetics posits nature itself, or the environment, as a proper object of **aesthetic appreciation**.

The sheer boundlessness of nature as an **aesthetic object** and the fact that the appreciator is situated within it require the reorientation of basic aesthetic categories, including a rejection of the traditional splicing of natural **beauty** with the picturesque (the painterly vision of beauty), a particular stress on experience as aesthetic **value**, an understanding of creation as detached from **artifactuality**, and the re-introduction of the **sublime** in relation to awe-inspiring natural processes. Two opposing views have been introduced: (1) **cognitivism**, which emphasizes the centrality of knowledge (scientific and other) to the aesthetic appreciation of nature; and (2) non-cognitivism, which emphasizes the immersive, emotionally engaging nature of the aesthetic appreciation of nature.

See **arousalism; emotions; emotivism**

Further reading: Berleant 1992; Budd 2002; Carlson 2000

epistemology: The study of the nature, sources, extent, and limits of knowledge (from the Greek *epistēmē* meaning knowledge) has been at the core of philosophy since antiquity. Traditionally, epistemology centers primarily on knowledge of facts, or propositional knowledge, although varieties of non-propositional knowledge, such as being acquainted with someone and possessing a skill, are also acknowledged. Knowledge is generally considered to be a species of belief, which is both true and warranted. While accounts of the property of warrant may vary considerably, it is commonly agreed that it is diametrically opposed to the idea of cognitive luck. That is, knowledge is true belief, but not mere true belief. The main issue in aesthetics pertaining to the concept of knowledge, thus construed, concerns the status of art as conduit to knowledge. This concern has emerged already in ancient Greek philosophy and marks a sharp disagreement between **Plato's** contention that art affords only an illusion of knowledge and **Aristotle's** contention that art is cognitively valuable and that this is part of its **value** as art. This original chasm, which is patently related to the problem of **truth** in art, still frames the current debate within Anglo-American aesthetics whether art affords us any propositional knowledge which is non-trivial and how this may relate to the notion of aesthetic value. Skepticism about such matters entails one or more of the following contentions: (1) works of art cannot give us much more than trivial truths; (2) such truths are not warranted and may be nothing more than a matter of cognitive luck; (3) the methods and purposes of art are not geared toward rational inquiry of reality; (4) whether or not a work of art affords knowledge is irrelevant to its aesthetic value. Consequently, art ought to be severed from the pretense of inquiry and from its claims of knowledge. Rebutting these contentions requires a fully fledged defense of **aesthetic cognitivism**. It is noteworthy that contemporary analytic aesthetics is also regularly concerned not only with this general problem but also with specific epistemological problems which are indigenous to the perceptual arts – for instance, the **innocent eye, photographic transparency,** the **seeing-as/seeing-in distinction,** and so on. Another general concern is the conceptual subordination of aesthetics as a field of philosophic inquiry to epistemology. Once again this concern has historical roots. At its very inception of aesthetics as an independent field of philosophy in the eighteenth century, **Baumgarten** envisioned it as the study of how the various mental contents pertaining to the fine arts enter at a foundational level into the very structure of knowledge. While this sweeping pronouncement of the task of aesthetics has lost its verve in the aftermath of

Kant, the idea that aesthetics somehow partakes in our conceptual inquiry into knowledge endured well into the second half of the twentieth century. Perhaps the most spectacular attempt to reintegrate aesthetics into epistemology is found in the work of **Goodman**. Finally it is noteworthy that, under the influence of **postmodernism**, continental aesthetics has grown particularly inimical to the close tie between aesthetic and epistemological considerations.

See **empiricism; mimesis; perception; science**

Further reading: Goodman 1976; Kieran and Lopes 2006

essentialism: The metaphysical doctrine that objects have essences and that their properties are not on a par **ontologically;** some of them are essential, whereas others are merely accidental. The essential properties are those which make the object what it is. Hence in order to give a real definition of the object, we need to give an account of its essential properties. Essentialism has been a part of Western metaphysical tradition since antiquity. While all metaphysicians accept the essential / accidental distinction in one form or another, they tend to disagree as to what 'essential' means precisely. With the exception of certain accounts of **beauty** in terms of essence (for example, **Plato**), the application of the essentialist doctrine to aesthetics remained limited for the most part to a specific concern: the **definition of art**. Early essentialist explications of the nature of art – from Plato and **Hegel** to **Tolstoy, Bell, Croce** and **Collingwood** – assumed that there must be some common nature or quality present in all art. Such attempts invariably failed because they hinged upon a property that not all works of art possess or else is not exclusive to works of art. In the aftermath of the empiricist attack on essentialism in the eighteenth century and its general endorsement by the twentieth-century analytic tradition, contemporary aesthetics has grown inimical to essentialist definitions of art to the point that by the second half of the twentieth-century **anti-essentialism** became almost common wisdom. It is noteworthy that **Danto** conspicuously downplayed **Wittgenstein's** anti-essentialist thrust when he constructed his influential essentialist theory of art. It is also noteworthy that the most viable contemporary form of essentialism is based on formal elaborations of Leibniz's idea that necessity is truth in all possible worlds, which were presented in the 1950s and 1960s by logicians like Saul Kripke, Jaakko Hintikka and Richard Montague. However, these ideas have had no effect on contemporary aesthetics as yet.

See **Aristotle; Bell; expression theory of art; functionalism; modern system of the arts; representation theory of art; structuralism**

Further reading: Davies 1991; Diffey 1973

ethicism see **moralism**

ethics: The relation of ethics to aesthetics consists of at least three distinct main tiers: (1) the relation between moral and aesthetic **values**; (2) the relation between moral and aesthetic **judgments**; and (3) the moral rights of artworks. The first tier consists of normative or evaluative issues such as whether a work of art can be morally bad, whether and how morally suspect works of art corrupt their audience or otherwise may cause harm to individuals or to the society, and in descriptive or analytic issues such as the very possibility of a relation between moral value and aesthetic value, whether and under which conditions an ethical flaw in works of art may also be aesthetic flaws, and what justifies the production and exhibition of immoral art. Under one guise or another, these issues have been debated since **Plato** until the present day. A denial of any relation between moral and aesthetic values may take the form of **autonomism**, which would justify morally suspect artworks on formalist grounds, or of **experimentalism**, which would opt for pragmatist grounds. The assertion of an essential link between moral and aesthetic values amounts to **moralism**. In its strictest form, moralism would even entail the claim that 'immoral art' is not art at all. The discussion concerning the relation between moral judgment and aesthetic judgment is typical to eighteenth-century aesthetics. The underlying premise here was that there must be a conceptual link or structural similarities between our judgments of the good and our judgment of the beautiful. Again, the idea of a conceptual kinship between the forms of the good, the perfect and the beautiful originated in Plato's theory of forms and preceded the rationalist position on the matter in early modern philosophy. Among **empiricist** philosophers, **Hume**, for example, derived his **taste theory** from his general account of morals in terms of feelings of approval or disproval, which occur spontaneously in anyone who makes customary imaginative associations. This discourse reached its apex in **Kant's** idea that the beautiful is the symbol of the morally good. The discussion concerning the moral rights of artworks originated in the second half of the twentieth century in conjunction with the growing general tendency in ethics to consider a vartiety of entities other than persons, including inanimate objects, as bearers of putative rights. The debate concerning artworks has been marred right at the outset by a difficulty in locating the rights in the artifacts themselves, rather than in the artists, who created them, or in the cultural community, which they inhabit. It is hard to conceive how one may develop an argument for the right of an artwork not to be injured or to suffer pain in any way, which would be neither metaphorical nor too inclusive to pertain to art specifically.

See **Aristotle; beauty; censorship; essentialism; formalism; law; pornography; Tolstoy**

Further reading: Gaut 2007

existentialism: A movement in continental philosophy, which rose to prominence in the aftermath of the Second World War, especially in France. No less a style of philosophizing than a body of philosophical doctrines, existentialism emphasizes the human experience of being in the world, often by examining various aspects of confrontation between human life and world. **Phenomenology** furnishes existentialism with adequate methodology for probing into human existence, in particular into such perennial themes as freedom, decision, and responsibility, as well as into related feelings of finitude, despair, guilt, and alienation, which have also become identified with existentialist art. Existentialist thinkers typically examine works of art as embodiments of human experiences in concrete life experiences, yet not in any **psychological**, causal sense, which they typically reject.

See **Heidegger; Nietzsche; Sartre; tragedy**

Further reading: Macquarrie 1972

experience, aesthetic: The idea that the perceptual experience and the state of mind appropriate to **aesthetic objects** is *sui generis* – introspectively identifiable, **phenomenologically** distinct, and **epistemologically** valuable – can be traced back most straightforwardly to **Kant**, who characterized aesthetic experience in terms of pleasurable **disinterestedness** and identified it as the determining ground of **aesthetic judgment**. The idea of aesthetic experience was theoretically employed at various times (1) to qualify the aesthetic domain phenomenologically by construing aesthetic experience as an essentially gratifying state of focused, reflexive attention, which is affectively absorbing, hence standing out from the ordinary flow of experiences; (2) to explain aesthetic **value** by construing it **functionally** as the volume or intensity of aesthetic experience; (3) to support **aesthetic cognitivism** by construing aesthetic experience as a transforming moment, wherein it provides extraordinary knowledge of the object experienced (for example, **Schopenhauer** contended that aesthetic experience gives us epistemic access to the object's form), or else, less metaphysically flamboyant, as a kind of non-inferential way of coming to know the object; (4) to identify and individuate artworks, conceived as the primary loci for aesthetic experience, hence to propagate an essentialist **definition of art**. These theoretical aspects of aesthetic experience have met with sustained criticism across the analytic-continental divide in twentieth-century aesthetics. The phenomenological aspect was criticized, most notably by **Dickie**, for being **ontologically** superfluous and for placing unwarranted emphasis on its purported unity or its purported **pleasurable** affective content. Consequently, the construal of aesthetic **value** as a function of aesthetic experience seems also unwarranted, since it patently fails to explain the aesthetic value of artworks which either do not elicit a phenomenologically unique experience at all (for example, **conceptual art**) or else elicit negative **emotions**, such as disgust or horror. The phenomenological immediacy of aesthetic experienced was challenged by **Gadamer**, who contended that aesthetic experience is not phenomenologically encapsulated, a timeless presence, but rather unifies the aesthetic object through a process of **understanding**. The definition of art in terms of aesthetic experience is open to the standard arguments against **essentialism**. Furthermore, unchecked, it may yield the theoretically dubious result – as in **Dewey's** attempt to bring art and life together – of re-categorizing all things aesthetic, including people and sunsets, as works of art. **Benjamin** argued that in the advent of the mechanical reproduction of art, aesthetic experience can no longer be used to define and demarcate the realm of (high) art. The purported centrality of the idea of aesthetic experience in aesthetic theory has generally become a distinct watershed between the analytic and the continental traditions in twentieth-century aesthetics. While the latter remains generally receptive to this idea (in particular in the field of **phenomenology**), the latter has grown largely inimical to it.

See **aestheticism; attitude, aesthetic; autonomy, aesthetic; Beardsley; Bell; concepts, aesthetic; environmental aesthetics**

Further reading: Beardsley 1982; Dewey 1959; Dickie 1974; Dufrenne 1973; Ingarden 1961; Schusterman 1997; Schusterman and Tomlin 2008

experimentalism: This is the view that learning is a process of experimental growth and that knowledge is achieved by reconstructing and reorganizing our experiences. In the context of art and morality, experimentalism is the view that **ethically** suspect works of art can still be both aesthetically and **epistemologically** rewarding. Insofar as experimentalism accepts that works of art can be morally flawed and denies that this reduces their value in any way, experimentalism coincides with moderate **autonomism**. Yet the experimentalist would hold in addition that works of art are means for the discovery of new modes of life and for the broadening of our aesthetic experience. This implies that morally provocative art is necessary for mental enrichment and that, short of the prevention of immediate harm to other people, **censorship** is detrimental to our need to learn. In other words, the prospects of knowledge should override the established norms of moral **education**. In this sense, experimentalism is a version of moderate immoralism, which states that an ethical flaw might be of aesthetic **value** in certain contexts. In practical terms, the experimentalist would prefer hurting the feelings of some over undermining the freedom of **expression**. However, while the boundaries of acceptable harm to others remain a moot issue, experimentalism remains on a slippery slope.

See **moralism; pornography**

Further reading: Dewey 1959

expression: In antiquity, expression in art was covered by the notion of **mimesis**. For instance, **Plato** believed that a certain musical mode represents a certain character trait. This conceptual overlap between expression and **representation** continued well into the formation of the **modern system of the arts**. Contemporary use of the term is much more restrictive. Expression in art comprises the kind of qualities and properties that we normally apply only to human beings: joyfulness, melancholy, courage, dreaminess, and so on. When expression is involved, we ascribe anthropomorphic **aesthetic properties** to the artwork. However, it is important to note the difference between expression and expressiveness. Expression presupposes a causal relation between the state of mind of the artist while creating the work and its final embodiment in the work. Expression is commonly understood precisely as the outward manifestation of such purported state of mind. By contrast, expressiveness inheres in the form of the artwork itself. Theories of expressiveness need to explain how the purported state of mind or **emotion** can impinge itself onto the work. **Langer,** for example, offered a symbolic theory to explain that. Common types of theories of expression include: (1) **arousalism,** (for example, **Tolstoy**) which explains expression in terms of a capacity of the work to arouse the appropriate emotions in the audience; (2) clarification theories (for example, **Croce, Collingwood** and **Dewey**), which explain expression in relation to artists' work on their **medium**; and (3) semantic theories, such as **Goodman's** theory of expression as **metaphoric** exemplification.

See **emotivism; expression theory of art; persona theory**

Further reading: Tormey 1971

expression theory of art: A generic name for **essentialist** theories of art, which hinge upon the **definition of art** as the **expression** of the artist's **emotions,** feelings and thoughts. According to such a theory, expression is a necessary condition for the kind of practices that we call art. Such theories are expressly **intentionalist**: the **meaning** of the artwork depends solely on what the artist presumably felt while creating his work. For that reason, such theories conceive art as a form of **communication,** wherein the artist communicates something of his inner world of experience by means of an artistic **medium** to the purported audience. Thus it must be assumed that the artist felt something while creating his work, and that this emotion was intentionally worked out, elaborated and clarified in the medium in order to make it manifest. Expression theories usually differ from one another **ontologically** by the way the artistic medium is defined (for example, mental, as in **Croce,** or physical as in **Tolstoy**), and by the way they construe expression (for example, in terms of clarification, as in **Collingwood**, or in terms of isomorphism, as in **Langer**). Expression theories enjoy some advantage over **representation theories of art**. First, historically speaking, they fit better with the **romanticist** move in the nineteenth century away from the imitation of nature toward self-expression, as well as with the styles of early **modernism** in art. Second, they seem to offer a better account of the **value** of art for us: the idea of art as expression allows art to be an instrument for searching the soul. Still expression theories have met with criticism for being too exclusive, leaving out other things that are art, but do not involve expression (for example, cases of **ornamentation**). Furthermore, expression theories tend to place unreasonable emphasis on assumptions concerning the **psychology** and biography of the artist. Simply put, we usually do not know whether the work has actually been produced in order to express something in particular, and sometimes the work is clearly expressive but there is no evidence of any intention on the part of the artist to express anything in particular. On other occasions – for example, when we encounter ready-mades or works that are based on **chance** operations – we happen to know that expression was not intended.

See **arousalism; conceptual art; Dewey**

Further reading: Collingwood 1964; Croce 1995; Dewey 1959; Langer 1953; Tolstoy 1960

F

family-resemblance: A term associated with **Wittgenstein's** later philosophical period. Wittgenstein maintains that some concepts – most notably, the concept of a game, and ultimately, **language** itself – are not applicable by virtue of a set of necessary and sufficient conditions. When we try to see what might be common to all games, for instance, we realize that just like a family, whose members resemble one another in many different ways, all the different things, which we call 'games', are united by an entire network of criss-crossing, overlapping similarities. The notion of family-resemblance is crucial to Wittgenstein's attack on **essentialism**. It has been utilized by **anti-essentialist** aestheticians during the second half of the twentieth century, who argued that essentialist **definitions of art** are bound to fail because art is a family-resemblance or an open concept, hence there can be no analytic definition for art.

See **Dickie; language-game; Ziff**

Further reading: Wittgenstein 2001

feminist aesthetics see **gendered aesthetics**

fiction: The word 'fiction' comes from the Latin verb *fingere*, which means to fashion or form. It is usually used to denote both the activity of inventive imagining, or the products of such an activity: imaginative **narratives** or objects (characters, places, and events). Fiction is normally contrasted with reality: engaging with a fictional world involves recognizing that its denizens have been excluded from the realm of actuality. One of the thorniest problems concerning fiction is the unsettled issue of the **ontological** status of fictional entities: what might the name 'Anna Karenina', for example, stand for? Classic strategies in analytic philosophy include construing such names as descriptions in disguise, or else as denoting a special, non-existing kind of objects. Both strategies typically generate a host of conceptual difficulties. This in itself is not a problem in aesthetics.

However, considering the fact that the representational artworks typically present some mixture of reality and fiction, understanding the relation between such different elements within a given artwork (literary or visual), and the relation of fictional entities to the actual world, including our very actual emotional responses to such entities remain an ongoing concern for any theory of artistic fiction. Emotional response to fiction gives rise to the **paradox of fiction**: feeling some **emotion** toward a fictional character while knowing that it does not exist. Another broad concern is the problem of distinguishing fictional narratives from non-fictional narratives. It is a testament to the power of fiction that fictional narratives sustain verisimilitude. This is precisely how **realism** works in **literature**: the **language** itself does not disclose the fictional status of the **text**. One strategy for distinguishing fictional from non-fictional narrative is to embrace some form of **intentionalism,** an appeal to the author's intention in fashioning the narrative in a certain way. An alternative influential suggestion comes from the **make-believe theory**: fictionality depends on the function of things like characters, places, and events as props for games of make-believe. Fiction is also often contrasted with **truth,** but this should be carefully qualified. For one, fiction is not mere falsehood (like an error). Furthermore, **aesthetic cognitivism** holds that precisely owing to the typical mélange of the imaginary and the real in any given work of fiction, it is also related to the actual world cognitively as a source for some factual information, as well as a means for re-categorizing or re-orienting our **understanding** of things, and for developing our moral sensibility.

See **epistemology; ethics; imagination; ontology**

Further reading: Currie 1990; Lamarque 1996; Walton 1990

film: Film is distinctly a **hybrid art form:** in the most standard cases it appears to be a successful marriage of **photography** and **theater** (which is a hybrid art form in its own right). However, this straightforward characterization generates some of the fundamental problems of the philosophy of film. First and foremost, the sheer hybridity and heterogeneity of film raises the question whether it is a form of art in itself, whether it has an essence. One classic approach was 'technological' **essentialism,** arguing that film is essentially different from a mere mechanical reproduction of reality (or theater) in its employment of distinct technical devices (close-ups, flashbacks, and various other editing techniques), which set the cinematic **narrative** apart. For instance, **Arnheim** argued that, very much like in **abstract** art, the unique technical features of the **medium** contribute to artistic **expression,** hence setting film apart from mere reproduction of reality. An alternative approach was to argue that the photographic component of film makes this art realist in a uniquely **epistemological** sense that sets it apart from **painting,** for instance. However, it has been argued that understanding film **realism** in terms of **photographic transparency** denies film of its status as a representational art, demoting it in effect to a mere reproductive craft. Finally, the collaborative effort, which is indigenous to filmmaking, raises the problem of authorship: whether the cinematographic work of art can be related to a single person, to wit, an author, in a way similar to works of **literature.** Answering in the affirmative, the **auteur theory** became influential for a while, promoting the careers of some film directors, but it remained challenged by contemporary practices in filmmaking.

See **Benjamin; fiction; illusion; medium; narrative; paradox of fiction; paradox of suspense**

Further reading: Arnheim 1964; Bazin 1967; Carroll 1996; Cavell 1979

forgery: Artistic forgery raises not only **ethical** issues, but also some weighty aesthetic issues. Artistic forgeries can be either a fake, that is, a seemingly indistinguishable duplicate of an original; or else a non-faked forgery, that is, an original, successfully emulating the recognizable **style** of a certain artist and consequently passing as an original of that artist. As a matter of fact, the latter case is more common than the former. The **autographic art/ allographic art distinction** affords a neat division between the various arts: while non-faked forgeries can occur in all the arts, only autographic arts can have fakes. In all cases, the important feature is the fact that the work's history of production has deliberately been misrepresented. Artistic forgery raises a difficulty for the view that aesthetic **value** depends on appearance alone, especially regarding fakes. As it happens, when a forgery is exposed, we tend to reject or devalue the work aesthetically, although in principle nothing in its appearance has changed. The only change was in our awareness of its true history of production. **Goodman** tried to solve this difficulty by arguing that even in the case of seemingly indistinguishable works, practice makes perfect. That is, knowing that one is a fake is aesthetically relevant since it prompts us to learn to see subtle differences eventually. And the more we know, the more we see.

See **aspect-perception; authenticity; *is* of artistic identification; ontology; pastiche; perception; properties, aesthetic**

Further reading: Dutton 1983

formalism: The thesis that: (1) any work of art has a formal aspect, which is commonly understood as the

arrangement of the work's various elements or their relation to one another; (2) the aesthetic **value** of the work is
determined solely by that form; and (3) the value of the
work is independent of other 'external' aspects of the
work, such as reference or utility. The notion of form
has had a distinguished, extensive, and diverse career in
the great metaphysical systems of Western philosophy.
Traditionally, form has been understood as the vehicle
of knowledge. That is, to know a thing is to comprehend
its form. Typically, theories of art, which in some sense
relate **aesthetic experience** to knowledge, give primacy to
form over other aspects of the work of art. This is clearly
the case in the **mimetic** theory of art as found in **Plato** and
Aristotle, for instance, but also in **Schopenhauer's** idea
that aesthetic experience pertaining to representations
in the visual arts is mediated by the forms of the objects
depicted, or in **Bell's** notion of **significant form**. As these
varied examples attest, the **ontological** status of artistic
form is a moot issue. The crucial question is whether form
is separable from the work, and hence may be shared in
principle with another work (that is, other elements), or
whether it consists in the elements as actually organized
in the work. The former Platonist option reifies form. The
latter renders form an indefinable property, as seen in
Bell's formalism, for example. Arguably, another important source for formalism is found in **Kant's** treatment of
the judgment of **beauty** in terms of formal purposiveness
and **disinterestedness**, which highlights the primacy of
pure form as harbinger of the aesthetic. The formalist
motivation to preserve the autonomy of aesthetic value
by insulating aesthetic value from aspects of the work of
art which bear extra-aesthetic reference – such as **expression, representation** or **function** – often involves rendering such aspects aesthetically irrelevant. For example,
Bell opposed form to pictorial content in **painting**, while

Hanslick opposed form to expression in music. However, this can be seen as a fallacious move: from the claim that a certain extra-aesthetic aspect of a work of art is not essential for aesthetic value, it does not necessarily follow that this aspect is aesthetically irrelevant.

See **autonomy, aesthetic; essentialism; Greenberg; properties, aesthetic**

Further reading: Bell 1958; Hanslick 1986; Isenberg 1973; Wollheim 2001

Frankfurt School: An interdisciplinary group of intellectuals associated with the Institute for Social Research, which was founded in Frankfurt in 1923, and later re-established in New York when the Nazi regime came to power in Germany. Among the leading figures of the Frankfurt School were social scientist Max Horkheimer, philosophers **Theodor Adorno** and **Herbert Marcuse**, psychologist Erich Fromm, and literary critic **Walter Benjamin**. Central to the Frankfurt School was the notion of a critical theory: a sophisticated attempt to carry on Karl Marx's project of transforming moral philosophy into social and political critique, linking theory and practice. The goal was to empower one toward self-emancipation from socially oppressive circumstances, that is, to strive toward rational society. Another common tenet in the Frankfurt School was the attempt to utilize some of **Freud's** analytic principles in the construal of a social psychology meant to link the individual person with his macro-social and macro-economic circumstances. In their aesthetic thinking, Adorno and Benjamin were in disagreement about the relation of art to the social realm, in particular to the instrumental domination of nature in the capitalist society. Adorno adhered to the notion of autonomous art standing against society as a critique, while Benjamin championed the immersion of new forms of art in technology and the consequent loss of the artifact's erstwhile singularity.

See **artifactuality; autonomy, aesthetic; culture; Marxism; modernism; politics; psychoanalysis; psychology; sociology**

Further reading: Jay 1973

Freud, Sigmund (1856–1939): Austrian neurologist, founder of **psychoanalysis**. He is particularly known for characterizing the human psyche in terms of a dynamic relation, or interplay between three distinct components: an unconscious repository of primal instinctual drives ('id'); a conscious part ('ego'), which strives to reconcile the demands of the 'id' with the external situation of the world; and its relatively independent counterpart ('superego'), which internalizes social and moral controls over the ego's functioning, primarily by means of parental influence. The dynamics of the superego and the id in Freud's theory is reminiscent of the **Apollonian/ Dionysian distinction** found in **Nietzsche**. Freud's view of art as therapeutically expressive behavior is reminiscent of **Aristotle's** theory of **catharsis**. Freud believed that since all the achievements of art come from the unconscious – the true psychic reality – art exemplifies the general psychoanalytic aim to penetrate through illusionary appearance into a hidden, repressed **truth**. Freud's ideas on art and artists had a tremendous, long-lasting influence on both popular and scholarly views on artistic creation and on **culture**.

See **Frankfurt School; Gombrich; Marcuse; Wollheim**
Further reading: Freud 1997 and 1999

functionalism: The idea that art serves a certain function or that it is normatively defined in terms of a certain function. The function of art may be **social, political,**

psychological, metaphysical, or aesthetic, broadly conceived. In the prescriptive sense, functionalism pertains to aesthetic **value**: the degree by which an artifact serves its proper function determines its value or its standing as a work of art altogether. Thus prescriptive functionalism implies instrumentalism with regards to aesthetic value: the proper function of a work of art is instrumental for achieving aesthetic value. Functionalism is opposed to **aestheticism**, the idea that art is autonomous, created and valued for its own sake. Functionalism may also coincide with **essentialism**: the ends, which art needs to serve, may be rendered essential to the very **definition of art**. Following the lead of **Beardsley**, functionalists in the second half of the twentieth century commonly maintain that the function of art is to provide **aesthetic experience**, which is inherently valuable. This position often falters in the face of **conceptual art**, or other forms of art, which denounce or undercut aesthetic experience. Functionalists may then either make the unappealing move of arguing that such things are not genuine works of art, or else attempt to show that they nonetheless involve aesthetic experience. Either way, contemporary functionalists face the theoretically daunting task of specifying an experience common to all works of art.

See **autonomy, aesthetic; Marxism**
Further reading: Davies 1991

G

Gadamer, Hans-Georg (1900–2002): German philosopher, a student of **Heidegger**, who became a key figure in the development of philosophical **hermeneutics** in the twentieth century. He is most famous for his attempt to rehabilitate the notion of prejudice as the inevitable condition for **interpreting** and **understanding**, and for envisioning the idea of 'the fusion of horizons', that is, the idea that understanding an artwork requires the overcoming of variance between the **truth** claimed by the artwork and that the interpreter believes to be the truth about the matter at hand. Gadamer's emphasis on the dialogical, interrogative, indeed playful nature of understanding is found also in his notion of *Spiel* (translated as play, or game), which exemplifies some affinity with **Kant** and **Schiller**. By that notion he referred to the immersive character of our aesthetic interaction with art: we are drawn into this game, absorbed in it. This experience of art is central to Gadamer's hermeneutics. He believed that its unique structure exemplifies the experience of **truth** and can be seen as a universal characteristic of human understanding in general. Gadamer pushed against **Kant's** tradition of **disinterestedness**. He believed that **aesthetic experience** cannot be cut off from the interest that we take in what we may learn from artworks about ourselves and about our lives, and how these insights may change us.

See **experience, aesthetic; interpretation; ontology**
Further reading: Gadamer 1976, 1986 and 1997

gaze: An instance of **postmodern** union between **existentialism, phenomenology** and **psychoanalysis**, this term denotes a highly complex idea pertaining to the power one may gain over another by means of cultivating a certain way of seeing, which is patently possessive. One person's glance may cause another person aware of himself as an object for the first person, and so, generally speaking, vision becomes tensely entangled in our desire and the desire of others. Thoughts of the gaze and what gives itself to vision, as pertaining to works of art and to the history of art, have played an important role in the attempt to construe the aesthetic as a kind of ideology of voyeurism, facilitating and cultivating the privileging of certain objects, their making and their viewing, as they are plucked out of the stream of life and become 'museumized'. The notion of the gaze is also central to the critical, politically aware stance, which typifies **gendered aesthetics**, especially recent feminist critiques of aesthetic theories.

See **museum; perception; politics; pornography; representation; Sartre**

Further reading: Jay 1994; Mulvey 2009

gendered aesthetics: Under this tentative label one might lump together a number of factions or categories which have become distinct within contemporary aesthetics – both continental, especially French, and Anglo-American – at least since the 1970s, pertaining to traditionally under-represented social groups – first and foremost, feminist aesthetics, but also gay and lesbian aesthetics. At the risk of overgeneralizing (and hence of appearing intellectually recalcitrant), one could say that these factions share most, if not all, of the following characteristics to various degrees. The overall theoretical approach acknowledges the fundamental idea that art is socially embedded, showing particular allegiance to the **postmodern** rejection of 'grand **narratives**', and to the idea that the history of ideas is in the last analysis a history of power. Historically speaking, all gendered aesthetics arose out of, and remain committed to, considerations pertaining to the social and political goals of their respective social groups. The presupposition that there is an intimate connection between sexual identity and artistic **expression** is coupled with the basic idea that artistic expression is instrumental for promoting (or undermining) **political** goals. With this inevitable adherence to some form of **functionalism** and **moralism,** comes also a built-in animosity toward **formalism.** Gendered aesthetics is commonly preoccupied with the definition, examination, and evaluation of gendered art, and with the re-introduction and promotion of alternative, gendered modes of expression in art, as well as in writing about art. This is shown very clearly in the writings of such successful writers as Luce Irigaray (1932–) and Hélène Cixous (1937–), who incorporated the stylistic opacity of the French postmodern **psychoanalytic** milieu into feminist critique. Gendered critiques of aesthetic theory and art history typically offer re-reading of the history of art and the history of aesthetics, which is designed to flesh out the biased nature of such narratives and unearth alternative narratives, which have been hitherto suppressed by pervasive patriarchalism or homophobia. The notion of the **gaze** often takes center stage here. To some extent one finds also skepticism regarding the very existence of a gendered aesthetic. Finally, there is some ambivalence in gendered aesthetics regarding the **value** of **pornography.** Certain gendered works of art – for example, the homoerotic **photography** of Robert Mapplethorpe – employ well calculated pornographic imagery in order to subvert and upset the possessive gaze of its purported audience. There is an ongoing debate within gendered aesthetics whether **censorship** of pornographic images delegitimizes sexual identity.

See **culture; representation; sociology; style**

Further reading: Castle 1993; Gever, Greyson and Parmar 1993; Hein and Korsmeyer 1993

genius: In aesthetics this concept remains closely associated with its historical role in **romanticism.** The way **Kant**

characterized genius was constitutive of that historical role. According to Kant, genius is the natural capacity to produce something which we adequately judge to be beautiful, but for which no rules can be given. Nor can the artist-genius himself explain how he creates. The genius person is endowed with exceptional creative powers, representing in a sense an altogether different order of human being. This characterization is eminently clear, for instance, in the writing of **Schopenhauer**, who maintained that the artist has an extraordinary capacity for **perception,** which is abnormally powerful and able to function in greater isolation from the will. In the twentieth century the romantic concept of genius has fallen into disrepute both in analytic aesthetics and in continental aesthetics.

See **beauty; Schiller**

Further reading: Kant 1952; Murray 1989

Gesamtkunstwerk: A term in German, often translated as 'total work of art' or 'unified work of art', which is chiefly associated with **Wagner's** thesis concerning the aesthetic nature and social **function** of the work of art of the future. The Gesamtkunstwerk is an ideal art form unifying **music,** poetry, and **painting** within the framework of drama. The idea did not originate with Wagner. Earlier **romantic** thinkers glorified the possible union of artistic media, so when Wagner wrote his essay 'The Artwork of the Future' in 1849, the idea of a total work of art was already something of a cliché. Wagner's utopian vision of the work of art of the future construed the total work of art as a historical inevitability. Harking back to the ancient unification of the arts in Greek drama and its religious function in ancient life, he argued that the ensuing separation of the arts into distinct media and genres had diminished their expressive force and is indicative of a society which has grown fragmented and divided. Wagner maintained that the Gesamtkunstwerk is bound to reverse this state of **cultural** decline by restoring integrity by means of artistic unity. He argued dialectically against **Lessing** that the radical separation of the arts must lead eventually to **medium** encroaching and to the realization of the natural drive of the sister arts toward unity. Wagner's Gesamtkunstwerk thesis is a culmination of the doctrine of **ut pictura poesis**. Wagner's own genre of music-drama, while breaking new grounds as a **hybrid art form**, nonetheless falls short of his theoretical conception of Gesamtkunstwerk in its explicit embrace of the supremacy of the musical medium, which no doubt bears witness to the influence of **Schopenhauer's** philosophy of music on Wagner.

See **absolute music; Aristotle; modern system of the arts; religion; theater**

Further reading: Wagner 1993

Gestalt theory: Derives from the German word for 'shape' or 'structure', this influential theory in the **psychology** of **perception** advances the claim that our perceptual experience of complex objects – such as facial expressions and melodies – is something distinct from, and irreducible to, the experience of a mere sum of sensory elements. Gestalt psychologists argue for the primacy of the perception of form, which is guided by the perceptual system through principles of organization, such as symmetry, similarity, proximity, congruity, and so on. They attempt to identify and experimentally investigate 'Gestalt qualities', namely, inherently structural features of our experience, including cases of **aspect-perception**. **Arnheim** carried out the most consistent and fruitful application of the principles of Gestalt theory to the study of art, arguing that the **meaning** of a work of art consists in its visual organization.

See **phenomenology**
Further reading: Arnheim 1974

Gombrich, Ernst (1909–2001): Austrian-born historian and theoretician of art, who was active primarily in England and in the USA, known for his influential work on the **psychological** and **cultural** foundations of the history of artistic **style**. In his celebrated book *Art and Illusion* (1960/1969), Gombrich sets out to solve what he calls 'the riddle of style', namely, the fact that while different artists, in different periods and cultures, have represented the world in different, often strikingly incompatible ways, their output can nonetheless be sequenced into cohesive historical epochs, which give us explanatory power. Central to Gombrich's account of **mimesis** and its stylistic history is his emphasis on the enduring contribution of the beholder, that is, on the theory-ladenness of **perception**, which underlies his famous rejection of the notion of an **innocent eye**. Gombrich's consideration is at once historical and psychological. On the one hand, his account of artistic activity in terms of 'schema and correction' – that is, as a process in which a picture, which conforms to a schema (certain invented pictorial techniques), is proposed as a faithful **representation** of the world, then tested against its model and consequently modified in light of perceived discrepancies – is inspired by Karl Popper's principle of falsification, betraying Gombrich's rationalist faith in the logic of artistic discovery. Gombrich's solution to the riddle of style is that mimesis is an ongoing, open-ended process of learning. He believed that experimental **psychology** has established that all seeing is **interpretation**, informed by **imagination**. He takes ambiguous figures, like the duck-rabbit, to be paradigmatic of the way we experience pictures in general: either seeing the marked surface or seeing the

depicted content, but not both. This aspectual parallel-
ism implies that mimesis is actually **illusion**. This idea
has met with searching criticism on various grounds,
most notably by **Wollheim**, who argued for a diametrically opposed view. In general, the idea that mimesis is
illusion seems to restrict the scope of **aesthetic experience**
unreasonably. Furthermore, Gombrich's position seems
to falter when confronted with **abstraction** in modern
art, since, strictly speaking, in terms of his dynamic
notion of pictorial discovery and in accordance with his
psychological premises, abstract art must be rendered
patently unsuccessful.

See **aspect-perception; resemblance; twofoldness**
Further reading: Gombrich 1982, 1985 and 1986

Goodman, Nelson (1906–98): American philosopher known
not only for his unique contribution to analytic aesthetics,
especially in his celebrated book *Languages of Art*, but
also for his important work in metaphysics, **epistemology** and the philosophy of **science**, most notably his 'new
riddle of induction' (also known as the 'grue paradox').
Goodman's aesthetics directly branches from his overarching philosophical quest to devise a general **understanding** of symbols – linguistic and non-linguistic – in
art, in science, and in ordinary life. For Goodman, works
of art are complex symbols, which belong to symbol
systems with determinate syntactic and semantic structures, and which behave like **language**. Understanding
works of art amounts to interpreting these symbols correctly; hence it has little or any relevance to traditional
questions of **beauty** or **aesthetic experience**. It is noteworthy that, in this general sense, Goodman's approach
coincides with the general philosophical thrust of **semiotics**. Indeed, Goodman maintained that the main task
of aesthetics is to determine, explore, and characterize

these symbol systems, and consequently to explain how they facilitate our understanding. In this sense, aesthetics essentially branches from epistemology, although it yields also important **ontological** corollaries such as the **autographic art/allographic art distinction**. Goodman's extensive discussion of depiction encapsulates many of his philosophical ideas. He argued that while pictures form a symbol system in just the sense that words do, pictorial symbol systems are more replete, and syntactically and semantically dense. This means that, contrary to written language, pictorial systems allow for an infinite number of possible symbols, and possible referents of those symbols, and that for a wide range of properties of the marks on the surface, the smallest difference in one of those properties affects what the symbol represents. For Goodman, symbols can denote or exemplify, or do both simultaneously. For instance, a painting of water lilies by Monet denotes certain water lilies, but it also exemplifies the artist's unique style or the artistic genre of impressionism. **Abstract** art and works of **music** typically exemplify (that is, the work refers to some of its own properties) without denoting anything. Goodman extends his notion of exemplification to account also for **expression** by means of his theory of **metaphor**. For Goodman, metaphoric transference consists in the transference of a given conceptual scheme to a new conceptual realm, which results in the re-classification of the latter according to the former. So in the metaphor 'man is a wolf', man is metaphorically a wolf, which means that man metaphorically exemplifies the property of being a wolf. By the same token, works of art exemplify metaphorically expressive properties.

See **cognitivism, aesthetic; conventionalism; representation**

Further reading: Goodman 1976

Greenberg, Clement (1909–94): American art critic, a major proponent of **modernism** in **painting**, which he construed in terms of **abstraction, medium** specificity and **self-reference**. Greenberg's **formalism** harked back to **Lessing's** medium purism and to **Kant's** idea of **disinterestedness** with some **Marxist** bend to boot. Greenberg contented that abstraction is historically necessitated by the integrity and the uniqueness of the material condition of the given artistic medium. Thus he championed around the mid-twentieth century the pioneering abstract expressionism of Jackson Pollock and rejected other painterly genres, such as surrealism, which he deemed literary hence impure. While Greenberg's critical stance has lost some of its luster in the wake of later developments in the **avant-garde**, it remained a classic locus for **postmodernist** discontent.

See **style**

Further reading: Greenberg 1971

H

Hanslick, Eduard (1825–1904): Austrian **music** critic, theorist, and historian, whose idea that music is essentially sonically moving forms is regarded as a standard interpretation of the idea of **absolute music**. His conviction that musical **meaning** cannot be construed in relation to extra-musical content has become a corner stone of contemporary musical **formalism**. A detractor of **Wagner**, he rejected not only the latter's indulgence in **romantic** excesses, but also the metaphysical and **psychological** core of his aesthetics. The centerpiece of Hanslick's aesthetics, which is contained mostly in his important book *On the Musically Beautiful* (1854), is his assault on the idea that the aim of music is the **representation**

of **emotions** and that this ultimately involves the **arousal** of **emotions** in the listener. Hanslick argued that there is no invariable causal connection between music and any specific emotion, and that definite emotions are intentional; hence they cannot be construed as the content of music. Music is too **abstract** in this respect for anchoring even the sheer dynamics of specific emotions. Indeed, we tend to associate the dynamic features of music with the felt dynamics of this or that emotion but, according to Hanslick, such associations are adventitious. Hanslick believed that musical content inheres only in mere form, which has no purpose beyond itself; hence **beauty** (pertaining to music) is autonomous, not a means for the representation of any extra-musical content.

See **autonomy, aesthetic; essentialism; expression; Langer**

Further reading: Hanslick 1986

happenings see **performance art**

Hegel, Georg Wilhelm Friedrich (1770–1831): German philosopher, one of the great figures of nineteenth-century philosophy, known for his all-encompassing absolute idealism: the idea that Spirit is ultimate reality and that history is progress toward self-consciousness of Spirit. Hegel's philosophy had an important influence on the formation of a number of different twentieth-century schools of philosophy. In aesthetics, it had a particularly long-lasting effect on continental movements such as **phenomenology, hermeneutics, Marxism,** and the **Frankfurt School,** largely through critical engagement with Hegel's **end of art thesis.** For Hegel, the subject matter of philosophy is the Absolute, which he understood as the nature of things, the whole of reality. Thus it is also the process of its own becoming toward an end, which fully defines its nature. Hegel defined the Absolute as Spirit, a self-thinking thought. Within this grand metaphysical system, art plays an important role. Hegel believed that art, like philosophy and religion, grasps the Absolute, only in sensuous form. Hence, for Hegel **beauty** is analogous to **truth**: it is the sensuous appearance of the idea of the whole, the unity of subjectivity and objectivity, which is expressed in the union of ideal content (a revelation of what Spirit is) with material embodiment. This is a development of the **romanticist** theme that beauty gives access to reality. Hegel differs from **Kant** in giving primacy to artistic beauty over natural beauty. The former kind is the immediate creation of Spirit, a self-reflection of Spirit. Hegel distinguishes between three types of art according to the specific type of relation between their ideal content and their sensuous form, which they exhibit. These types of art correspond to different historical periods: (1) symbolic art (ancient Hindu and Egyptian art), in which the sensuous element predominates over the ideal content; (2) classical art (ancient Greek art), in which both elements are united in harmony; and (3) romantic art (the art of Christianity), in which Spirit overflows its sensuous embodiment. Hegel entertained the possibility of the end of art with regards to romantic art, wherein he diagnoses a transition from the aesthetic to religious consciousness. Following this general division, Hegel devised a hierarchy of the fine arts according to their respective adherence to varying ratios between the two elements.

See **cognitivism, aesthetic; ontology; tragedy**

Further reading: Hegel 1975

Heidegger, Martin (1889–1976): German philosopher, a leading figure in **phenomenology**, **hermeneutics** and **existentialism**, whose reputation has been tainted by his open support for Hitler and the Nazi regime during the 1930s. His best known work in aesthetics is an essay titled *The Origin of the Work of Art* (1935/1950). In this work Heidegger probed into the essence of art itself, describing it as a unique kind of 'disclosure'. Disclosure (as opposed to concealment) is a specialized term in Heidegger's **ontology**, referring to the initial conditions which allow things to come into being or be made to appear before consciousness. Heidegger maintained that art, especially poetic art, allows us to witness the tension between concealment and disclosure: it opens for us a realm wherein we can see things, and at the same time resists explication. Heidegger called this the 'conflict of world and earth'. The artwork moves the earth into the open of a world and keeps it there. For Heidegger, this is the nature of **truth** in art. He famously discussed Van Gogh's **painting** of old peasant shoes, aiming to show that the painting reveals more about those shoes and about the world which they inhabit, than any direct examination would do.

See **end of art thesis**

Further reading: Heidegger 1971

hermeneutics: Named after Hermes, the interpreter of the divine message to humankind in ancient Greek mythology, hermeneutics is known as the art and theory of **interpretation**. In its beginnings in the sixteenth century, hermeneutics was concerned with retrieving the original **meaning** of sacred **texts**, but over the course of its development it acquired a much broader significance. In the twentieth century hermeneutics became one of the major schools of continental philosophy associated with **Heidegger** and **Gadamer**. Contemporary hermeneutics approaches problems pertaining to textual interpretation from the vantage point of an interpreter who is fundamentally embedded in history; his existence is significantly enabled and determined by **cultural** conditions. The interaction between the interpreter and the text is part of the history of what is understood; hence any interpretation is culturally mediated by the historically constructed prejudices which constitute the interpreter's practice. An important concept in this context is the 'hermeneutical circle'. The circularity of interpretation concerns the relation of part and whole: the interpretation of each part depends on the interpretation of the whole. For instance, the meaning of a part of a **painting** depends on the whole of the paining, but also the meaning of a particular work of art depends on the whole cultural system of which it is a part. The hermeneutical circle has been generalized to apply to all human knowledge. This means that textual interpretation, including the interpretation of art, ultimately reveals the finite and situated character of all human knowing.

See **intentionalism; language; Margolis; Ricoeur; understanding**

Further reading: Gadamer 1976

Hume, David (1711–76): Scottish philosopher whose work brought British **empiricism** to an apex and had an enduring effect on moral philosophy, **epistemology**, and aesthetics well into the twentieth century. In his essay 'Of the Standard of Taste' (1757), a seminal text in the annals of aesthetics, Hume advanced a **subjectivist** theory of **aesthetic judgment**. He accepted **Hutcheson's** idea that describing an object as beautiful amounts to making a claim about the tendency of the object to elicit a certain **pleasurable** response. Hume maintained that **beauty** is in the mind; it arises from sentiment, it is not a property of any external object (although it is causally linked to certain qualities in the objects). He nonetheless resisted the trap of dismissing taste as a matter of sheer idiosyncratic preference. Hume believed that there is a universal standard of taste: rules of composition which govern excellence in art. Such rules can be discovered through experience and are supposed to be universally pleasing in all countries and ages. However, Hume maintained, performing an aesthetic judgment under such a standard of taste requires well trained, competent judges endowed with delicate, well-developed taste, as well as suitable conditions which would eliminate bias arising from the caprice of fashion and the mistakes of ignorance. In sum, for Hume beauty is indeed in the eye of the beholder, but the beholder needs to be a competent judge, and the judgment is universally valid only under certain restricting conditions. When these necessary requirements are not met, sameness of sentiment is not guaranteed, and this explains the actual variation in taste, which is accidental (Hume believed), not a result of any defect in human nature. In twentieth-century aesthetics, Hume's contention that the rules of art are akin to laws of nature, to be discovered by **scientific** observation, has lost its appeal in light of **Wittgenstein's** argument against reducing explanations in aesthetics to explanations in **psychology**. It is noteworthy that Hume also made an important contribution to the understanding of the **paradox of tragedy** in his essay 'Of Tragedy'.

See **emotivism; Kant; perception; taste theories; tragedy**
Further reading: Hume 1987

Hutcheson, Francis (1694–1746): Scottish moral philosopher, born Irish, who is known also for his contribution to early modern aesthetics. Following John Locke's model of the perception of secondary qualities (for example, color), Hutcheson postulated that our sense of **beauty** is internal, consisting of an ability to have **pleasure** aroused in the mind. Beauty is pleasure raised by the sense of beauty. It is an idea, an internal object, which can be traced back to the **perception** of external objects exemplifying a certain complex property, which he described as uniformity in variety. Aspects of Hutcheson's theory were later employed by **Hume** in his account of the standard of taste.

See **judgment, aesthetic; empiricism; subjectivism; taste theories**

Further reading: Hutcheson 1973

hybrid art forms: Some works of art are clearly a product of two or more previously existing, concrete art forms, artistic techniques, or even technologies. The idea goes back to **Aristotle's** description of the heterogeneous origins and components of **tragedy**. Other examples abound: **Wagner's** music dramas combine **music** and dramatic **narrative; film** typically combines **theater** and **photography;** kinetic sculpture combines **sculpture** and **dance,** and so on. New art forms, such as computer and **new media** art, often exemplify particularly complex and diverse origins in distinct technologies, activities, and concerns, some of which involve unusual, even controversial artistic **media,** for example, tissue culture technologies. Such examples fly in the face of medium **purism,** for instance of the type which had been advocated by **Lessing,** and later by **Langer,** and to some extent also by **Arnheim.** In response to Lessing's stress on medium differentiation, Wagner envisioned the idea of a **Gesamtkunstwerk.** One may be reluctant to give in to this metaphysically extravagant idea of an oceanic art form. Langer argued that each art has a primary apparition which is constitutive of that art. For example, the primary apparition of **painting** is virtual space, and that of music is virtual time. In composing different orders of art, all except one will cease to appear as what they are. Still, one is compelled to disavow **Langer's** notorious conclusion that there are no happy marriages in art – only successful rape. At least in artistic successful instances, the hybrid whole seems to have creative, critical, and cognitive significance, and **understanding** these artworks depends on appreciating exactly how the hybrid emerged from previously existing artistic activities and concerns, and how the aesthetic **value** of the work might be related to medium interaction, interpenetration and mutual recalcitrance. Deliberate artistic choices such as to present dramatic narrative by musical means, as in Richard Strauss' tone poems, or to create music for the eyes, as in Hans Richter's experimental cinema, are significant not just vis-à-vis the history of **style**, but also in terms of their conditions of meaningfulness. Furthermore, if we yield to something like the thesis of the 'death of the author', which has garnered prominence in continental aesthetics since **Barthes**, then the idea that the hybrid status of an artwork is intrinsically related to its history of emergence and reception becomes only more pronounced.

See **appreciation, aesthetic; ontology; pastiche; performance art; synaesthesia**

Further reading: Arnheim 1964; Langer 1957; Levinson 1984

I

illusion: An illusion is a false belief concerning something actually perceived. We also speak of illusion when a vivid mental image occurs as a result of imagining something, which is not really there. In either senses, the very possibility of illusion presents a problem for **epistemology**, since it exemplifies the fundamental contrast between appearance and reality. In aesthetics we may distinguish between two levels of discussion pertaining to the notion of illusion: (1) art in general as illusion; (2) the meaning, scope, and function of illusion in the various **perceptual** arts. The broad sense is best represented in the twentieth century by **Gombrich's** theory of art as illusion. A necessary corollary to Gombrich's contention that all depiction is illusory is the rejection of **mimetic** art as a conduit of reality, that is, naive **realism**. Gombrich maintained that there is no **innocent eye**. In the narrow sense, we may observe the relative status of visual and aural illusions within the context of their respective artistic media. In the case of **painting,** if we preclude Gombrich's position, then illusion is relegated to the relatively minor artistic practice of trompe l'oeil (from French: trick the eye) effects, such as painted curtains. Still trompe l'oeil paintings pose an interesting philosophical problem by making it moot whether representational seeing necessitates or excludes simultaneous attention to the marked surface and the pictorial content. In the case of **music**, we can speak of illusion generally, concerning the fundamental phenomenon of musical motion, wherein we perceive movement without being able to specify its object, or locally, concerning the relatively minor compositional practice of musical reproduction, such as the use of a wind machine in program music. The art of **film** may be regarded as the only art which is illusionary in a fully fledged sense. An obvious reason for that is the fact that the very notion of a moving image is facilitated by an optical illusion. However, while the cinematic illusion is clearly perceptual, it is not cognitive, bearing consequences of an entirely different sort. For instance, seeing a monster approaching on screen does not entail the belief that there is one in front of us in reality, hence we do not flee the cinema.

In fact, it yields a situation akin to the **paradox of tragedy**.

See **imagination; psychology; representation; resemblance; twofoldness; Wollheim**

Further reading: Gombrich 1986

imagination: The term denotes a mental faculty, but also an activity: the ability to form and experience images of things and to think creatively. Art is a thoroughly creative endeavor, so imagination under its various guises permeates all aspects of creating, performing, and experiencing art. Imagination is intentional: whether I imagine an apple, or that I need to go home, or what it is like to be a millionaire, all these exercises of the imagination are about objects, events or situations, which can be either actual or fictional. Imaginative action – for example, when children ride a broom pretending it is a horse – is also intentional. Of course, this is important in aesthetics precisely because so much of art is built on **fiction**: prose, poetry, drama, **film**, figurative **painting**, and so on. The artist employs imagination while conceiving of fictional possibilities, and the audience employs imagination in **understanding** them. Moreover, experiential imagining – that is, imagining what it is like to roam in a fictional world or to be in others' shoes – may elicit intense emotional response. This gives rise to the **paradox of fiction**, which consists of the conceptual oddity of feeling some **emotion** toward a fictional character while knowing that it does not exist. Image formation is often compared to **perception**. Imagining an apple seems to be akin to seeing an apple: it can be vivid, and it always situates the one who imagines in some spatial relation to the intentional object. However, as **Wittgenstein** pointed out, imagining is voluntary, subject to one's will, while perception is not. This **phenomenological**

difference is important for understanding the permeation of perception by imagination, or **aspect-perception**, when a certain object can be perceived under more than one aspect. Aspect-perception, or rather seeing-in, was notably used by **Wollheim** in order to account for pictorial **representation**.

See **Burke; Collingwood; Croce; improvisation; Kant; make-believe theory; narrative; paradox of suspense; persona theory; seeing-as/seeing-in distinction; twofoldness**

Further reading: Scruton 1974; Walton 1990; Warnock 1976

imitation see **mimesis**

immoralism see **experimentalism**

improvisation: Spontaneous, **imaginative** yet mindful artistic creation through performance, which is indigenous to all the performing arts, and by extension also to artistic processes which result in products of visual and literary arts (consider, for instance, action **painting**, and experiments in automatic or other non-linear forms of writing). The concept is quite broad and open. In principle it can be applied to anything between the limiting cases of, on the one hand, works whose performance is totally determined, hence **ontologically** identified solely by their **notation** (for example, certain types of electronic **music**) and, on the other hand, works which are created extempore by mere **chance** operations (John Cage's notorious '4′33″' comes to mind here). Still one should be careful not to collapse the notion of **interpretation** as normally applied to performance practice into the notion of improvisation. Improvisation is not merely a radical form of interpretation, and not all instances of interpretation are simply improvisational. In general, the concept of improvisation is safely applied to the immediate composition of a new work by its performers, or to the elaboration, embellishment, variation, or adjustment of an existing framework (for example, the treatment of show tunes in jazz standards, or of character and plot types in the Italian genre of *Commedia dell'arte*, or the use of social **narratives** in stand-up comedy). The difference within this spectrum is a matter of degree in the performer's reliance on clearly defined, previously existing works or practices. The main philosophical issue here is ontological: either the nature, the identity, and the mode of coming into being of the newly improvised work, or else the possibility of performance in the absence of works. While we acknowledge that an improvisation can be considered as an **aesthetic object**, suitable for contemplation and open to **aesthetic appreciation**, it still marks an ontological shift from an emphasis on the ways in which notation determines performance to the skill and creativity of the performing artist, and also a shift from the idea of a work as a product to the idea of a work as a process. Thus, if one tends to define a work of performing art strictly in terms of performance **authenticity**, then improvisation as such could be relegated to a special ontological kind, namely, performance in the absence of a work. Alternatively, improvisation broadens the concept of a work to include exciting, fleeting moments of art coming together.

See **dance; performance art; theater**

Further reading: Alperson 1984; Thom 1993

indiscernibles see *is* of artistic identification

innocent eye: The thesis, chiefly attributed to the eminent British art critic John Ruskin (1819–1900), that the history of **mimesis** is a gradual process of clearing up the artist's recognition and **interpretation** of the world from presuppositions, which obstruct what actually impinges upon the mind when viewing the world. In this sense, the term denotes an ideal kind of **perception** – unaffected by epistemic notions, such as knowledge and belief – which is said to be the hallmark of mimesis. Purportedly, this historical process reached its apex in the **paintings** of J. M. W. Turner and the French impressionists. **Gombrich** is highly critical of the ideal of the innocent eye. While he accepted that our perception of the world is informed by what we know about it, by our ordinary expectations and conjectures, he denied that perception can be disengaged from such presuppositions. He argued that seeing – hence mimetic art – is irredeemably dependent upon knowing, including the adherence to conventions of **style**.

See **epistemology; phenomenology; psychology; representation; resemblance**

Further reading: Gombrich 1986

institutional theory of art: A theory associated chiefly with the work of **Dickie**, which consists in an early (*Art and the Aesthetics*, 1974) and a revised version (*The Art Circle*, 1984) of the theory. The institutional theory of art is an attempt to construe a **definition of art** which would circumvent the fallacies of **essentialism** without succumbing to anti-essentialist skepticism regarding the prospect and promise of such a project. Dickie's initial insight, following some early critique of **anti-essentialism** as well as **Danto's** idea of the '*is* of artistic identification', was that art might be definable by non-exhibited properties, such as **artifactuality**. Like traditional theories of art, both versions of Dickie's institutional theory assume that works of art are artifacts, yet they place the work of art within a richer context, a multi-placed network of social practices, that is, the **artworld**. Furthermore, Dickie worked out both versions with the practices of twentieth-century art in mind, in particular the emergence of **conceptual art** – for instance, ready-mades and found art. The two versions offer different accounts of how works of art are made possible within the artworld. The early version puts great emphasis on the notion of conferred status: the status of a candidate for appreciation is conferred upon an artifact by a person acting on behalf of the artworld – normally, an artist – thereby turning it into a work of art. Several major criticisms had been leveled against Dickie's early theory. It has been argued that (1) the theory rests on an unfounded legalistic approach to the artworld, and that it mistakenly uses the language of formal institutions in order to describe its largely informal constellation; (2) that Dickie cannot avoid, as he would have liked, the concept of an **aesthetic appreciation**, which is based on the perceptible **properties** of the object; (3) that Dickie's definition of art is circular. The later version of the institutional theory was designed to meet these and other objections. Abandoning altogether the notions of 'status conferral' and 'acting on behalf', and replacing the problematic concept of appreciation with the more neutral concept of presentation, the theory now defines a work of art as an artifact of a kind created to be presented to an artworld public. It then goes on to define (1) an artist as a person who participates with **understanding** in the making of a work of art; (2) a public as a set of persons, the members of which are prepared in some degree to understand an object presented to them; (3) the artworld as the totality of all artworld systems; and (4) an art-world system as a framework for the presentation of a work of art by an artist to an artworld public. This definition of art remains circular, although, Dickie maintains, not fatally so, owing to its emphasis on understanding, hence on the presupposition of knowledge, practical and theoretical. In other words, these definitions pertain to the way we learn about art, and, assuming that art-making involves an intricate, co-relative structure that cannot be described straightforwardly, they inform us of the inflected nature of art.

See **animal art; law; museum; sociology**
Further reading: Dickie 1974 and 1984

intentional fallacy: A term introduced by **Beardsley** in the course of his attack on **intentionalism**. It denotes the tendency to refer to the artist's intentions in the **interpretation** and evaluation of works of art, literary and other. According to Beardsley, the artist's intentions, insofar as we understand them as mental entities, are neither available nor desirable as a standard for the evaluation of artistic success, even in the extreme case where the artist judges his own work. Beardsley's argument hinged on a distinction between two entities: the artist's mind, which is private, and the work of art, which is open to public scrutiny. Evaluation and interpretation pertain only to the latter. Any reference to the former, hence the **psychological** or biographical study of external evidence belonging to the former, is irrelevant. Still the strength of the argument depends on a successful defense of the thesis that intentional attitudes are mental entities, and on the viability of a sharp distinction between the artwork and the mind and life of its creator, which are not guaranteed in any sense.

See **contextualism; New Criticism**
Further reading: Beardsley and Wimsatt 1946

intentionalism: The view that the meaning of a work of art is the one intended by the artist, and that the successful **interpretation** of the work is a matter of capturing that intended **meaning**. The **definition of art** most suitable for intentionalism is art as a form of **communication**. **Expression** theories of art, such as those offered by **Tolstoy**, **Croce** and **Collingwood**, are patently intentionalist. In its simple form, intentionalism can be resisted on the basis of **Beardsley's** idea of the **intentional fallacy**. The intentionalist can be accused of confusing the speaker's meaning with **text** meaning, wrongly assuming that resorting to the former could resolve ambiguities in the latter. In continental aesthetics, intentionalism has been rejected almost across the board by **Marxists**, **structuralists** and **poststructuralists**. Analytic aesthetics remained interested in the prospects of more sophisticated versions of intentionalism, in particular hypothetical intentionalism, which reframes the intention of the artist in terms of our best hypothetical attribution of his intention formed from the position of the intended audience.

See **New Criticism; understanding; Wollheim**
Further reading: Iseminger 1992

interpretation: The term denotes both a thoughtful, creative activity in which an object (the artwork, or a part thereof) is interpreted, and a product of that activity, which is something purportedly different from the artwork (an **understanding** of the artwork, an ability to grasp its artistic **value**, a disclosure of its **meaning**, or an ascription of meaning). In order to realize what interpretation is in any given context, we need a complete grasp of what an artwork is, of the nature of the process, and of the status of the product. Here we find a cluster of interrelated issues, which also underscore some deep philosophical differences (most distinctly seen during the second half of the twentieth century) between mainstream analytic aesthetics and continental aesthetics, in particular **hermeneutics** and **poststructuralism**. It has been suggested that interpreting an artwork is different from describing its features. However, this presupposes that the features of the artwork can be described without being interpreted. The **ontological** assumption here is that the artwork is an independent, stable, well demarcated thing, autonomous of the activity of interpretation. It also presupposes that the activity of interpretation is in a sense **empirical**: we detect the features of the artwork and they in turn constrain admissible interpretations of the work. Consequently, interpretations can be said to be true or false. This was, for instance, **Beardsley's** position. We can locate **Gadamer** on the extreme other pole of the philosophical conception of interpretation: if we maintain that an interpretation is an 'ontological event', which constitutes its object, then the artwork is actually altered by the history of its interpretations. The difference between Beardsley and Gadamer also represents another important distinction between monism and pluralism (some prefer the terms 'singularism' and 'multiplism') concerning the aims of interpretation. Monism asserts that interpretation aims at a single true, well worked out interpretation of the artwork. Pluralism asserts that interpretation aims at a multiplicity of admissible interpretations. The monist usually runs into difficulty upon trying to explain how he knows that his interpretation is the only true one: it seems impossible to ground an uncontroversial standard for establishing truth and falsity for any particular interpretation. Still a common monist strategy is to resort to **intentionalism,** an appeal to authorial intention. Poststructualists typically side with the pluralists owing to the former's vehement rejection of both authorial intention and the idea that **texts** constrain admissible interpretations. They also happily embrace the possibility of the coexistence of equally admissible, yet incompatible or incommensurate, interpretations. It is noteworthy that the notion of interpretation in the performing arts (**music**, standard **theater** performance, and especially **dance**) poses an additional complexity since, in standard cases, performance is itself a live interpretation of a score or a play. Here a difficulty arises from the incompleteness of the **notation** (in music and dance) or the text (in theater). Since the performance is underdetermined by the notation or the text, the performance token (the performance as interpretation) will always have properties that exceed its respective type.

See **appreciation, aesthetic; authenticity; Barthes; intertextuality; judgment, aesthetic; language; Margolis; metaphor; narrative; New Criticism; semiotics; structuralism; titles; truth; type/token distinction; Wollheim**

Further reading: Beardsley 1970; Gadamer 1997; Iseminger 1992; Margolis 1989

intertextuality: The idea that every **text** is a mosaic of quotations drawn from other texts (visual, verbal, or even **musical**), which the author finds available in her **cultural** surroundings. The idea that all texts are intertextual problematizes the very notion of a text. It renders a text as a plurality, a signifying system made of, and interspersed with, other signifying systems with no sharp boundaries between inner and outer (that is, **language** as a whole). It follows that a text cannot have a single **meaning**, and there can never be one true **interpretation** of it. This idea became closely associated with Julia Kristeva's (1941–) unique contribution to **semiotics**, although it has origins elsewhere in literary criticism, most notably in the work of Mikhail Bakhtin (1895–1975) and **Barthes**. Intertextuality is commonly evoked in media studies, and in the interpretation of works of art, which openly refer to, or quote from, other works. However, it is noteworthy that the term is often used in a loose sense simply to denote some sort of literary influence, with no **poststructuralist** presumption whatsoever.

See **medium; truth; understanding**

Further reading: Graham 2000

is **of artistic identification:** The idea, presented by **Danto** in his seminal paper 'The **Artworld**' (1964), that what makes a certain object a work of art (but not another object, which happens to look exactly like it) is its being embedded in a context of artistic theory, not its mere appearance. That is, if we are willing to say that a urinal or a bottle rack – ordinary objects such as Duchamp's ready-mades – *are* artworks, then this is not a matter of mere predication, but rather a manifestation of another sense of the word 'is': the *is* of artistic identification. Danto's argument – often also dubbed the visually-indistinguishable-pairs argument – proceeds as follows. When we are faced with an ordinary object, which has been designated as art, there is nothing about it which sets it apart **phenomenologically** from its non-art counterpart. There are no perceivable **properties** which would distinguish art from non-art. Hence the identification and experience of certain ordinary objects as art must hinge upon a conceptual or theoretical shift, presupposing that a properly informed audience is ready to manifest a new **understanding**, which had emerged within in the artworld. While this sort of 'transcendental' mode of reasoning may not be acceptable without reservation, the argument does highlight the theoretical difficulty involved in maintaining the traditional presupposition of **artifactuality** in the face of certain twentieth-century artistic practices, primarily **conceptual art**. Danto's conclusion prompted **Dickie** to develop his **institutional theory of art** in order to account for the unique conceptual dynamics of the artworld.

See **attitude, aesthetic; definition of art; perception**
Further reading: Danto 1964

J

judgment, aesthetic: Aesthetic judgment is a **value** judgment. It is different from moral judgment in important ways. It is not uncommon that two apparently competent critics may offer incompatible judgments for the same artwork. The plurality of judgments is inherent in the subject matter of aesthetics and in an important sense it can be rationally tolerated. This is not the case in moral judgment: divergent judgment invites censure and correction. Furthermore, divergent aesthetic judgments can be, and often are, tolerated indifferently. No action is implied or expected, since the judgment merely indicates some potential in the **aesthetic object**. Again, this is not the case in moral judgment: it is expected to be consistent with some behavior. These characteristics of the aesthetic judgment underscore the central issue pertaining to aesthetic judgment: the nature of its validity and grounding. Theories of aesthetic judgment usually run the gamut from **subjectivism**, which relates aesthetic judgment to the attitude of the critic, to **objectivism**, which relates aesthetic judgment to the properties of the object. Two very important attempts along this continuum to give aesthetic judgment universal validity were made by **Hume** and **Kant**. It is noteworthy that the enduring significance of Kant's view is in the acknowledgment of the normative character of the aesthetic judgment.

See **beauty; experience, aesthetic; pleasure; properties, aesthetic**
Further reading: Hume 1987; Kant 1952

Kant, Immanuel (1724–1804): German philosopher regarded as the greatest thinker of the eighteenth century and one of the towering figures of Western philosophy, who maintained that the general structure of our experience is cast a priori by the mind itself, and that we can have a certain general knowledge of that. His *Critique of Judgment* (1790), the third in his trilogy of *Critiques*, is regarded as a masterpiece of aesthetic theory, whose enduring influence is still felt in both continental and analytic aesthetics. In that work, which both unifies Kant's overarching critical project and culminates some of the major themes in eighteenth-century aesthetics, Kant argued that **aesthetic judgments** (judgments of taste) are subjective, based on feelings of **pleasure**, yet universally valid, lending themselves to interpersonal agreement. Kant thought that he could achieve that by stressing the normative aspect of such judgment, and by grounding it in certain cognitive capacities shared by all. Thus Kant tried to resolve the tension between the British **empiricist** tradition, represented by **Burke, Hutcheson** and **Hume**, which construed the judgment of **beauty** as making a claim about our feeling of pleasure, and the rationalist tradition, represented by **Baumgarten**, which construed the judgment of beauty in terms of our **perception** of certain objective properties. For Kant, the judgment of beauty is a reflective judgment: a judgment in which we seek a new concept, rather than applying a known concept to something. Kant accepted that the judgment of beauty is subjectively grounded in feelings of pleasure; however, he contended that this is pleasure of a distinctive kind: it is disinterested, unrelated to any desire for the object. Kant maintained that such disinterested judgments are asserted with a universal voice: they are universally valid, not because they are provable, but because, being disinterested, they ought to be shared by anyone who perceives the object. In this normative sense, they are also necessary. The content of such judgments is formal: it is the recognition of the form of purposiveness, without ascribing any purpose that the object is presupposed to satisfy. Disinterested pleasure is taken in the perceived form of the object. Kant grounded these requirements of the judgment of beauty in our cognition: disinterested pleasure is the experience of the free, harmonious play of the two faculties that yield perceptual knowledge: **imagination** and **understanding**. When these two faculties harmonize, the former remains unconstrained by the latter; and so beauty is perceived, unitary and coherent, but not under any particular concept. Kant maintained that the operations of these faculties are essentially uniform for all people. Kant incorporated other important themes into his aesthetic theory. These include his discussion of the aesthetic judgment of the **sublime**, the capacity of **genius** to transcend concepts in the production of artworks, and the connection between aesthetic judgment and moral feeling. These ideas became the cornerstones of **romanticism**. Kant's aesthetics had a tremendous influence on the aesthetic theories of later philosophers, most notably **Schiller**, **Hegel**, **Schopenhauer** and **Nietzsche**. His idea of **disinterestedness** had particular longevity as the quintessential characteristic of the **aesthetic attitude** well into the twentieth century. Kant's underscoring of the formal aspect of the judgment of beauty was an important precursor for the later rise of **formalism** in aesthetics.

See **ethics; Gadamer; objectivism; subjectivism; taste theories**
Further reading: Kant 1952

kitsch: This derogatory German term (of unclear linguistic origins) is commonly applied to artifacts which are considered to be pretentious, vulgar, or otherwise designed to please and flatter the masses by means of promulgating false, self-congratulatory sentiments. With the exception of occasional exploitations of kitsch in **avant-garde** art (for example, the works of Jeff Koons), kitsch objects – which may be everything from tacky Monet coffee mugs to fake Greek colonnades – are usually fixtures in our ordinary life, and hence related to methods of mechanical reproduction and to the social dynamics of mass production and consumption. This may explain why kitsch seems to be merely grafted upon genuine art. A typical kitsch object exploits generic **emotional** themes – sadness, serenity, love, and so on – or plays at being **beautiful** in a manner which is instantly and effortlessly identifiable. The unreflective, conventional take on such themes, associated with kitsch, renders them universal in the sense of appealing to the audience's most common denominators; hence, arguably, it fails to enhance or expand the audience's sensitivities or knowledge about these matters. This actually secures the rhetorical efficacy of kitsch when it is harnessed to **political** causes. Kitsch seldom seems particularly **imaginative** or susceptible to aesthetic characterizations, and it is usually taken to negate **truth** in art, as well as creativity and **profundity**.
See **definition of art**
Further reading: Kulka 1996

knowledge see **epistemology**

L

Langer, Susanne (1895–1985): American philosopher known for her broad philosophical interests in the humanities, including her singular contribution to the Anglo-American philosophy of **music** around the mid-twentieth century. Langer's aesthetics is informed, on the one hand, by Ernst Cassirer's philosophy of symbolic forms, and, on the other, by **Wittgenstein's** early picture theory of meaning. To an extent, Langer's approach is reminiscent of **semiotics**, although her clear adherence to **aesthetic cognitivism** sharply sets her apart. According to Langer, through symbolism we represent, organize, and make sense of various features of our world. Art consists in transforming human feelings and **emotions** into symbolic forms, and in this sense music is said to be paradigmatic. Langer argued that music and our emotions are isomorphic. Thus she belongs to a philosophical lineage which begins **Aristotle** and continues through **Schopenhauer** to **Hanslick**. Following Wittgenstein, she couched this isomorphism in logical terms: the semblances of emotive life supervene on the arrangement of the formal properties of the music. Thus isomorphism is supposed to secure not only musical **meaning**, but also its **value** and **profundity**. In effect, Langer idiosyncratically harnesses Wittgenstein's erstwhile theory of logical form to produce a version of the **expression theory of art** along lines that were familiar from **Collingwood** and **Croce**. Still, Langer's theory is open to criticism on account of its vagueness with regard to the exact nature of the emergence of semblances from formal properties, and the relation of the former to definite emotions.

See **formalism; representation; sculpture**
Further reading: Langer 1953 and 1957

language: Aesthetics relates to language on four different planes of philosophical concern, which intertwine in the most philosophically intricate ways. The first and perhaps the most obvious plane is the philosophic study and criticism of art forms and works of art which consist, partly or wholly, in a linguistic **medium**. The second, closely related to the first, is the employment of tools and insights derived from advances in the philosophy of language or in linguistics. The third is the analogy of art as language – the view that art is structured, or behaves in some sense, like language, or that it relates to the mind or to the world in the way that language does. The fourth is the analogy of language as art – the 'linguistification' of **aesthetic experience**. With regard to the second and third planes, it would be safe to say that the linguistic turn in twentieth-century philosophy had far-reaching implications for both the Anglo-American and the continental traditions, and that in both traditions we have seen philosophers engaged in fully fledged aesthetic theories of art as language, albeit strikingly different from one another: for instance, **Collingwood**, **Goodman** (both Anglo-American), **Barthes** and **Gadamer** (both continental). It is noteworthy that the analogy of art as language is found also in the empirical **sciences**, as well as in related disciplines such as musicology. A striking example would be the recent Chomsky-inspired generative theory of tonal **music**. With regards to the fourth concern, which arguably harks back to **Hegel**, the discrepancy between the analytic and the continental traditions in aesthetics comes to a head. Combined with another far-reaching idea, that of language as a universal medium, which both mediates and shapes what we think, the idea that philosophy is fundamentally a critique of language yields the bold assertion that aesthetic experience does not come to us pure, but is molded linguistically, its texture determined by the language we use. This idea has been promoted quite radically by continental aesthetics, in particular within its **poststructuralist** and feminist strains. This idea also underlies the great theoretical interest that continental thinkers have in the philosophical and artistic significance of **metaphor**, in its power to transgress conceptual and experiential borders, and to reveal novel, insightful perspectives. On this purported middle-ground between art and philosophy, we find some of the most distinguished thinkers of the continental tradition, who even strive to write their own philosophy as art, rendering language as a medium which, through creative manipulation and transgression, can show us the construction of thought. It is important to note that some of the most fundamental concepts currently used in aesthetics – such as **understanding, interpretation, meaning, narrative**, and **text** – traverse all four planes of philosophical concern, and so typically inherit all the conceptual complexity and worry that is the mark of genuine philosophy.

See **communication; deconstruction; Derrida; gendered aesthetics; hermeneutics; intertexuality; language-game; New Criticism; poststructuralism; Ricoeur; Saussure; self-reference; semiotics; structuralism; titles; Wittgenstein**

Further reading: Hagberg 1998

language-game: A term associated with **Wittgenstein's** later philosophical period. Wittgenstein maintained that the aim of philosophy is the grammatical investigation of our uses of **language** hence philosophy is purely descriptive. He used the term 'language-game' as a methodological tool to describe, delineate, and contrast both actual and hypothetical mundane uses of language in the mercurial context of human practice. For Wittgenstein, the meaning of a word is its use in a concrete language-game, and all language-games are of equal standing. In Wittgenstein's use of the term, language-game neither serves as a technical term, denoting some sort of entity, nor pertains to any theory of language, which Wittgenstein believes cannot be founded. It serves to highlight the fact that language is a rule-guided activity, and that it pertains to human life and play, interwoven with and embedded in a form of life. The notion of 'game' itself is a prime example of what Wittgenstein calls a **family-resemblance** concept. The indeterminacy, which is inherent in certain language-games, and the conceptual impossibility, according to Wittgenstein, of securing a transcendental viewpoint, from which one can survey and rank all language-games, attracted various writers of **poststructuralist** or **deconstructionist** conviction.

See **appreciation, aesthetic; postmodernism**

Further reading: Wittgenstein 2001

law: Legal issues pertain to aesthetics mostly owing to the fact that works of art are enmeshed in ordinary life as commodities, as well as means of **communication** and **expression**. Art law requires a **definition of art**. While a working definition could always be agreed upon, the thorny philosophical problem underlying the very attempt to define what art is, which has been aggravated by the advent of **conceptual art** in the twentieth century, remains unsettled. Issues like copyright, trademark, moral right, and ownership in the arts, and the various infringements thereof, hinge upon fundamental problems in the **ontology** of art, including the relation between an artist and his work, the nature of **artifactuality** and the authorship of **texts**, and such ontological distinctions as original, copy, and **forgery, type/token, singular/multiple**, and so on. Ontological conundrums in the arts, and their legal counterparts, seem to flourish with technological advancements in mechanical and especially digital reproduction and manipulation of texts, images, and sounds. Another important concern for art law is the relation between art, **ethics**, and **politics**, especially regarding such perennial matters as the freedom of speech, artistic freedom, governmental funding of art, and in general any sort of governmental regulation of the practice and exhibition of art. The central problem here is justifying **censorship** in art, whether on political, religious, or other normative grounds, as in the case of **pornography**, for example. In this context, art law can be seen as the institutionalized recognition of the power of art to challenge the established normative order.

See **analog/digital distinction; museum; new media; sociology**

Further reading: Merryman, Elsen and Urice 2007

Lessing, Gotthold Ephraim (1729–1871): German philosopher, critic and dramatist whose main contribution to aesthetics is his treatise *Laocoön: An Essay on the Limits of Painting and Poetry* (1766). In *Laocoön*, Lessing argues that **beauty** is not determined by moral considerations, and that visual art and poetry cannot be assimilated to one another. According to Lessing, poetry and visual art are subject to different laws of artistic production and must therefore kept apart. Lessing's theory is **mimetic**: art **represents** reality, and there should be a natural relationship between sign and signified. Thus, poetry, which uses temporally successive signs – that is, words – must deal with objects that follow each other in time – that is, events. Visual art, which uses spatially coexistent signs – that is, colors and shapes – must deal with objects that coexist in space – that is, bodies. Furthermore, Lessing distinguishes between a 'natural' sign, which **resembles**

its object, and an 'arbitrary' sign, which connects to its object by mere **convention**. Thus, according to Lessing, poetry ought to strive to convert its 'arbitrary' signs – that is, words – into 'natural' ones – that is, dramatic action. Lessing's stress on purely aesthetic standards preceded the aesthetics of **Kant**. **Wagner's** thesis of the **Gesamtkunstwerk** can be seen as an attempt to counter the main thrust of Lessing's theory.

See **medium; mimesis; ut pictura poesis**
Further reading: Lessing 1984

literature: The art of literature is primarily the art of **language**, but that makes it very heterogeneous in terms of what kind of things are done, or can be done with the words, and how. The term 'literature' is normally used to refer at least to standard cases of poetry, drama and prose **fiction**. But more often than not, it is also stretched to cover other things, some of which are quite extravagant, from historical texts, through William Burroughs' literary cut-ups, to self-generating digital poetry. Literature faces the problem of demarcation on two fronts. First, as the Viennese cultural critic and writer Karl Kraus (1874–1936) wittily pointed out, the unfortunate thing is that verbal art works with the material that the rabble handles every day. That is why (he thought) literature is beyond help. Literature cannot be defined as the sum total of its rhetorical devices, and so we face the continuity of literature with various non-literary genres (diaries, reports, and so on) and the mundane uses of language in general. It is noteworthy that Kraus himself exploited this continuity in his own literary work. Furthermore, literature cannot be adequately identified with fiction. This openness of the concept of literature renders it particularly susceptible to **anti-essentialist** arguments. In response, attempts have been made to provide an institutional definition of literature. Second, the emphasis in continental aesthetics, in **structuralism** and even more pronouncedly in **poststructuralism** (including its **Marxist** and feminist varieties) on construing literature as **text**, rather than as 'work', involves not only corresponding shifts in the related notions of literary **meaning** and **interpretation**, but also the subordination of literature to wider ideational frameworks, strategies and goals.

See **Barthes; cognitivism, aesthetic; definition of art; gendered aesthetics; institutional theory of art; intentional fallacy; intentionalism; metaphor; mimesis; narrative; New Criticism; new media; paradox of fiction; pastiche; postmodernism; realism; self-reference; theater; ut pictura poesis**

Further reading: Barthes 1977; Lamarque and Olsen 1996; Sartre 1988

M

make-believe theory: This comprehensive theory of the representational arts, which has been advanced by the contemporary American philosopher Kendall Walton (1939–), hinges on the instructive analogy between children's games and our multifarious engagements with **representation** in traditionally **mimetic** arts such as **painting** and **literature**, but also in **music**, and even in decorative arts. The notion of **imagination** (including self-imagining) is fundamental to the make-believe theory: objects may prompt our acts of imagination, in which **fictional** truths (propositions that, in a given social context, are imagined to be true) are generated about the objects, about the world which they inhabit, and about us vis-à-vis the objects. Representations are designed to serve as props in certain sorts of games of make-believe. The difference between depiction and literary representation is in the nature of the game: the former is a representation whose function is to serve as a prop in relatively rich and vivid perceptual games of make-believe in which are to imagine of our perceptual acts that the objects of those acts are things that the depiction represents. Literary representation does not involve such perceptual games. Either way, according to the make-believe theory, the core of representational-ity is not denotation, as **Goodman** argued, for instance. With regards to literature, this has the welcome result of quietening down standard **ontological** and semantic misgivings regarding the existence of fictional entities. Another theoretical advantage is the way in which the make-believe theory seamlessly brings in considerations pertaining to our **psychological** and **emotional** involve-ment with representations. Still, with regard to the per-ceptual arts, the need to postulate a **phenomenological** blend of imagination and **perception** results in some conceptual ambiguity regarding the purported relation between the two. In particular, in **abstract** perceptual arts such as music, this seems to lead to considering music merely as a screen for projecting one's personal fantasies.

See **ornamentation; paradox of fiction; truth**
Further reading: Walton 1990

Marcuse, Herbert (1898–1979): German philosopher, a member of the circle of philosophers, social scientists, and cultural critics known as the **Frankfurt School**. Marcuse's work is known for its attempt to imbue **Marxism** with the ideas of **Freud**, in particular in his important book *Eros and Civilization* (1955). In this book, Marcuse set himself apart from the general **cul-tural** pessimism of the other members of the Frankfurt

School, most notably **Adorno**, who maintained that the task of critical theory is by and large negative: to unmask the unjust character of existing society. Marcuse argued that Freud's notion of instinctual repression as a means of survival is relative to the needs of different societies at different historical circumstances. Thus he envisaged the prospect of social revolution and the utopist escape from suffering and repression. Aesthetic reflection is of crucial importance in Marcuse's utopist vision: human freedom is attainable through artistic **beauty**, which is by its very nature is always in conflict with the socially given. However, when the conflict is over upon the attainment of utopia, when art fulfills itself as social reality, the role of art is over. Hence, for Marcuse, utopia means the **end of art**.

See **Hegel; modernism; politics; sociology**
Further reading: Marcuse 1955 and 1978

Margolis, Joseph (1924–): Contemporary American philosopher whose persistent work within Anglo-American aesthetics, in particular relating to the fields of **interpretation** and the **ontology** of art, sets him distinctly apart by virtue of its uncommon affinity with certain **hermeneutic** and **poststructuralist** views. Margolis' characteristic mélange of relativism and pragmatism is best captured in his important contention that works of art are physically embodied and culturally emergent entities. This means that the identity and **meaning** of a work of art are unstable because they are culturally constituted. Since the practice of interpretation is also culturally mediated, any interpretation of the **aesthetic properties** of an art work ultimately involves constituting those properties as subject matter for interpretation. For Margolis, the idea that there can be only one true interpretation of a work undercuts the very idea of art.

Margolis' critics occasionally voice their concern that this position may risk a slippery slope to some sort of inconsistent **subjectivism**.

See **text; truth**

Further reading: Margolis 1980 and 1999

Marxism: The term loosely designates any system of thought or philosophical approach to social criticism derived to various extents from the work of the German social philosopher and economic theorist Karl Marx (1818–83). While Marx himself wrote relatively little on art or aesthetics, certain aspects of his theory of history, a materialist reversal of **Hegel's** idealism, in which he relates the rise and fall of societies to the furthering and impediment of human productive power, have had a long-lasting influence on twentieth-century aesthetics. Marx's general idea, popularized by his close collaborator Friedrich Engels (1820–95), was that the higher human activities and institutions, such as art, belong to the cultural 'superstructure', which is related to a material 'base' of socio-historical and economic conditions. While the exact nature and dynamics of the relation between 'superstructure' and 'base' remains a moot issue, this general framework is shared by all Marxist views on art. Consequently, Marxist aesthetics is patently **contextualist** and hostile to **formalism**, especially with regards to **beauty**, and to any form of **aestheticism**. It renders the artistic activity inseparable from, hence expressive of, its historical and utilitarian circumstances. Thus Marxist aesthetics typically rejects the idea of **disinterestedness** also.

See **Adorno; Benjamin; Frankfurt School; Greenberg; Kant; Marcuse; modernism; politics; sociology**

Further reading: Eagleton 1990; Marcuse 1978; Solomon 1973

meaning: While we often say quite rightly that works of art have meaning, or at least that they are meaningful, the use of the term across the field of aesthetic theory tends to be elusive and multifarious. There may be several inter-related reasons for this. To speak of meaning, one needs first to locate the basis of meaning either in thought – that is, the artist's mind or that of the audience – or in the relevant public mode of **representation** as related also to its carrying artistic **medium**. Of course, this necessarily presupposes a certain relation between thought and representation. It is noteworthy that the history of ideas has seen the shifting of paradigms between the classical tradition – for which thought precedes **language** and other forms of representation, rendering the latter as a vehicle of the former, hence deriving the meaning of vehicle from the representative powers of thought itself – and the post-Kantian inclination to reverse this dependency on the effect of making thought itself dependent on its linguistic or otherwise outer representation. Also, one needs to determine whether or not meaning is some sort of semantic relation between the work of art and something external to it (that is, objects, event, properties – the 'world' broadly construed). Wittgenstein, for instance, suggested that the meaning of a word pertains to its use, and so the concept of meaning is to some extent displaced by the concept of **understanding**. In this sense, what a work of art means pertains to our understanding of it, how this understanding is manifested and justified. Such considerations bear significant implications for the scope and nature of **interpretation** of a work of art, insofar as interpretation is conceived in terms of the fleshing out of meaning. Aestheticians and other philosophers writing on art may differ significantly across these intertwined ideational lines due to their adhering to different theories of meaning. However, one can observe a general tendency in contemporary aesthetics to locate meaning in the work of art itself on both sides of the so-called analytic-continental divide, often in order to avoid some form of **intentionalism**, or as a result of some other intellectual commitment to rendering the work of art as a **text**.

See **Barthes; Beardsley; Collingwood; communication; Croce; Danto; Derrida; Gadamer; Goodman; hermeneutics; intentional fallacy; interpretation; Kant; Langer; Margolis; metaphor; New Criticism; poststructuralism; semiotics; structuralism; Tolstoy; truth; Wittgenstein**

Further reading: Hagberg 1998

medium: Literally meaning something which stands between two other things, the notion of medium implies also the possibility of transference of something from one side to the other, or mediation between the two sides. Hence the idea of medium patently gives rise also to the idea of content, i.e. that which is transferred by the medium. This straightforward sense implies medium indifference, that is, the possibility of communicating the same content by different means. This notion is found most commonly in science, but also in **communication**, in spite of some adherence to conceptually self-defeating notions such as the one encapsulated in Marshall McLuhan's slogan that the medium is the message. The identification and characterization of a medium are **ontologically** relative both to the things conjoined and to the mediated content. This is particularly relevant to the case of medium in art. For instance, in **music** we can refer to various things as a medium: the composer, the performers and their instruments, the work, the **interpretation**, the sound, the air in the concert hall, and so on. An art medium can be a physical thing (for example, paint or stone) or else it can consist of the sensory qualities which inhere in matter (for example, color or pitch), including manners of execution of such **perceptual** qualities. **Conceptual art** seems particularly problematic in this sense, since it undercuts precisely such determinants. Alternatively, an art medium can also consist of a system of signs, linguistic or other. Arguably, the nature of the medium is essential to the existence and appreciation of the artwork. Hence the idea of medium indifference in art seems to be counter-intuitive. Indeed, unless one conceives the work of art in mentalist terms – like **Collingwood**, for instance – or else in a strict empiricist sense as an **aesthetic object,** like **Beardsley**, there is no sense in denying that, at least in common artistic practice, **understanding** and **appreciating** a work of art involve considering the artist's choice of a physical medium, the way in which the medium enters into the artist's creative process, and the qualities of the medium in reference to its responsiveness or recalcitrance towards the artist's manner of interacting with it. Such considerations suggest the idea of **twofoldness**. A related issue concerns medium differentiation or medium specificity, that is, the idea that content is to some extent a function of its carrying medium. If we maintain that each art form has a specific nature determined by the uniqueness of its medium – as did **Lessing**, for example – then we might reach the doctrine of medium purity, which is a form of **essentialism**. Medium purity is implausibly restrictive insofar as it does not allow **hybrid art forms**.

See **formalism; Greenberg; new media**

Further reading: Lessing 1984; Margolis 1980; Wollheim 1980

metaphor: The lexical meaning of the Greek verb *metaphérein* (to transfer, or to carry over) points not only at the special dynamics of metaphor, but also at the difficulty of explaining how exactly metaphor does its magic. Metaphor is primarily a linguistic creature, an instance of non-literal, figurative use of **language**, in which some sort of creative transference of **meaning** takes place. What sort of transference, what makes it creative, how it is related, if at all, to **truth** and knowledge, and whether metaphors are semantic at all – all these issues remain moot. Metaphor is most indigenous to poetry, **literature**, or to any other distinctly verbal art, and also to philosophy itself. It has even been argued that our entire 'literal' language is actually entrenched in clusters of conceptual metaphors, which define its structure and the inferences we draw from that structure. It is still common to extend the notion of metaphor also to the non-verbal arts. For instance, it has been suggested that certain cases of the use of photomontage in film ought to be acknowledged as genuine visual metaphors. It is also noteworthy that **Goodman's** theory of metaphoric exemplification patently extends across the arts. Theories of metaphor usually run the gamut from decisively deflationary theories, which deny that metaphor has any meaning other than its literal meaning and maintain that metaphors are merely pragmatic devices used to achieve a certain effect, to fully fledged creationist theories, such as **Ricoeur's**. Along this theoretical spectrum we can distinguish between four major types of theories:

(1) comparison (or substitution) theories, like **Aristotle's**, which treats metaphor as a condensed simile. Such theories commonly fail to explain the conceptual tension and novelty so typical of metaphors.

(2) **Emotive** theories, which displace metaphoric meaning by **emotional** response. Such theories run into difficulty when required to explain how such

displacement takes place, and also when faced with the cognitive difference between otherwise nonsensical metaphoric combinations of words.

(3) Tension (or interaction) theories, which deny that the concepts conjoined in a metaphor are related by similarity, and maintain that the conceptual confrontation within metaphor forges a new metaphoric meaning, which is irreducible to their previous meanings. Such theories are creationist and can explain metaphoric novelty, but they hinge on the controversial viability of metaphoric truth.

(4) Speech act theories, which explain metaphoric meaning from the vantage point of a much broader theory of **communication**.

See **Beardsley; cognitivism, aesthetic; interpretation; understanding**
Further reading: Johnson 1981; Ortony 1993

mimesis: A Greek word often translated as 'imitation', and depending on context also as 'copy', '**representation**', or 'impersonation'. It is commonly used in reference to an artistic or literary representation of the real world – mostly objects and events, but also character-traits and **emotions** – and it has been traditionally employed to define the very essence of art. In general, the term 'mimesis' is used when one thing is modeled on, or presented by, another, but the exact meaning of this relation remains theory-laden. Understanding the relation as bearing on the **truthfulness** of the mimetic product was at the heart of the disagreement between **Plato** and **Aristotle** concerning the cognitive **value** of art. The idea of the truth-conferring nature of mimesis, for example by means of **resemblance**, was criticized in the twentieth century by **Goodman**, who maintained that mimesis presupposes **convention**. During the seventeenth and eighteenth centuries, mimesis was commonly given a relatively narrow interpretation as the imitation of nature, including human character and emotions. This became the founding principle of the **modern system of the arts**. Against this backdrop it is noteworthy that **Lessing** importantly brought considerations pertaining to artistic **medium** to bear on the issue of mimesis, and this resulted in an argument for the need to differentiate between the mimetic arts with respect to their mimetic capabilities. In the twentieth century the term 'mimesis' received some highly specialized interpretations, for example, in the various theories of the **Frankfurt School**, and perhaps more influentially, as part of **Derrida's** conception of **deconstruction**.

See **cognitivism, aesthetic; definition of art; Gombrich; make-believe theory**

Further reading: Halliwell 2002

modern system of the arts: Named after a classic essay by the eminent historian of ideas Paul Oskar Kristeller (1905–99), this is the widely accepted historical thesis that the birth of aesthetics in the eighteenth century occurred in conjunction with the decisive formation of a system of fine arts, which originally included exclusively and irreducibly five privileged members: **painting, sculpture, architecture, music** and poetry. Other arts, such as **dance, theater** and prose **literature**, were added only retroactively. This historical process culminated in Charles Batteux's (1713–80) suggestion to set the principle of **mimesis** as constitutive of the fine arts, understood as imitation of **beautiful** nature. The importance of this thesis is in setting up a watershed between the purported **autonomy** of the **modern** arts, now contrasted with the crafts and **science**, and the ideas of the ancient Greeks and Romans, which had no such unified conception of art, and did not separate the various arts from utilitarian objectives, or from one another.

See **Aristotle; ornamentation; Plato**

Further reading: Kristeller 1980

modernism: In aesthetics the term 'modernism' generally refers to a complex, somewhat disorderly constellation of philosophical ideas, constitutive and critical, some of which are traceable back to the eighteenth century. Depending on context, it may also refer to certain artistic practices and movements, which began to emerge across the fine arts in late nineteenth century, first in Europe and later also in the USA, becoming indigenous to the first half of the twentieth century up until the 1960s. Modernism is often conflated with the term 'modernity', which is normally reserved for denoting specifically the cultural condition or epoch within which modernist ideas, practices, and constitutive events became increasingly manifest. The tenets of modernism in aesthetics are of varied origins and any shortlist would inevitably be far from exhaustive. Furthermore, since they function as ultimate presuppositions, that is – as assumptions to the effect that various ensuing issues can be raised and answered – they have yielded not only contrasting philosophical responses but also contrasting artistic manifestations – celebratory on some occasions and anguished on other. Modernism is often seen as the culmination of the so-called 'project of the Enlightenment' with its rationalist thrust toward **truth** and systematization, as well as its firm belief in the prospects of progress, technology and innovation. Some foundational ideas in the history of aesthetics arose in this spirit, for example: **Lessing's** arguments for **medium** purity, **Kant's** ideas of **aesthetic autonomy** and **disinterestedness**, and **Hegel's** quest for truth in art. Other ideas followed: growing awareness of the medium in art led to **formalism**, to **aestheticism**, and to an emphasis on **self-reference** in art; anti-realism, which has grown more pronounced in **science**, led to increasing preoccupation with modes and methods of **representation**. Some of the most distinct artifacts and practices that have become part and parcel of the modernist milieu in art, and the theoretical responses to them, can be analyzed in terms of either an emulation of, or a reaction against, these perennial themes. The urge to create new artistic objects and new ways of seeing is eminently clear not only in the way the visual arts challenged received methods of representation – for example, in cubism – but also in the fracturing of the tonal idiom in twentieth-century music, and also in some of the literary experiments of the past century from Virginia Woolf's stream-of-consciousness writing to William Burroughs' cut-up method for producing new kinds of prose and **film**. At times such phenomena reflected also the state of cultural shock and antagonism toward the effects of technological advances and social transformations, which ran parallel to such enjoyment of experimentality. A rift opened between high art – especially institutionalized **avant-garde** – and popular **culture**. Sentiments of alienation, repression, and distortion were given voice and shape in art, but also in theory, for instance, in the deep ambivalence of the **Frankfurt School** thinkers towards the idea of aesthetic autonomy. Eventually, the ultimate presuppositions of modernism themselves became, at least arguably, the primary focus of **postmodernist** critique over the past three decades, thus becoming also sharply delineated and susceptible to further scrutiny. Insofar as aesthetics is committed to the compartmentalized autonomy of art and the aesthetic, and to foundationalist theorizing about this exclusive domain, it would be fair to say that aesthetics has been, at least since its eighteenth-century inauguration, largely a modernist affair. This is evident across the so-called analytic-continental divide, although analytic aesthetics in particular remained by and large overwhelmingly modernist especially with regards to its firm belief in the coherence and comprehensibility of its purported subject matter as well as its belief in the fundamental, philosophically far-reaching idea of the fixity of **text**.

See **abstraction; Adorno; autonomism; Beardsley; Bell; Bloomsbury Group; conceptual art; Derrida; Greenberg; Hegel; Kant; Marcuse; Marxism; modern system of the arts; narrative; New Criticism; phenomenology**

Further reading: Eysteinsson 1990

Moore, George Edward (1873–1958): British philosopher, a major figure in early analytic philosophy. His best known work in **value** theory is the *Principia Ethica* (1903), which contains the bulk of Moore's writing on aesthetics. He argued that the appreciation of what is beautiful in art or nature is one of the two unmixed goods (the other being personal affection) which are intrinsically valuable. According to Moore, this cannot be doubted rationally. **Beauty**, like goodness, is a simple yet indefinable and unanalyzable non-natural property – that is, a property intuited by the mind, hence non-empirical – and any attempt to analyze it would inevitably involve a **naturalistic fallacy**, namely, the identification of beauty with something else. This view is complemented by a theory of sense-data. For Moore, the crucial criterion of reality is one's immediate experience, and he maintains that our entire knowledge of the world must be traced back to its source in immediate experience. The object of experience, the sense-datum, is an objective entity, a part of objective reality, which impinges directly on our consciousness. Thus, according to Moore, an experience of beauty is an experience of some objective entity, and the way to approach this object of experience is to focus on the experience itself, on the given. From this follows a sense of theoretical **aestheticism**. Moore's views had a tremendous influence on the members of the **Bloomsbury Group,** in particular on **Bell,** who attempted to spell out a fully fledged **formalist** theory of art along Moorean lines. Moore's ideas also played an important part, albeit indirectly and by way of reaction, on the formation of **Wittgenstein's** ideas on aesthetics during his second sojourn in Cambridge.

See **epistemology; essentialism; objectivism; open question argument; properties, aesthetic**

Further reading: Moore 1993

moralism: The view that works of art (1) have a moral dimension; (2) can be morally evaluated; and (3) their aesthetic **value** depends on their moral status. Thus, moralism is squarely opposed to **autonomism** and to **formalism.** It is also opposed to **experimentalism** insofar as the latter allows an inverse relation between immorality and aesthetic value (hence it amounts to moderate immoralism). Full-blooded moralism – for example, in **Plato** and **Tolstoy** – is absolutist and **essentialist,** consequently excluding too many artworks which would otherwise qualify as great. As such, it is susceptible to arguments aimed at **essentialism.** Any such extreme version of moralism seems to lose its force when applied to purely **abstract** works of art, unless one is willing to argue on independent grounds that amoral art is by that very token also immoral. This kind of criticism has been leveled against **aestheticism.** A moderate, pluralist version of moralism would be more lax about the three aforementioned characteristics. A moderate moralist might hold that a work of art may have a moral dimension and could be morally evaluated, if its **narrative** is conducive to moral reasoning, or if it otherwise elicits an appropriate cognitive-affective response from its audience. This position may also be applicable to abstract works of art. Moderate moralism tends to embrace **cognitivism**. That is, it assumes that if we engage with works of art, they actually teach us moral **truths** and how we ought morally to feel.

See **autonomy, aesthetic; censorship; ethics**

Further reading: Gaut 1998; Kieran 1996; Tolstoy 1960

museum: Derived from the Greek word *mouseion*, which originally denoted a place holy to the Muses, the term came in modern times to denote an institution – often embodied in a designated building – for the exhibition, preservation and study of artworks (and other objects) as well as for a whole range of related social, educational, and cultural functions. From the perspective of the **institutional theory of art**, museums play a crucial, indispensible role as a framework for the presentation of a work of art by an artist to an **artworld** public, hence in the admission of an object into the realm of art. Such admission may yield both aesthetic and legal consequences, as in the case of **forgery,** for instance. Ordinarily, the museum is taken, albeit not without reservation, to embody the principles of **aesthetic autonomy** and **disinterestedness** by virtue of the actual segregation of certain artifacts from the desires, purposes, and utilities which inhabit ordinary life. Critiques of aesthetic autonomy are thus *ipso facto* critiques of this view of the museum. For example, this can be seen indirectly in the problematic relation between the museum and the **avant-garde,** whose unruly adherence to the principle of aesthetic autonomy tends to conflict with the institutionalized sense of that same principle as epitomized in the museum. A more direct critique of the notion of the museum can be found in **postmodern** theory and artistic practice, in particular in the attempt to unearth and dismantle the 'museumizing' **gaze**, that is, the historical-theoretical **narrative**, which enables the petrifaction, reorientation, and redefinition of life within the orderly, **epistemologically** oppressive confinement of the museum space.

See **culture; education, aesthetic; law; sociology**
Further reading: Hein 2000

music: While some reference to music, its nature, and its effect can be found in the works of the great philosophers since antiquity, and throughout the ages, it seems that music gained its unprecedented prominence as a unique subject matter for philosophical contemplation only fairly recently, beginning in **romanticism,** and most conspicuously in the metaphysics of **Schopenhauer**. Twentieth-century philosophy of music manifests the typical disjunction between the continental approach, which examines music from the vantage point of an often grand-scale, culturally situated, critical aesthetic theory (for example, **Adorno**), and the analytic approach, which tends to compartmentalize the philosophic inquiry into the nature, properties, and effect of music. Contemporary Anglo-American philosophy of music revolves around a number of well defined general themes: **ontology, representation, expression,** and **understanding**. The ontology of music as a performing art is informed both by the status of most musical works as multiple, and by further complications pertaining to advances in music technology (for example, sampling and other post-production manipulations of previously existing material related to the **analog/digital distinction**). The latter is a reason for differentiating the ontology of standard, common-practice, so-called 'classical' music from the ontology of rock and other kinds of popular music, which arguably bears some resemblance to the ontology of **film**. Either way, the prevalent problems in the ontology of music pertain to the existence and identity of the musical work. These problems can be addressed by means of the standard **type/token distinction**, but there remains a difficulty in identifying the musical type. Since the musical work has an intentional character, the musical type cannot be situated unambiguously in the realm of physical sound without losing precisely that which makes a given sound-pattern music for us. It is also difficult to relegate the musical type to some wholly **abstract**, eternal realm without falling prey to the vagaries of **Platonism**. A third alternative – identifying the work with the score – is bound to fail for reasons which would sound trivial to any performing musician: in most cases what the performer does is never fully commanded by the score. The philosophical issues pertaining to representation and expression in music hinge upon the general view that music is **mimetic**, and that musical **meaning** should be construed as a relation between the music and extra-musical content. This general view is related in turn to the view of music as **language** – that is, the attempt to understand the phenomena of music in syntactic and semantic terms. Typically, those who tend to resist the analogy between music and language – such as proponents of musical **formalism** (for example, **Hanslick**) – would flatly deny that pure instrumental music, so-called **absolute music,** can be either about features of external reality or else about the **emotions**, although musical features may **resemble** both to some extent (for example, birdsong or the expressive contour of a human sigh) to some extent. The main reason is the failure of music, being mere aural syntax, to pin down some particular object or the relevant attitudes. Nor, others argue, does musical

understanding require apprehending thoughts about any particular subject. Such objections may be met within the framework of a **make-believe theory** although formalists would still insist that the idea of make-believe inevitably renders the musical experience impure, as it were, using music as a screen for projecting one's own fictional **narrative**. The expressive character of, for example, sad music can be explained in non-representational terms most readily as a case of the music making us literally sad. However, **arousalism** generally fails to account for other obvious cases, in which recognizing intense **emotions** in the music is quite compatible with not being emotionally moved by the music. Alternative cognitivist approaches include: (1) regarding the expressive properties of music as a case of exemplification, as **Goodman** does, but this entails the possibility of reference in music; (2) regarding such properties as resembling human emotional or as being isomorphic to human emotion, but this entails a commitment to the idea that music is essentially mimetic; (3) adhering to the **persona theory**. While the latter option seems more promising in enabling us to account for the particular interest of expressive properties to the listener, it risks dabbling in speculative metaphysics.

See **affective fallacy; authenticity; cognitivism, aesthetic; Gesamtkunstwerk; Goodman; illusion; improvisation; interpretation; Langer; Nietzsche; notation; profundity; properties, aesthetic; Wagner**

Further reading: Adorno 2002; Kivy 2002; Ridley 2004; Scruton 1997

narrative: A narrative consists of the way, and the means by which, we tell a story. Narrative is not restricted to a particular form, or **medium**, it can be fictional or real, or any combination of the two. It does presuppose some logical structure – the occurrence of change from one state of affairs to another – but it also presents itself as open for further alteration, or retelling. In this general sense, narrative is pervasive and omnipresent in our lives: folk tales, novels, gossip, newscasts, rituals, and movies are all narratives, and some would argue that history itself and even **science** are narratives too. As a universal phenomenon, narrative is studied not only by philosophy, but also by the social sciences, and it has become the object of a specialized interdisciplinary field called 'narratology' which bears close connection to **semiotics** and **hermeneutics**. In aesthetics, the notion of narrative is applicable across the board, most naturally with regards to **literature, theater,** and **film,** where it is specifically considered in relation to the issue of **fiction,** in particular with the problem whether, and in what sense, fictional narratives differ from non-fictional narratives. Narrative is also relevant to the visual arts, where it pertains mostly to the issue of **representation,** and even to **music,** where it is commonly related to the issue of **expression** and specifically to the problem of **absolute music.** Some of the common presuppositions of narrative are of particular importance in aesthetics. For example, the distinction between narrative (the product) and narration (the telling) invites the postulation of the narrator as a fictional entity. Such a move is essential, for instance, to the **persona theory** in music. Another distinction, between the narrator and her audience, is important for discussion of the nature of fictional narratives insofar as one wishes to locate fictionality in the **imaginative** license granted to the audience. Narrative is also considered with regards to aesthetic **value.** It has been argued that the value that we attach to certain artworks – for example, moral **truth** in novels – requires the kind of unfolding that is narrative.

See **anthropology; Barthes; interpretation; Ricoeur; text; understanding**

Further reading: Booth 1983; Chatman 1980

naturalistic fallacy: A term introduced by **Moore** in his *Principia Ethica* (1903), pertaining to the philosophical tendency to identify something which is indefinable and unanalyzable with something else. Moore contended that this fallacy has been as commonly committed with regard to **beauty** as with regard to good. Since, for Moore, beauty, like the good, is a simple indefinable property, to commit a naturalistic fallacy is to reduce aesthetic propositions to either **psychological** propositions or definitions as to how people use words.

See **open question argument; properties, aesthetic**

Further reading: Moore 1993

New Criticism: A diverse group of scholars – including, among others, poet T. S. Eliot, literary critics I. A. Richards and William K. Wimsatt, and philosopher **Monroe Beardsley** – who dominated Anglo-American literary criticism in the 1940s and early 1950s. The term also denotes their method of choice, which was premised on the idea that the poetic **text** in itself – isolated from the conditions of its production or the effect of its public reception – is the proper subject matter of critical analysis. This main idea was expressed in Wimsatt and Beardsley's well known arguments against what they dubbed respectively the **intentional fallacy** and the **affective fallacy**. The New Critics focused their efforts on textual explication, the study of rhetorical devices and the various structural features of the poetic text. This was complemented by a matching **epistemology**: the New Critics also maintained that the poetic text instantiates **meaning** and knowledge. Both concerns are reflected, for instance, in Beardsley's theory of **metaphor**, wherein the philosophical significance of this trope is explicated as interplay between two levels of meaning: the central meaning of the word and its marginal meaning, consisting of those properties that the word suggests or connotes. While the critical agenda of the New Critics has become somewhat dated, some of their most significant tenets still flourish under various guises. The blatant anti-positivism of the new critics was gleefully picked up by **poststructuralists,** who similarly wish to deny the possibility of any resolute reading of a text. For one, there is a striking kinship between the challenge that the New Critics posed to the idea of authorship and the sentiments concerning the purported 'death of the author', which have been voiced, for instance, by **Barthes.** The New Critics' sensitivity to subtle interdependencies of structure and content, and to the manner in which such intricacies may disclose latent levels of meaning remain as relevant as ever in **gendered aesthetics.**

See **autonomy, aesthetic; deconstruction; Derrida; interpretation; postmodernism**

Further reading: Beardsley and Wimsatt 1946 and 1949; Brooks 1947; Brooks and Warren 1960; Ransom 1941

new media: A blanket description for a whole range of different objects, processes, and social practices, which have been growing increasingly intertwined and which already pertain almost equally to the domains of **communication,** entertainment, and lifestyle. What we ordinarily count as new media may consist of one or more of the following standard categories: (1) computer-mediated communications, primarily e-mail, chat rooms, voice image transmissions, the web and mobile telephony;

(2) digital technologies for distributing and consuming, primarily media texts characterized by interactivity and hypertext formats, such as the world-wide-web, CD-ROM, DVD and the various platforms for computer games; (3) **virtual reality**, which runs the gamut from computer-mediated representations to fully immersive simulated spaces; and (4) a whole range of transformations and dislocations of established media in, for example, **photography**, television, and **film**. New media challenge aesthetic theory on various fronts. First, the varied origins of new media technologies in realms as remote from one another as military cybernetics, the entertainment industry, early twentieth-century avant-garde art and computer technology necessarily give rise to **medium** hybridity and to artistic conceptualism. Digital reproduction itself has important **ontological** ramifications, since it dissolves the distinction between original and copy. Thus, unless transferred and fixed into an analog medium, a digital artifact is a multiple work. The automatization of digital processes – for instance, in self-generating texts and forms or in hypertext artifacts – introduces **chance** into certain new media artifacts, and further upsets such notions as **artifactuality**, authorship, the **autographic art/allographic art distinction**, and **narrative**. Furthermore, arguably digital interactivity is performative, that is, the interaction with the new media artifact becomes itself an **aesthetic object**.

See **analog/digital distinction; conceptual art; definition of art; hybrid art forms; performance art; single/ multiple distinction**

Further reading: Binkley 1997; Lopes 2009; Manovich 2000; Saltz 1997; Vesna 2007

Nietzsche, Friedrich (1844–1900): German philosopher, poet, and cultural critic, also an occasional composer of some **music** for piano. His radical philosophical ideas, such as the death of god, the *Übermensch*, and the perspectival character of all knowledge, as well as his highly stylized literary mode of philosophical exposition, had an immense influence throughout the twentieth century on various schools of thought, such as **existentialism** and **postmodernism**. His thinking also had a substantial impact on the arts, most notably on the composer Gustav Mahler, as well as on **Freud** and the emergence of **psychoanalysis**. Much in Nietzsche's varied philosophical writing on art is directly connected to his troubled association with **Schopenhauer** and **Wagner**. His early essay, *The Birth of Tragedy* (1872), is the work of a young admirer. Nietzsche not only followed Schopenhauer's metaphysics of the Will, but also embraced the view that art is valuable for survival amid the horrors of human existence. The important question is always what art can do. He moved beyond Schopenhauer by utilizing the **Apollonian/Dionysian distinction** to develop a critical diagnosis of European **culture**, which he believed to be bereft of a will to live, and to explain how art affirms life. Wagner's art emerged victorious in this essay as the great contemporary promise for cultural regeneration. In later years, as Nietzsche grew increasingly disillusioned with Schopenhauer's asceticism, and his friendship with Wagner went sour, he penned a series of polemic essays against Wagner's belabored music and depleted Schopenhauerian aesthetics. In particular, Nietzsche rejected Schopenhauer's characterization of the **aesthetic experience** in terms of the cognitive import of **disinterestedness**, emphasizing instead the creative, frenzied drive of the artist, which he attached to his notion of a higher humanity. Nietzsche's later philosophy of art shows a deepening of some of the original, anti-cognitivist themes in *The Birth of Tragedy*, including the creative, transfiguring powers of art, the existential justification for aestheticizing or beautifying life, and, crucially in this context, the contrast between **beauty** and **truth**, and hence the vitality of art as opposed to the lethargic effect of **science**.

See **genius; Gesamtkunstwerk; poststructuralism; profundity; romanticism; sublime; tragedy**

Further reading: Nietzsche 1967

notation: In Western tradition, the history and development of performing arts such as **music** and **dance** is inseparable from the development of the relevant notational systems for performance, and common practice in such arts would be unrecognizable in the absence of notation. Indeed the most significant changes in twentieth-century art music are connected with the invention of new means of notation or with the obliteration of standard notational practices. Arts that admit notation are commonly allographic (it is noteworthy that not all allographic arts are based on notation), the exception being notation that admits **chance** operations or otherwise does not determine a fixed sequence. According to **Goodman**, notation must be syntactically disjoined and articulated. This means that each mark in the notational system must belong to no more than one character and cannot be associated otherwise. In contra-distinction, **text** in natural **language** is not fully disjointed and articulate, allowing common ambiguities, hence it fails to be a notation. Thus notation and pictorial **representation**, which is dense and replete, are on the opposite sides of Goodman's spectrum. Interestingly, this corresponds to the **analog/digital distinction**. Owing to its aforementioned syntactic nature, notation patently underdetermines performance, insofar as the performance involves the **interpretation** of the relevant notation by human performers. This is even more pronounced in dance than in music, and at any rate more pronounced in non-standard notational systems, which lack the conventional foundation of common practice. Hence the problem of **authenticity** arises, not only in the performing arts but also regarding the faithful rendition of other kinds of allographic works, for example, in **architecture**.

See **autographic art/allographic art distinction; ontology**

Further reading: Goodman 1976

objectivism: The view that **aesthetic judgments** pertain to, and are measured against, qualities and their particular arrangement, which we perceive to exist in the given object. For the objectivist, a judgment is justified to the extent that we can establish that the object indeed possesses those qualities and relations. If so, it is true. Objectivism is a form of universalism about **aesthetic properties**. To affirm that a work of art is beautiful is to imply that anyone who judges it correctly ought to find it beautiful as well. Thus, objectivism is diametrically opposed to **subjectivism**, which locates the determination of beauty in the personal feelings of the spectator. Still, objectivists may acknowledge that such feelings can accompany the aesthetic judgment without being intrinsic to it. Objectivism typically involves difficulties in settling matters of **beauty** (or any other aesthetic property) and aesthetic **value** merely by referring to descriptive features of the artwork. Objectivist accounts of **beauty** have been around since **Plato**, for whom beauty was a pure objective form intuited by the mind, and **Aristotle**, who contended that the chief forms of beauty are inherent in mathematics, for example, order, symmetry and definiteness. Objectivism was also a staple of early modern rationalist accounts of beauty and was also prominent in **Baumgarten's** aesthetics in the eighteenth century. In the twentieth century, **perceptual** objectivism was notably expounded by **Sibley**.

See **truth**

Further reading: Sibley 2006

objects, aesthetic: Circularly stated, aesthetic objects are the objects of **aesthetic experience**. Often the term is used as a placeholder for the artwork, but the idea remains theory-laden. The nature of the object depends on the given definitions for the artistic **medium** and the aesthetic experience. Thus an aesthetic object can be a physical object (for example, in imitation theories), a **perceptual** object (for example, in **Beardsley**), or an ideal object (for example, in **Croce** and **Collingwood**).

See **attitude, aesthetic; expression theory of art; ontology; representation theory of art**

Further reading: Beardsley 1981; Ingarden 1961

ontology: Ontology is the philosophic study of what there is. It is one of the most fundamental, broad fields of philosophic inquiry. It is generally concerned with showing that certain entities exist, with explaining their mode of existence, and with describing the most general features and relation of such entities. Aesthetic theories may be informed and even shaped by general ontological commitments. For instance, **Plato's** indictment of the arts derived its force from his ontology of forms. **Schopenhauer** believed that **music** is the most superior art of all because it is an immediate reflection of the metaphysical Will, understood as ultimate reality. Deep differences in ontological commitment between mainstream analytic aesthetics and **hermeneutics** result in radically different theories of art interpretation. And so forth. The ontology of art is a specialized branch of aesthetics which studies the existence of artworks in the most general terms. Some artworks seem to exist in a different way compared to other artworks. An oil **painting** by Rembrandt is a physical thing, a singular specimen which will be lost forever if stolen or burnt, while a Mozart symphony is most readily understood as a sound-type, existing in many actual performances, consecutive or simultaneous, brilliant or pedestrian, each of which is a genuine Mozart. The ontology of art in the analytic tradition is predominantly descriptive: it usually attempts to capture such conceptual differences and divisions among the arts within a unified theory.

See **artifactuality; authenticity; autographic art/ allographic art distinction; contextualism; essentialism; forgery; formalism; medium; notation; objects, aesthetic; singular/multiple distinction; titles; type/token distinction**

Further reading: Currie 1989; Goodman 1976; Wollheim 1980; Wolterstorff 1980

open question argument: An argument devised by **Moore** in his *Principia Ethica* (1903) in order to show that ultimately any attempt to define a fundamental value is bound to fail since such terms, for example 'good', denote simple yet indefinable objects. Moore argued that for any tentative definition of 'good' – call it 'D' – we can ask meaningfully whether 'D' is good, and argued that this question would remain an open question. For instance, if we define 'good' as '**pleasure**, it remains an open, independently meaningful question whether some pleasure is good. Moore's argument and its **essentialist** conclusion was adapted to aesthetics by **Bell**, who attempted to show that **significant form** is a fundamental aesthetic **value** which, while impinging directly on our consciousness, remains indefinable.

See **beauty; naturalistic fallacy; properties, aesthetic**
Further reading: Moore 1993

ornamentation: Decorative artifacts – Oriental rugs, flowery wallpaper, rococo embellishments, and so on – have a distinctly **abstract** quality, often consisting of, but importantly not limited to, complex repetitive patterns. While ornamentation has a long history, having been employed since ancient times and in many **cultures**, the decorative arts were initially left out of the **modern system of the arts** owing to their non-representational character, and they traditionally did not garner the same respect in aesthetics as the 'official' fine arts. Recent studies of ornamentation, most notably by **Gombrich** and **Arnheim**, focused mainly on the **psychological** mechanisms and the evolutionary and cognitive **value** underlying the human interest in striking a fine balance between the regular (expected) and the irregular (unexpected). Ornamentation manifests and rewards our efforts to make sense of our environment by actively superimposing an order on the existing order of things. The **make-believe theory** offers a philosophically broader understanding of ornamentation in terms of psychologically inhibited participation in games of make-believe. Ornamental representations, even ornamental elements in bona fide representations, draw our attention to the actual patterns or elements, and away from vivid **imagining**. This framework affords not only a consideration of the full range of ornamental phenomena, but also of the pervasive coexistence of ornamentation and **representation** in the fine arts, and the **self-referential** character of ornamentation.

See **mimesis**

Further reading: Arnheim 1968; Gombrich 1979; Walton 1990

P

painting: When one thinks of the most standard case of a painting – say, Da Vinci's *Mona Lisa* – the first thing that strikes one's mind is its sheer **artifactuality**. Such a work of art seems to be the paradigmatic instance of an ontologically **singular** and autographic work. Indeed the main philosophical issues pertaining to the art of painting are related to this general **ontological** characterization. Ontological conundrums concerning **forgery** and **authenticity** are most obvious in this sense, but one can also consider the **intentionalist** temptation to construe what the painter does on the canvas as some form of **communication**. Moreover, even more puzzles are generated when these characteristics are disrupted or undermined, whether by the introduction of mechanical reproduction into the art of painting, as **Benjamin** observed, or when the deliberate introduction of **chance** operations attempts to undercut the artist's intention (for example, action painting) or even artifactuality altogether. The *Mona Lisa* is also a figurative painting. In it we see that lady with the mystic smile. In analytic aesthetics, most of the contemporary theories which concern painting are competing theories of pictorial **representation** or theories of pictorial **perception**, ranging from **Bell's** theory of **significant form** to **Wollheim's** theory of **twofoldness**. All these theories try to give a proper account of experiences like the one with *Mona Lisa*. Of course, the disruption of figurativity by means of **abstraction**, for instance, which has become a hallmark of twentieth-century modern painting, generate some more puzzles concerning the possibility of non-representational painting. For example, theories like Wollheim's and the **make-believe theory** attempted to include non-representational painting under the aegis of a representational theory of painting. It is noteworthy that contemporary continental aesthetics offers a different variety of theoretical concerns and approaches to painting. For example, **semiotic** analyses of visual **texts, phenomenological** analyses of the visual field, and the overall concern of **hermeneutics** with the ontology of painting given our historically situated conditions of knowing.

See **Arnheim; autographic art/allographic art distinction; Barthes; Gombrich; Heidegger; illusion; mimesis; photography; resemblance; significant form**

Further reading: Wollheim 1987

paradox of acting: Named after the famous essay by the French philosopher, novelist and playwright Denis Diderot (1713–84), who described the unequal acting of players who play from the heart. The paradox emerges from Diderot's suggestion that great actors should move us emotionally without being moved themselves, that is, without actually experiencing the **emotions** they are portraying as characters on the stage.

See **expression; imagination; make-believe theory; theater**

Further reading: Diderot 1965

paradox of fiction: We may really fall in love with Anna Karenina, or with Sherlock Holmes. Both are fictional entities and we do not believe that they really exist. But if we accept that **emotions** are intentional and that to love someone logically presupposes believing that the object of our emotion actually exists, then we run into a paradox. The paradox of fiction is engendered by our difficulty to explain our real emotional response to **fiction**. To resolve the paradox we need to deny either (1) that we really fall in love with Anna or Sherlock (for instance, by trying to show that what we actually feel is some alternative state of mind, which does not entail real existence), or (2) that loving Anna or Sherlock logically requires that we believe that they really exist (for instance, by conceptually weakening this requirement); or (3) that we do not believe that they exist (for instance, by showing that we are psychologically in the grip of the fictional **narrative** to the extent that we suspend our disbelief or perhaps become irrational in some sense). It is noteworthy that the **make-believe theory** has generally proven quite successful in providing a solid resolution (of the first type aforementioned): our **psychological** participation in sufficiently elaborate games of make-believe could get us close enough to feeling real emotion for fictional entities.

See **imagination; representation**
Further reading: Hjort and Laver 1997

paradox of suspense: A familiar experience among movie buffs is the thrill which accompanies each viewing of a familiar suspense scene. The paradox of suspense arises from the inconsistency of three individually acceptable propositions: (1) the experience of suspense in **fiction** requires uncertainty on the part of the viewers; (2) familiarity with the **narrative's** outcome eliminates uncertainty; (3) viewers experience suspense in fiction when they are familiar with the narrative's outcome. It has been suggested that it is possible to resolve the paradox by interpreting the notion of uncertainty in proposition (1) modally. That is, in order to experience suspense, it is enough that the viewer merely entertains uncertainty, **imagining** how the narrative's outcome could be different.

See **emotions; film**
Further reading: Carroll 2001

paradox of tragedy: Watching Oedipus piercing his eyes on the stage is pleasurable, although in real life we would have been sickened by the sight. The paradox of **tragedy** is brought about by the difficulty of explaining how the experience of pain and horror elicited by the tragic events is also experienced as **pleasure**, and furthermore, why we hold such art to be particularly aesthetically valuable. The paradox can be evaded by denying that such art does not really arose negative **emotions**, or else by denying that the negative emotions are unpleasant or objectionable. Alternatively, the two most commonly cited solutions are **Aristotle's** theory of **catharsis**, which suggests that enduring the horror is ultimately rewarded psychologically and socially, and **Hume's** idea in his essay *Of Tragedy* that the negative emotions are over-whelmed and converted by the concurrent pleasure that we experience, leaving an altogether positive experience. The paradox of tragedy can be generalized to apply to other cases of negative emotion in art, most notably in horror **films.**

See **arousalism; fiction; imagination; psychology; theater; value**

Further reading: Aristotle 1995; Carroll 1990; Hume 1987

pastiche: The term originates from the French *pastiche* and also from the Italian *pasticcio*, and it usually denotes a work – literary, visual, or musical – which imitates a distinct **style**, replicates the content of another work, or otherwise consists of a medley of some other works of art or parts thereof. It is often used in a pejorative sense, indicating a lack of **imagination** or creativity. For this reason, as well as for its common lack of critical and cognitive significance, a pastiche fails to be a genuine **hybrid art form.** Still, pastiche has some obvious **value**

for decorative arts, and it has often been used effectively in parody. It is also quite common in **new media** art. **Postmodern** thought, itself an occasional pastiche, has sought to rehabilitate the idea of pastiche as some sort of playful practice of 'double-coding', hence **meaningful** and creative after all, especially in **architecture**. However, it is not clear at all whether pastiche rises to the level of artistic **self-reference**.

See **forgery; ornamentation**

Further reading: Rose 1991

perception: The study of perception is indigenous to **psychology**, philosophy of mind, **epistemology** and **phenomenology** – **science** studies it empirically while philosophy does so conceptually under various guises. Aspects of all these different modes of inquiry into the nature of perception, its conceptual structure, and its underlying processes inform considerations of some of the central issues in aesthetics, such as **aesthetic properties** and **aesthetic appreciation**. Theories of **aesthetic attitude** from **Kant** onwards are commonly couched in perceptual terms as they aim to demarcate a unique species of aesthetic perception. **Bell's** theory of **significant form** epitomizes the idea of aesthetic perception. Theories of **representation** pertaining to the perceptual arts (primarily the visual arts and **music**) may incorporate, and often are shaped by, current empirical knowledge and conceptual and phenomenological analyses of perception. To adduce a few examples: **Gombrich's** rejection of the 'myth of the **innocent eye**' and his theory of pictorial representation as a form of **illusion** hinged on the idea that perception is permeated by cognition, while **Arnheim's** theory capitalized on the findings of **Gestalt theory**. **Wollheim's** treatment of the phenomenon of seeing-in underscores the intentional character of the kind of seeing appropriate to pictures. In the philosophy of music, the **ontological** disagreement between **formalism** and **contextualism** manifested itself at some point in two contrasting views of the structure of musical perception: namely, synoptic apprehension of musical form as opposed to following a concatenation of bite-size phenomenal units of musical experience.

See **aspect-perception; photographic transparency; science; seeing-as/seeing-in distinction; synaesthesia**

Further reading: Arnheim 1974; Bell 1958; Gombrich 1986

performance art: A contemporary, radical **hybrid art form,** closely associated with **conceptual art,** often combining distinct elements of **theater, music, dance,** and various visual arts, in which the performing artist becomes not only a participant in her own art, but on occasion also its corporeal subject matter. Performance art is open-ended, not restricted by content, **medium,** or any standard considerations pertaining to performance time and space. It may take the shape of anything from the most mundane activities to brutal self-mutilation. Typically, performance art deliberately disrupts conventional boundaries. For example, in happenings the traditional distinctions between performers and audience, and between performance and public space, are eliminated, and the formal aspects of **narrative** are being undercut by **chance** operations. The result not only upsets the **ontological** categorization of the given work, but also the very idea of an **aesthetic object,** which arguably necessitates some measure of **disinterestedness.** These aesthetic characteristics actually serve the often **politically** embedded nature of such events. Furthermore, performance art aims at breaking the distinction between the artist and her work, often by using the body as the physical medium of the art work. This iconoclastic focus on the body and its image has been propelled by feminist and other types of **gendered aesthetics**.

See **improvisation; postmodernism**

Further reading: Goldberg 1995

persona theory: Officially referred to as 'the persona theory of musical expressiveness', this is a contemporary attempt to carry over the idea that composition is founded on the basic act of dramatic impersonation from literary theory to the philosophy of **music**. The basic idea, common to all advocates of this theory, is that human emotional behavior and response is the most appropriate model for the musical **expression** of **emotions**. The idea that our response to music is akin to our response to people, that music has in a sense a human physiognomy, has been explored by **Wittgenstein**, who put it to interesting philosophical use in his later work. However, his original philosophical foray should not be confused with the current persona theory, which postulates an indefinite person-like entity as a focus for our emotional response to music, and so is bound to entangle itself with **ontological** questions concerning the identity and nature of this hypothetical entity. According to the persona theory, as we hear sadness, for instance, in the music, we actually imagine a hypothetical musical persona who expresses her sorrow, and we identify or sympathize with her. For that reason, sad music can make us sad on occasion, although this does not entail simple **arousalism**. The persona theory is not just a theory of musical expressiveness, but also a theory of musical **meaning** and **value**. The **imaginary** engagement with the musical persona in a given piece of music is supposed to give us access to what the music actually means and why it is of such value to the listener. In this respect, the theory is a response to the **formalist's** inability to give a strong account of the interest that we take in pure instrumental music, so-called **absolute music**, and why we deem it emotionally relevant or **profound**. It is also a response to the **make-believe theory**, which is bound to reduce expressiveness to **representation**. The persona theory is open to misgivings concerning the viability of attributing literary mechanisms of emotional identification or any concrete extra-musical **narrative** to pure instrumental music. It also raises important issues concerning the role of the composer's warrant to engage with the music in such a way, hence concerning the general problem of the relevance of the artist's intention to a proper **understanding** of the work of art.

See **contextualism; intentionalism**

Further reading: Kivy 2009; Levinson 2006; Robinson 2005

phenomenology: As the name attests, this is the systematic philosophical study of phenomena, or appearances. However, the term conflates a whole array of different doctrines and methodologies, which cannot be reduced to any single conclusive set of concerns. The main proponents of phenomenology in the twentieth century were Husserl, **Heidegger, Sartre** and Merleau-Ponty, so phenomenology bears close relations to both **hermeneutics** and **existentialism**. In general, phenomenology presents itself as a critique of traditional philosophy. To achieve the real task of philosophy, a radical change of attitude must be performed, moving away from the objectified **meanings** of things, as presented by **science**, to their meanings as immediately experience in the 'lived-world', that is, the world as we act in it, prior to any theorizing about it. In phenomenology this is called 'reduction' or 'epoché'. Phenomenologists also subscribe to the doctrine of intentionality. Ideas like the description and analysis of immediate experiences, as well as the intentionality of consciousness, are not foreign to analytic aesthetics, and can be fruitfully employed without subscribing to any particular phenomenological program. For instance, arguably some aspects of the aesthetics of **Beardsley** and **Wollheim** are distinctly phenomenological. Still other staples of continental phenomenology, and its ensuing aesthetic theory, such as the peculiar concern for the question of the meaning of Being (most notably in Heidegger's work), have had very little influence on analytic aesthetics.

See **epistemology; experience, aesthetic; perception**
Further reading: Dufrenne 1973; Heidegger 1971

photographic transparency: The thesis that visually attending to a photograph enables us to literally see things that are remote from us in time and space, for example, distant places and dead relatives. **Photography** is said to be transparent in an epistemic sense: photographs are counterfactually dependent on the scenes that they depict, which means that for any given photograph, had the scene been different, the photograph of it should have had a different look; furthermore, this counterfactual dependence is not mediated by the intentions of the photographer. The importance of the transparency thesis lies not only in its bold account of photographic **realism**, relegating photographs to other artificial means of seeing-aids like mirrors and telescopes, but also by setting a sharp epistemic difference between photography and **painting**. Paintings are epistemically opaque by these standards even at their most realistic. We simply do not see through them. Moreover, the thesis may be conducive to anti-realism about **representation**: contrary to photographs, bona fide representations stand in intentional relation to what they represent, so **understanding** them requires recognizing the manner in which they embody a certain thought. Objections to the transparency thesis have included insisting that the photographic practice, indeed the photographic process itself, is replete with distortions, and it is patently in the full control of the photographer, inevitably colored by her interests and attitudes. The counterintuitive grouping of photographs with such visual aids as mirrors and telescopes is resisted by arguing that, contrary to ordinary seeing, photographs do not convey information about the spatial and temporal relations between the object seen and ourselves. It is noteworthy that the transparency thesis is at odds with digital photography, which while being an epitome of photographic realism in any ordinary sense, would still be regarded as epistemically opaque, very much like painting, if we consider the fundamental technological malleability of this **medium**.

See **analog/digital distinction; epistemology; film; new media; perception**

Further reading: Currie 1991; Scruton 1983; Snyder and Allen 1975; Walton 1984

photography: A relatively young art, less than 150 years old, photography began its life in optico-chemical technology but its **medium** is already being transformed by recent digital technology. The exact nature of this transformation and its effect on mainstay problems in the **ontology** and **epistemology** of photography is a matter of ongoing debate and speculation. A central tenet in the philosophy of photography, which is traceable to the original work of French theorist and critic André Bazin (1918–58), is the **essentialist** definition of photography in terms of a special, causal ontological link of the photograph to its subject matter. Arguably, due to its mechanical means of production, photography is automatic and objective, and this eliminates the artist's intention from the medium. This is where photography differs most dramatically from realistic **painting**: photographs are connected to reality in a way that paintings can never be. These ontological sentiments can be found both in analytic and in continental aesthetics, most notably in **Barthes'** distinction between the *studium* of a photograph, which relates to its **cultural** encoding, and its *punctum*, which is what rises out of the photograph to pierce the viewer. From this ontological characterization follows the **photographic transparency** thesis, which remains one of the most hotly debated topics in field. The thesis has the important, albeit contested, implication that, contrary to painting, photography – at least 'ideal' photography, untainted by pre- or post-production manipulations – does not involve **representation**. Still, the very essentialist foundation of the philosophy of photography has been questioned on account of the multiplicity of cultural uses, artistic and other, for photographic technology, and the subordination of the various photographic media to such cultural needs. Indeed, as opposed to painting, photography is already well integrated into our dynamic living environment. As in the case of other forms of **new media** art, digital photography may be pushing aesthetic theory against what **Dewey** called the 'museum conception of art'.

See **analog/digital distinction; automatism; intentionalism; realism**

Further reading: Barthes 1981; Bazin 1967; Maynard 1997; Scruton 1983; Snyder and Allen 1975; Walton 1984

Plato (427–347 BC): Ancient Greek philosopher, a student of Socrates and the teacher of **Aristotle**. Plato's ideas had an immense, long-lasting influence on the formation and course of Western philosophy. Plato's harsh indictment of the arts, which culminated in his call for the exile of poets from the ideal city-state in Book X of his *Republic*, is informed by his grand metaphysics of pure forms, by his hands-on experience with the rhetorical efficacy of artistic imagery, and by some overarching pessimism concerning human nature, which he famously captured in his bleak tale of the cave. Plato believed that genuine knowledge can only be secured by means of intellectual apprehension of pure forms (for example, 'squareness', 'horseness'), and that while things in the perceptible world cannot be in themselves sources of real knowledge, they are knowable insofar as they partake in their respective pure forms. Plato defines this relation between a concrete thing and its pure form as **mimesis** in the specific sense of mirroring or image-making. Thus any concrete table is a copy or imitation of an original, which is the pure form of 'tableness', wherein **truth** resides, and any further **representation** of the concrete table, whether pictorially or verbally, is bound to produce a mere copy of a copy, twice removed from truth. Plato's **epistemological** argument is complemented by his **psychological** observation in Books II and III of the *Republic* that the arts exert a pervasive influence on the emotional make-up of human beings, therefore careful monitoring of the exposure of the public to the effects of certain types of poetry or **music** is required in order to ensure virtuous **education**. Plato's ultimate conclusion is both anti-cognitivist and moralist: mimetic art is patently fallacious, its public use is bound to have erroneous results; therefore it should be censored. Plato's enduring influence on the philosophic **understanding** of art and artists has been many-sided. While giving initial form to the idea of **censorship** in art, his discussion of the arts in the

Republic, despite its largely negative conclusions, opened up possibilities for re-thinking the relations between art and truth, and between art and the **emotions**. His musings on the divine madness of the inspired poet, in the *Ion* and the *Phaedrus*, planted seeds which later emerged in full bloom in the **romanticist** idolizing of the **genius**. Furthermore, the characteristic tension within Plato's dialogic **style** between what he says and how he says it, between the explicit doctrine and the artistic form that sustains it, can be considered as a subtle beginning for a profound theme in Western philosophy, that of art as a way of doing philosophy.

See **beauty; cognitivism, aesthetic; language; moralism**
Further reading: Plato 1997

pleasure, aesthetic: The notion of aesthetic pleasure is well entrenched in the history of aesthetics since the eighteenth century. It has been repeatedly regarded as the quintessential experience which is valuable for its own sake, qualified to serve as the locus for aesthetic **value**. Aesthetic pleasure was central to **taste theories**, which defined the faculty of taste as a capacity for taking this kind of pleasure in sense experiences with beautiful things. The **phenomenological** qualification of aesthetic pleasure in terms of **disinterestedness** came with **Kant**, and it has endured in one form or another as the hallmark of the **aesthetic attitude** well into the twentieth century. For instance, **Bell** characterized the experience of **significant form** as a kind of disinterested pleasure which he called 'aesthetic emotion' (although it lacks the essential characteristics of any real emotion), and **Beardsley** referred to the aesthetic pleasure that we take in either the formal qualities of the artwork or in its regional characters (that is, qualities which result from the characteristics of the parts of the work and the relationships among them).

See **beauty; Hume; judgment, aesthetic; open question argument; paradox of tragedy**

Further reading: Beardsley 1981; Bell 1958; Hume 1987; Kant 1952

point of view: When we look at a **photograph** or a realistic **painting**, we see what is represented in the picture from a concrete point of view, which does not coincide with our actual point of view vis-à-vis the two-dimensional **representation** before us. This **fictional** point of view is an **aesthetic property** of the picture, and the very possibility of its existence sets standard depictions apart from **abstract** or **ornamental** representations, including **music**, which do not give us enough **perceptual** cues for the generation of a fictional point of view. It also sets them apart from three-dimensional objects, for example, **sculptures**, which do not mandate any particular fictional point of view, and **texts**, which may mandate a fictional point of view, but only by means of belabored, dense descriptions, and never as part of a perceptual game of **make-believe**.

See **medium; realism**

Further reading: Walton 1990

politics: The idea that art is related to politics presupposes that art is socially embedded, and that one cannot fully appreciate its **value** without observing how creating art and presenting it in the public domain are integral to the structure of society. As such, this presupposition negates the principle of **aesthetic autonomy**. Yet such ideas have ancient philosophical roots in **Plato's** demand to expel all poets from his ideal state as well as in **Aristotle's** favorable view of artistic **mimesis** as indigenous to the rationality of human beings, hence as politically constitutive of human beings. The connection between aesthetic and politics resides primarily in the various functional relations which may obtain between works of art and political goals. Art may be conducive to, or detrimental to, certain political goals, and depending on the case, the result would be the promotion and recruiting of such art, or else its persecution and censoring. Recent history abounds with extreme examples of both scenarios, the most blatant of which is probably the concurrent exhibition of 'Degenerate Art' and 'Great German Art' by the Nazi regime in 1937. When art is systematically created and manipulated for the sole purpose of serving political goals or otherwise 'aestheticizing' politics, this would be a case of propaganda, which often involves shameless employment of **kitsch**. In such cases, the problem regarding the **definition of art** becomes acute. In general, the relation between art and politics involves some underlying issues concerning the **meaning** of artworks, their aesthetic **value**, and the boundaries of admissible **interpretation**. Imbuing art with political meaning seems to require a preliminary general defense of **functionalism** and **moralism**, hence a rejection of various forms of **formalism** and **aestheticism**, which may prove more difficult when it comes to attributing political meaning to works of **abstract** art including pure instrumental **music**. Moreover, reading political content into works of art on the basis of the artist's personal circumstances might involve the **intentional fallacy**. Other difficulties arise concerning the provocative or even potentially hurtful nature of certain political art works, in particular those which invite censorship in liberal societies. Here we may inquire whether such 'politically evil' works can be of aesthetic value or specifically **beautiful** despite their blatant immorality. Finally, politics and aesthetics are patently related in most variants of continental aesthetics, which generally embody social or **cultural** criticism in one form or another. It is no wonder, for instance, that the very notion of aesthetic autonomy is highly problematic within the framework of **Adorno's** aesthetics.

See **Barthes; Benjamin; censorship; communication; ethics; existentialism; experimentalism; Frankfurt School; gendered aesthetics; law; Marxism; moralism; performance art; postmodernism; Sartre; semiotics; sociology**

Further reading: Eagleton 1990; Edelman 1995

pornography: An explicit, detailed, and often belabored or perverted depiction in **text,** imagery or performance of sexual activity and the genitals, in which the subjects are sexually objectified and exploited, and whose primary function is to arouse its audience sexually. Pornography is generally considered to be morally wrong, and in most societies it is a prime subject for stringent **censorship,** although there is considerable dispute about why this is so, and what justifies legislating against it. While the production and consumption of pornography is generally defended in liberal societies as an exercise in free speech, it is commonly argued that pornography is morally damaging for its audience, that its production often involves the infliction of physical harm, and that it depreciates certain groups within society, most notably women, hence actually offending against the principle of freedom of speech. The notion of pornographic art is oxymoronic insofar as pornography is exclusively defined in terms of its sordid function, hence patently lacking any reference to an artistic **medium.** Still, successful works of art may incorporate elements of **style,** content, or **cultural** convention which are recognizably pornographic. Arguably, in such cases the pornographic material is re-contextualized in such a way as to interfere with its primary function and to contribute, despite its alleged immoral character, to the overall artistic **value** of the work.

See ethics; gaze; gendered aesthetics; law; performance art; representation; sociology

Further reading: Dworkin 1985; Kieran 2001; Williams 1981

postmodernism: A cluster of multifarious reactions – theoretical, political, and artistic, sometimes all at the same time – not only to modern philosophy and its perennial presuppositions, but also to modern life broadly construed. Postmodernism is closely associated with continental thought, in particular with the onset of French poststructuralism, but its intellectual roots are quite diverse and, at least arguably, may include Wittgenstein's notion of language-games, Thomas Kuhn's theory of scientific revolutions and the ensuing interest in the sociological grounding of knowledge. Over the past three decades it has become widespread also in Anglo-American academia, in particular in literary, social, and cultural studies, and also in art and media theory. No less a style of philosophizing or a mode of exposition and expression, which was anticipated to some extent by Nietzsche, than a matter of intellectual history, postmodern thinking is patently obsessed with modernity qua cultural epoch and with its varied modernist manifestations, also in art, and on the whole it is deeply anti-Platonic. Postmodernism generally seeks, quite gleefully at times, to undercut foundationalism, essentialism, and realism on all fronts. Its ingrained suspicion concerning intellectually oppressive meta-narratives, together with its social constructivism, have led postmodernism to reject any privileged claim for knowledge, including such foundational theses as the very distinction between epistemology and the sociology of knowledge, the idea that knowledge involves veridical representation, the correspondence theory of truth, and in general the entire dream, set up by the Enlightenment, of knowledge as a coherent, canonical, explanatory system. While most of these critical issues have been raised and confronted already within the tradition of **modernism**, and also in analytic philosophy, the ultimate result according to postmodernism is a diametrically opposed view of reason itself as socially biased, historical, ethno-centric, and pervasively gendered; hence as patently oppressive rather than liberating. This is reflected in the critical recourse of some postmodern thinkers to **psychoanalysis**. The relation between postmodernism and aesthetics was bound to be highly problematic insofar as the sovereignty of the latter as well as its essential ties to modernism are concerned. It is noteworthy that, in a sense, **architecture** served as an intellectual cradle, so to speak, for postmodern thinking. This makes some genetic sense given the intimate enmeshment of architectural designs in the stream of life, which shelters them from the 'museumizing' **gaze** so harshly criticized in postmodern thinking about art. In general, postmodernism rejects all the grand historical narratives and epistemic structures underlying traditional, modernist aesthetics on both sides of the so-called continental-analytic divide. Since the history of ideas is to be conceived in terms of a history of power struggles, then any release ought to take the form of contextualizing, diversifying, and in a sense flattening of the discourse concerning works of art, their construction, and definition, in order to recapture their enmeshment in life. This is reflected, among other things, in the willingness of postmodernism to embrace the bizarre and the surreal, as commonly seen in contemporary **performance art**, as well as in its tendency to refract through various **gendered aesthetics**. However, whether postmodern aesthetics merely amounts to replacing one set of values for another or to a genuine 'trans-valuation of all values', as **Nietzsche** put it, remains a moot issue.

See anti-essentialism; deconstruction; Derrida; language; literature; museum; pastiche; Plato; politics; sublime; text

Further reading: Jameson 1991; Lyotard 1991

poststructuralism: A late twentieth-century philosophical development mainly in the continental tradition, which had a major impact on the formation and proliferation of contemporary postmodernism. Poststructuralism was essentially a reaction against structuralism but also an extension of it. Poststructuralist critics, most notably Derrida, challenged the purported self-sufficiency and stability which the structuralists attributed to systems of signs, as well as the structuralists' adherence to rigid, clear-cut, conceptual dichotomies for explicating those systems. While poststructurlism retained the structuralist contention that systems of signs are not constituted cognitively – that is, by some sort of a mental feat of a subject – they targeted the Cartesian faith in a logical foundation. The method of deconstruction was introduced in order to undermine such belief in the internal coherence of such systems. It is noteworthy that skepticism about the notion of a subject or about the veracity of representations had been around long before poststructuralism, and that anti-Cartesian themes in the philosophy of language concerning language-games and the indeterminacy of meaning, among other things, have been explored, seriously and deeply, also in analytic philosophy. Arguably, it is the novelty and rigor of the poststructuralists' focus on the analysis of texts – in particular the canons of Western metaphysics – which has created a genuine impact: deeply problematizing the notion of text in its relation to the ideas of meaning and interpretation, and of course, truth. Poststructuralists strive to show that texts are unstable linguistic structures; their meaning is never pre-fixed by authorial intention, even when there is evidence to the contrary, or delineated in any logically prior manner. Undercutting the very idea of privileged meaning opens up the text to a myriad of conflicting meanings, which in turn undercuts the traditional sense of interpretation as the systematic unearthing of meaning, truth, and knowledge. In other words, the practice of interpretation amounts to nothing more than free-style elaborating on the text, and in effect rendering itself as a text in its own right, to wit, an original creation, on a par with the text being interpreted. Evidently, such dynamics of instability, and the particular delight one takes in it, became a hallmark of ensuing literary theory and criticism. However, the poststructuralist literary ravaging of philosophical theories is *ipso facto* detrimental also to aesthetic theory, insofar as the latter traditionally aims at establishing necessary and sufficient conditions for privileged **value** judgments.

See **Barthes; cognitivism, aesthetic; gendered aesthetics; intertextuality; literature; Margolis; New Criticism**
Further reading: Culler 1982

profundity: An elusive, emotionally related aesthetic quality sometimes ascribed to certain works of art of uncommon human depth. It is supposed to be categorically distinct from both **beauty** and the **sublime**: ugliness in art can be profound, and profound art need not overwhelm us. Its elusiveness is in part a matter of linguistic ambiguity: it is both descriptive and evaluative. As such, 'profundity' might simply be a euphemism for adhering to a certain cultural canon: Bach is profound whereas the Beatles are not, or vice versa. It is distinctly also a **metaphor**, related to notions of depth, hence its meaning is always partly shaded, negatively related to what can be seen. An uncontroversial example for the idea of profundity in art would be the **tragedy**, in particular the crucial moment of **catharsis** which has repeatedly been described (for example, by **Schopenhauer** and early **Nietzsche**) precisely in those visually-negative terms, wherein, quite paradoxically it seems, we could gain access to genuine, deep knowledge about human existence. However, exactly what is profound in tragedy, or in any other such case – whether it is the prime **representation** of the 'metaphysical will' or something else – is always contingent upon the proposed definition and function of art within the given system of metaphysics. Thus the descriptive use of the term 'profundity' tends to beg the question. This can be seen, albeit indirectly, in the preoccupation of analytic aesthetics in recent years with the problem of profundity in pure instrumental **music**, which on the one hand still enjoys the romantic status of being the most profound art of all, but on the other hand allegedly evades any extra-musical content, which could serve as the bearer of profundity. The crux of this current debate is the possibility of musical 'aboutness', of relating **absolute music** to extra-musical content. Whatever makes any such purported content profound in the first place is passed over in silence.

See **cognitivism, aesthetic; culture; emotions; properties, aesthetic; romanticism; truth**

Further reading: Harrell 1992

properties, aesthetic: In general, properties are qualities, attributes, characteristics, and features of things. We ascribe aesthetic properties to works of art (also to natural objects) when we exercise our powers of discrimination on them. The contemporary discussion of aesthetic properties began with **Sibley** and remains a main concern for analytic philosophy. While **beauty** is perhaps a classic example of an aesthetic property, the first general thing to observe about aesthetic properties is their sheer variety. They include **emotional** properties (sad, joyful), **perceptible** (rhythmic) as well as non-perceptible properties (strange), anthropomorphic (sluggish) and formal properties (balanced), evaluative properties (beautiful), and many more. Importantly, the **language** that we use in order to ascribe aesthetic properties tends to be **metaphoric**, especially in the case of emotional and anthropomorphic properties. Aesthetic properties supervene on non-aesthetic, quantitative or physical properties (for example, length, shape) but also on secondary qualities such as color. The existence of the former depends on the existence of the latter, but it was Sibley's important point that the existence of the latter is never a sufficient condition for the existence of the former. Owing to their tertiary, emergent status, aesthetic properties commonly involve the **ontological** difficulty of determining whether these properties are real, objective properties of objects, or else that they merely amount to an ascription to external objects of our own attitudes and feelings. Still, the public character of the aesthetic discourse – that is, the fact that we can openly reason about what we see or hear in a work of art, and moreover allow others to see or hear for themselves by drawing their attention to aesthetic properties – seems to suggest that while aesthetic properties are not objective in any physical sense, they are still not mere projections.

See **appreciation, aesthetic; attitude;** *is* **of artistic identification; judgment, aesthetic; objectivism; realism; subjectivism; taste theories; value**

Further reading: Hermerén 1988; Sibley 2006

psychoanalysis: The clinical study of the mind and its development, and of human interaction and **culture**, which originated chiefly and most fully in the work of **Freud**.

Traditionally, psychoanalysis presupposes a dichotomy between the outer phenomenal realm of conscious, conceptualizable awareness and the inner realm of unconscious motivation, which cannot be fully known. The analysis of personality hinges upon conflict, namely, repression, which prevents unconscious material from reaching consciousness; hence the exploration of inner psychological reality requires breaking through wilful, albeit unconscious, defenses. **Interpretation** in psychoanalysis specifically denotes a method for bringing unconscious material into consciousness by means of lifting repression. Psychoanalytic interpretation aims at integrating these two mental realms in such a way as to generate meaningful continuities and contradictions. This often calls for elaborate ideational reconstruction of the inter-relationships between latent and manifest contents. Works of art, no less than dreams, are seen primarily as products of unconscious processes – that is, they are seen as the aestheticizing of unconscious material – so the psychoanalytic theory of art tends to recognize the effects of repression in every aspect of art-making and its use. Consequently, in line with its intellectual roots in the work of **Nietzsche**, psychoanalysis suggests also a theory of culture as the social embodiment of repression. Psychoanalysis has exerted considerable influence over twentieth-century aesthetics, primarily in the continental tradition, for instance in the aesthetics of the **Frankfurt School**, most notably in the work of **Marcuse**, and also in the work of various **postmodern** thinkers. Still one can observe consistent psychoanalytic influence on the work of **Wollheim**.

See **Apollonian/Dionysian distinction; catharsis; gaze; gendered aesthetics; pleasure; psychology**

Further reading: Kris 1952; Kuhns 1983; Rose 1980; Wollheim 1973

psychology: Psychology studies the experiences and behavior of organisms, primarily human beings. Insofar as art – its objects, its products, and the experiences it may involve – play an important role in human life, it is a legitimate object of psychological study. The concerns of art psychology, or empirical aesthetics, coincide with some major topics which also concern philosophical aesthetics: **perception, imagination,** and **aesthetic experience.** Yet while psychology normally employs the empirical methods of the physical sciences, it faces two general difficulties. First, scientific **understanding** in psychology may not guarantee prediction and control of the phenomena explained. This is clearly the case regarding art, insofar as a given work of art is **ontologically** unique. Second, since the ontological status of the mind, one of the primary objects of psychological study, has been, and still remains, a highly debatable issue, its empirical study is patently theory-laden. Again, this is clearly the case regarding art, insofar as **aesthetic properties** are mind-dependent. Furthermore, the relevance of experimental psychology to aesthetic theory remains a moot issue. While solid facts are invaluable to the soundness of any aesthetic theory, it has been argued, most notably by **Wittgenstein,** that causal empirical explanations conceptually misconstrue aesthetic phenomena; hence, that aesthetics is not a sub-field of psychology. Another line of argumentation is due to **Kant**'s contention that **aesthetic judgments** are normative, rather than empirical. Indeed experimental psychology tends to be ambivalent with regard to the notion of aesthetic **value.** Still the case of psychoanalytic theories of art is somewhat different. **Psychoanalysis** is not only descriptive but also, and perhaps more importantly, therapeutic. It is primarily concerned with works of art qua products of human creativity, hence with the interpretation of works of art in terms of edifices of unconscious motives.

See **Arnheim; Gestalt theory; Gombrich; pleasure; synaesthesia**

Further reading: Arnheim 1974; Berlyne 1974; Gombrich 1986; Kreitler and Kreitler 1972; Locher Martindale and Dorfman 2006

ready-made see **conceptual art**

realism: In aesthetics the term realism usually means the quality of verisimilitude in an artwork, and also a distinct artistic **style**. In **literature**, a realist text often includes elaborate descriptions of ordinary daily life, locations, and events (also accurate descriptions, if reference is made to real locations and events), in a particularly plausible **narrative**. In **theater**, a realist performance (either of a realist play or of a non-realist play) is usually characterized by real-life stage setting and by real-life gestures on the part of the players, who assume the attitude known as the 'fourth wall', that is, they act on stage as if they are unaware of the presence of an audience. Realism in photography and in film is particularly related to the **photographic transparency** thesis. Realism in painting amounts to the ability of the viewer to recognize what is depicted. The notion of resemblance was traditionally adduced in order to explain pictorial realism. However, resemblance fell out of favor in the twentieth century owing to **Gombrich's** theory of pictorial style, in particular his arguments against what he called the 'myth of the **innocent eye**', and **Goodman's** later suggestion that realism is ensued by familiarity with pictorial conventions.

See **Arnheim; conventionalism; fiction; mimesis; representation; truth**

Further reading: Gombrich 1986; Goodman 1976

representation: In aesthetics representation is commonly regarded as an intentional relation, which presupposes a certain conceptual set-up. First, we need the artist, the one who creates the representation, and his audience, those who understand his work. Now x (for example, a picture) represents y (for example, an object, a person, an event) when the artist intends x to stand (in some sense) for y, and when the audience realizes that y is intended to stand for x. The appeal to the artist's intention is usually designed to rule out allegedly illegitimate instances such as seeing faces in clouds or other kinds of idiosyncratic experiences that a spectator may have. However, the appeal to the artist's intention is strongly contested by theories which explicitly assimilate representational **meaning** into **textual** meaning and so undermine authorial intention, for example, **semiotics**. Most theories of representation in aesthetics are theories of pictorial representation, or depiction. Such theories were applied also to purported cases of musical representation (for example, the rolling thunder in Beethoven's 'pastoral' symphony) with some measure of success. Literary representation is by and large lexicographic, so it is best handled by theories which capitalize on the sweeping analogy of art as **language**, such as semiotics and **conventionalism**. The main types of theories of representation are: (1) the **resemblance** theory, which is the oldest and perhaps the most intuitively appealing of all; (2) the **illusion** theory, which has been advanced by **Gombrich**; (3) **conventionalism**, whose most notable proponent was **Goodman**; (4) semiotics; (5) the seeing-in theory, whose most notable proponent was **Wollheim**;

(6) the **make-believe theory**. Recent accounts of musical representation utilized a variant of the seeing-in theory, although it met with the objection that there is no phenomenon of 'hearing-in' which is analogical to 'seeing-in'. Another viable account was offered by Kendall Walton in his **make-believe theory**.

See **Aristotle; innocent eye; intentionalism; literature; mimesis; music; photography; Plato; seeing-as/seeing-in disctinction; twofoldness**

Further reading: Gombrich 1986; Goodman 1976; Walton 1990; Wollheim 1980

representation theory of art: A generic name for **essentialist** theories of art which hinge upon the **definition of art** as **representation**. According to such a theory, representation is a necessary condition for the kind of practices that we call art. The scope of such theory, the range of practices and objects that it can be applied to, and its consequent exposure to counter-examples and its resistance to criticism, depend on the exact definition of representation adhered to in each case and on its conceptual sophistication. In this context, representation has been understood as **mimesis** since antiquity, and this conception played an instrumental part in the formation of the **modern system of the arts**, persisting well into the nineteenth century. However, mimesis in the sense of the imitation of nature had always limited applicability to **literature** and **music**, as well as to non-representational arts like **architecture** and the decorative arts. The visual arts veered away from the imitation of nature toward experiments in distortion and **abstraction** around the turn of the twentieth century, the representation theory of art was bound to fall out of favor. Over the past century modern art has furnished a broad array of counter-examples for this theory, rendering it particularly vulnerable to **anti-essentialism**.

See **Aristotle; ornamentation; Plato**
Further reading: Aristotle 1995; Kristeller 1980; Plato 1997

resemblance: As a theory of pictorial **representation**, the appeal to resemblance amounts to saying that pictures represent simply by looking very much like what they depict. This idea is intuitively appealing, and it has enjoyed a long venerable history. **Plato's** idea of **mimesis** precisely put pictures in a relation of mirroring what they depict. But this idea is also unclear in itself, because 'looking like' can mean anything, hence postulating resemblance between a picture and that which is depicted in the picture is always undermined by the difficulty of saying exactly in what respect the two resemble each other. The idea of resemblance was famously attacked by **Goodman** on account of the discrepancy between the logic of resemblance and the logic of representation. There are cases of resemblance without representation (for example, twins), and cases of resemblance, which are also representations without being pictorial representations (for example, a fabric sample), and cases of representations which resemble one another more than they resemble that which is depicted in them. Furthermore, there are pictorial representations which cannot possibly resemble what they depict, because it is purely **fictional** or a type (for example, a picture of an imaginary flower). Finally, while resemblance is a symmetric, reflexive relation, representation is neither. A picture of Elvis Presley may resemble Elvis, and so Elvis also resembled his picture, but it is not the case that he represented his picture. Also, Elvis surely resembled himself, but that again is not an instance of representation.

See **innocent eye; realism; representation theory of art**
Further reading: Goodman 1976

Ricoeur, Paul (1913–2005): French philosopher, one of the great exponents of **hermeneutics**, whose thoughtful, open-minded approach inspired the intellectual exchange of ideas between analytic and continental philosophy. Ricoeur's theory of **metaphor** is of particular interest to the philosophic study of the arts owing to its important emphasis on the creative, **imaginative** workings of **language**. His theory of metaphor is essentially a tension, or interaction theory: when a metaphor is coined, the conflicting concepts and contexts which the metaphor yokes together blend and keep apart simultaneously within the sentence as a whole, and this tense dynamics imparts new **meaning** onto language. A genuine vehicle for **truth** and knowledge, what such a living metaphor teaches us about the world cannot be exhausted by literal paraphrase. For Ricoeur, this is how metaphor vividly regenerates and replenishes language. Ricoeur has also made important contributions to the study of **narrative**, which he considered as yet another fountain of youth for language. In particular, he argued for the kinship between **fictional** narratives and allegedly real historical narratives.

See **cognitivism, aesthetic; interpretation**
Further reading: Ricoeur 1977

romanticism: A name for a historical literary-philosophical movement which emerged in the late eighteenth century in Germany spreading across Europe, and also for a constellation of artistic **styles** in **music**, **literature** and the visual arts distinctive of the nineteenth century, which is often dubbed the 'romantic period'. Romanticism forged itself against the emphasis placed by the Enlightenment on reason and order, and against the faith in scientific and technological progress which came with it. The romantic prophylaxis against the sense of alienation, which modernity brought about, was an attempt to unify human experience and to restore the unity of humankind and nature. Feeding on the idea of **aesthetic autonomy**, which was strongly interpreted as the license of art as a distinct realm of human experience and knowledge, romantic thinkers put their faith in the transmogrifying power of art to educate human beings, to acculturate and motivate human action, and to reform morals. In a sense, romantic aesthetics strove to render the whole of human life as art. The primacy of art over **science** as the highest form of human **expression** followed from the belief that **aesthetic experience** can unlock vast areas of human experience neglected by the rational mind. Romanticism decisively placed emotion and intuition before reason, arguing for the primacy of the irrational over the rational. These ideas had a tremendous influence on the arts. The romantic urge to recover the **beauty**, mystery and spirituality of nature in the aftermath of science and technology found its way to landscape **painting**, as well as to the expansive tone poems which became typical of the romantic period in music. The emphasis on subjective experience and self-expression, powered by the characterization of the artist as **genius**, contributed to the freeing-up of **classicist** formal constraints on the various arts (with the notable exception of **sculpture**). The addition of the category of the **sublime** has opened up the realm of the aesthetic way beyond classicist conceptions of beauty into the dark recesses of human experience. This manifested itself in increasing artistic engagement with overpowering, often violent, and even morbid experiences and situations.

See **absolute music**; **Baumgarten**; **classicism**; **culture**; **education, aesthetic**; **Gesamtkunstwerk**; **Kant**; **modernism**; **Nietzsche**; **profundity**; **Schiller**; **Schopenhauer**; **style**; **Wagner**

Further reading: Seyhan 1992

S

Sartre, Jean-Paul (1905–80): French philosopher, Nobel laureate writer, and political activist, a major figure in French **phenomenology** and **existentialism**. Sartre's main interest in art – as a novelist, playwright, critic, and theorist – was propelled by his fundamental idea that existence precedes essence. Engagement with the world through commitment, decision, action, and active transformation embodies what we are, and discloses our moral status. Thus 'how should one act?' is always the fundamental question. For Sartre, artistic creation, in particular writing, in which he excelled, is itself a form of experience shaping action: endowing with significance an event or an object that would otherwise remain unseen by casting it into an artistic **medium**. The unique **ethical** tenor of Sartre's existentialism comes across most clearly in his idea that the authentic artist should freely render her medium transparent (in the sense of not obfuscating the human condition by drawing attention to itself) so the audience may assume full responsibility for the object which has been laid bare before them. Correspondingly, the role of the critic is to examine and assess this interplay between **imaginative** freedom and the human condition, which constitutes the artist's unique point of view. In light of this **ontological** requirement, Sartre considered prose (but not poetry) to be the most potent art of all.

See **authenticity; gaze; Heidegger; Nietzsche; theater; tragedy**

Further reading: Sartre 1988

Saussure, Ferdinand de (1857–1913): Swiss linguist best known for his singular theoretical contribution to structural linguistics, which propelled the advance of **structuralism** and **semiotics** and their consequent application to the study of artworks and other **cultural** phenomena. In his seminal posthumous work, *Course in General Linguistics* (1916), Saussure laid out the distinction between *la langue*, which denotes **language** as a social institution (for example, English or French), and *la parole*, which denotes the variety of speech events. Only the former notion, which is abstract and logically prior to the latter, is a proper subject matter for the scientific study of language. According to Saussure, language is a static, synchronic, and coherent system of signs to which we respond in more or less predictable ways. Signs consist in a **conventionalist** relation between a signifier (usually, a word) and a signifier (a concept). The sign derives its linguistic value from this bond and its position in the system of language as a whole. Any straightforward application of Saussure's model to art must presuppose a **formalist** view of art as language and the viability of construing works of art in terms of objective, self-contained, and self-regulating systems of signs. Resistance to this formalist rigidity has become the crux of **poststructuralist** critique in continental aesthetics.

See **Barthes; text**

Further reading: Culler 1986

Schiller, Friedrich (1759–1805): German poet, playwright, and philosopher, author of the famous 'Ode to Joy', which is featured at the conclusion of Beethoven's ninth symphony. Schiller's best known work in aesthetics consists of a series of twenty-seven letters titled *On the Aesthetic Education of Man* (1795), which he wrote to his patron, the Duke of Augustenburg. In this work Schiller decisively transgressed **Kant's** separation of the realm of the good and the beautiful in a manner that became distinctive of the **romanticist** quest for an ideal humanity, free from the intellectual and social maladies of modernity, which can only be achieved through the redemptive powers of art. His famous dictum that 'only through **beauty** man makes his way to freedom' encapsulates this vision of binding aesthetics together with **ethics** and **politics**, and it was vividly complemented by his firm personal belief in the primacy of the artist over the philosopher. A centerpiece of Schille's conception of beauty is his distinction between two fundamental drives in human nature: the intellectual (formal), which is subject to moral laws, and the material (sensible), which is subject to physical needs. Schiller maintained that this human duality can be resolved by the impulse to play, which is the same as **aesthetic experience**. In play we fuse the sensory, material life with form, thus arriving at 'living form' which is beauty. The artistic creation of beauty is playful in that the artist is no longer subject to the constraints of either moral duty or physical need. Schiller believed that we can be fully human only when we play, that is, only when we bring about beauty.

See **education, aesthetic; Gadamer; genius**
Further reading: Schiller 1967

Schopenhauer, Arthur (1788–1860): German non-academic philosopher, most notable for his philosophy of **music**, as well as for his immediate influence on **Wagner** and **Nietzsche**. Schopenhauer's best known work is *The World as Will and Representation* (1818/1844) where his philosophy of art, featuring some of the most distinct themes of **romanticism**, is fully integrated into his system of metaphysics. Schopenhauer followed **Kant's** distinction between the world of phenomena, which is accessible to reason, and the world as it is 'in itself', but he proceeded to characterize this irrational, metaphysically foundational realm of the world as 'Will': a blind force which is ultimate reality. Schopenhauer believed that we are acquainted with the Will-governed world through its individuation into a multiplicity of empirical manifestation, or 'representations', but also irrationally in our immediate awareness of ourselves acting in the world. He coupled this metaphysical picture with existential pessimism, portraying human life as prolonged misery and servitude. In this context, **aesthetic experience** assumes its great importance for Schopenhauer. Drawing on a bold reading of Kant's idea of **disinterestedness**, Schopenhauer suggested that aesthetic experience affords a momentary release from the torment of the 'Wheel of Ixion' that is life as we are able to suspend our attachments to things in the world. This release opens up the possibility for Will-less, hence objective apprehension of things. For Schopenhauer, the artistic **genius** serves a particular purpose by utilizing his abnormal powers of objective apprehension for endowing others with aesthetic experience, thus imparting the genuine knowledge that art enshrines. According to Schopenhauer, the arts differ from one another with respect to their cognitive **value**. **Tragedy** is ranked first among the **representational** arts. But music occupies a league of its own, since it formally mirrors the metaphysical Will itself. For Schopenhauer, music is the most cognitive art of all. Schopenhauer's philosophy of art had some influence on **Wittgenstein**, especially during his early period, and also on **Langer**, who emulated Schopenhauer's idea of isomorphism in her account of musical **expression**. Contemporary analytic philosophy of music became more hospitable to Schopenhauer's ideas on music only recently.

See **cognitivism, aesthetic; profundity; truth**

Further reading: Schopenhauer 1969

science: Aesthetics and science are undeniably related, but such relations are multifarious, often conceptually subtle, and partly obfuscated by the course of intellectual history. It should be noted that from its inception in the eighteenth century onwards, against the background of the formation of the **modern system of the arts**, aesthetics has been pulling away from science, claiming its own domain and modes of inquiry, and at times even claiming its own domain of **truth**. This broad historical trajectory became exceedingly manifest upon the rise of **romanticism** when the gulf between artistic imagination and scientific logic grew unbridgeable. In a belated twist of intellectual history, **postmodernism** promised to close this gap by admitting that both art and science are on a par as social constructs. Be that as it may, we can still observe in contemporary aesthetics some concrete moments of interlacing with science. First and foremost, there is an entire field of empirical aesthetics, which is the study of the arts by means of the theories and methods of **psychology** as well as other scientific behavioral sciences. Philosophical aesthetics tends to be suspicious towards what sometimes seem like dated, overly positivist, conceptual apparatus on the part of empirical aesthetics, which for obvious methodological reasons tend to equate the aesthetic simply with **pleasure** or with what people prefer. Still, analytic aesthetics has been traditionally receptive to scientific rigor and has a keen interest in such concepts as **imagination** and **perception**, which are of mutual interest also to cognitive science, linguistics, and psychology. Finally, aesthetics has a long-standing interest in the notion of **medium** as a direct interface between science, technology, and art. Technological innovations and scientific discoveries can shape artistic **representation** (for example, the development of perspective in painting) and give rise to new artistic media (for example, **photography, film** and **new media** art), which in turn open up new vistas for aesthetic inquiry.

See **Arnheim; Gombrich; Saussure; Wittgenstein**

Further reading: Currie 1995; Kemp 1990; Raffman 1993

sculpture: In comparison to art history and **anthropology,** aesthetics has shown relatively little interest in the art of sculpture. Sculpture shares many of its general philosophical characteristics and concerns with **painting.** Taken as a primarily visual art, sculpture is regarded as **representational** art, although it also lends itself to **abstraction.** It is a quintessentially autographic art, but it also lends itself to mechanical reproduction, so a sculpture can be a multiple work. It also lends itself to artistic hybridity – for example, kinetic sculpture, which can be understood as a hybrid of the forms of sculpture and **dance.** It is reasonable, then, to attribute the philosophical uniqueness of sculpture to other distinct characteristics of its **medium:** a sculpture is normally a three-dimensional structure of solid material, occupying physical space in a way that constrains or otherwise structures the observer's movement in that space. This means that sculpture is essentially also a tactual art: it concurrently engages our sense of touch, either actually, by touching the sculpture, or by way of somatic **imagining.** It is noteworthy, that the latter option may apply also to borderline cases of sculpture, such as James Turrell's light installations or other **new media** art involving holograms. Arguably, appreciating such 'immaterial sculptures' involves also imagining what it would feel like if in some possible world we could touch it. Furthermore, since a sculpture normally puts no restriction on our **point of view,** appreciating a sculpture involves moving around it and gathering different perspectives of it. Thus a consideration of the actual viewing environment as part of the **aesthetic experience** appropriate to sculpture seems warranted. This point has been emphasized by **Langer** in one of the few sustained philosophical discussions of sculpture in recent literature. Langer maintained that sculpture creates and consists in what she calls 'virtual space', which is organized around the observer's possible movements and actions.

See **appreciation, aesthetic; architecture; autographic art/allographic art distinction; hybrid art forms; perception; singular/multiple distinction**

Further reading: Langer 1953; Read 1961; Vance 1995

seeing-as/seeing-in distinction: **Wollheim's** theory of pictorial **representation** explains pictures in terms of mental construction as a certain relation between mental events. We conceptualize pictorial content by means of a **phenomenologically** peculiar species of seeing. Wollheim's erstwhile suggestion was to couch this seeing appropriate to representations in terms of seeing-as, following **Wittgenstein's** discussion of **aspect-perception**. However, Wollheim later changed his mind, arguing that seeing-as falls short of elucidating representational seeing, which seems to involve a closely related phenomenon which he dubs 'seeing-in'. That is, rather than seeing a marked surface *as* a woman, we see a woman *in* a marked surface. Seeing-in is triggered by certain differentiated surfaces. Wollheim's argument in favor of the switch from seeing-as to seeing-in is threefold: (1) the range of things that we can see-in includes both particulars and states of affairs, hence it is broader than the range of the things that we can see-as; (2) seeing-as must meet the requirement of localization, whereas seeing-in does not; (3) seeing-in permits unlimited simultaneous attention to what is seen and to the features of the medium, whereas seeing-as does not. Such considerations render seeing-in applicable to other **perceptual** arts as well. For example, it has been suggested that it would be possible to utilize Wollheim's conception to explain **musical** representation in terms of the phenomenon of hearing-in. While Wollheim insists that seeing-in logically precedes representation, he does not offer a full account of this **psychological** ability. This is an obvious shortcoming of his theory.

See **experience, aesthetic; painting; twofoldness**
Further reading: Wollheim 1980 and 1987

self-reference: A work of art may be self-referential in one or more of the following senses: (1) containing a copy of itself or another work within the same **medium** (for example, a picture within a picture, or a story within a story); (2) referring to the work itself (for example, a story acknowledging that it is indeed a story, or a **theater** performance encroaching upon its audience, or even M. C. Escher's famous **painting** of the self-drawing hands); (3) referring to its own **style, medium,** performance practice or **cultural** situation (for example, historically authentic performances, or ready-mades, such as Marcel Duchamp's notorious *Fountain*). While self-reference in art is infrequent, and may even be regarded as a mark of artistic sophistication, it is rampant and unpalatably self-congratulatory in the popular media, for instance, in so-called 'reality' genres on television. Insofar as we have difficulties in defining what a work is (in relevant cases), self-reference – that is, the work being about itself – may prove to be a second-order problem for the **ontology** of art. In non-literary arts – for example, visual arts and the performing arts in general – we may construe self-reference also as an **aesthetic**

property of the work, understanding it in both a **perceptual** and a **cognitivist** sense. From a historical point of view, it is noteworthy that, as an aesthetic property, self-reference has become a hallmark of **modernism** in art. With regards to **language**, self-reference normally denotes a sentence which refers to itself or its own referent. Such self-reference patently yields a variety of paradoxes, the most famous of which is undoubtedly the 'liar paradox' (consider the sentence 'This sentence is not true'). Still, the fact remains that our ordinary use of such sentences in ordinary speech, or indeed their use in **literature**, is relatively minor. Literary works of art may certainly be self-referential in the aforementioned senses without bending one's mind. Indeed, **metaphors** are prime examples for self-referential language, which is not paradoxical in any strict sense. It is noteworthy that **postmodern** thought tends to make an expansive use of the term self-reference as it applies to language, in effect arguing that in the last analysis all **texts** are patently **intertextual** and *ipso facto* self-referential, and so within this hermetically verbose environment the air of paradox is inescapable. In this respect, **Derrida's** treatment of the term metaphor as being metaphoric itself is exemplary.

See **authenticity; conceptual art; make-believe theory; meaning; ornamentation; representation; semiotics; understanding**

Further reading: Foucault 1983; Miller 1996

semiotics: Derived from the Greek word for 'sign' (*semeion*), semiotics is the standard term for the theory and analysis of signs as commonly applied to a broad range of cultural phenomena, from works of high **literature**, visual art and **films** to the most mundane artifacts and practices of popular **culture,** which are all regarded as various modes of **communication**. Contemporary semiotics was founded on **Saussure's** structural linguistics as well as the general theory of signs propounded by American philosopher Charles Sanders Peirce (1839–1913), who famously suggested differentiating between three types of reference: (1) 'iconic' for cases which solely depend on resemblance (for example, when a picture looks like its object); (2) 'indexical' for cases in which one thing points at, or implies the existence of another thing (for example, when smoke implies fire); (3) 'symbolic' for cases which solely depend on convention (for example, a flag of a nation). These categories are not mutually exclusive. For instance, a picture of smoke is both iconic (it resembles smoke) and indexical (it implies the existence of fire). The term 'semiotics' is often used interchangeably with the term 'semiology', which has been originally suggested by Saussure, although the latter is best reserved for applications which strictly follow Saussure's brand of scientific linguistics. In the aftermath of **poststructuralism**, semiotics now boasts a much broader and lax spectrum of goals and methodologies. It may seek to contextualize signs, thereby fleshing out, often by means of undercutting the contested primacy of authorship, hidden **narratives**, which ultimately shape or reconstruct the ideational reception of its audience. Alternatively, embracing radical relativism, semiotics stresses the openendedness of any **interpretation** and the indeterminacy of **meaning**. In any case, semiotics, although highly instructive as an approach to the history of art and to literary criticism, is nonetheless at odds with aesthetics, insofar as it tends to collapse **aesthetic judgment** into mere rhetoric. This can be seen most clearly in **deconstructionist** approaches to **texts**.

See **anthropology; artifactuality; Barthes; gendered aesthetics; Goodman; intertextuality; Langer; language; sociology; structuralism; understanding**

Further reading: Barthes 1977; Eco 1979; Kristeva 1980

Sibley, Frank (1923–96): British philosopher, and an early champion of analytic aesthetics, best known for his attempt to distinguish the aesthetic domain – reflected in our use of **aesthetic concepts** and aesthetic reasoning – from the non-aesthetic. Sibley argued that the language we use to describe the **aesthetic properties** of a certain object (for example, adjectives such as 'balanced', 'luminous' or 'graceful') depends on, but is not reducible to, the perceptually corresponding physicalist language that we use to describe its features (for example, 'blue', 'square' or 'curved'). In both cases the **language** is perceptual, but while an appropriate use of the latter requires merely good eyesight, an appropriate use of the latter requires a more discerning power: namely, **taste**. Furthermore, whereas the justification of the non-aesthetic assertions is a matter of correct inference from general non-aesthetic propositions, the justification of aesthetic assertions amounts to employing particular non-aesthetic propositions as examples. For example, we say that a certain composition of shapes is balanced, because there is a blue round shape on the upper right-hand side. Such reasoning is actually an invitation to perceive the property of balance in the composition, not an inference from its physicalist properties. Sibley importantly argued that such language is objective insofar as, like the language of color, it depends on an agreement in judgments. Sibley's emphasis on the role of aesthetic reasoning in prompting the **perception** of aesthetic properties has important implications for criticism as well as for **aesthetic education**. However, it has been argued against Sibley that he has not been able to show that all aesthetic concepts are indeed not condition-governed or that this is what actually qualifies them as aesthetic.

See **beauty; judgment, aesthetic; objectivism; Wittgenstein**

Further reading: Sibley 2006

significant form: A term that has become associated with **Bell's formalist** theory of art in his book *Art* (1914). It denotes what Bell takes to be the essence of all art. Significant form supervenes on the formal features of the work of art, such as, in the case of painting, the particular arrangement of lines and colors, and their interrelations. It elicits an **aesthetic experience**, for which Bell uses the misnomer 'aesthetic emotion'. In fact, significant form is the object of aesthetic experience, hence it is both an object of immediate experience and, metaphysically speaking, a part of physical reality itself (insofar as it can impinge directly on the mind). Given Bell's philosophical indebtedness to **Moore's** experiential realism, it is reasonable to conclude that Bell's notion of significant form is an aesthetic equivalent to Moore's notion of sense-data. The **ontological** duality of significant form clearly suggests such an affinity. While the notion of significant form applies quite naturally to visual art and to music, it seems to pose difficulties when applied to verbal art. Indeed, Bell remained quite ambivalent regarding the status of **literature** as a pure art.

See **definition of art; essentialism**

Further reading: Bell 1958

singular/multiple distinction: A widely accepted, albeit not entirely uncontested, distinction in analytic **ontology** of art between artworks that are unique, occurring at only one place at one time, and artworks which may occur in different places at the same time. Typical examples of singular artworks include oil **paintings** and **sculptures**

curved in stone. Typical examples of multiple artworks include novels, plays, and films.

See **music; new media; photography**

Further reading: Currie 1989; Wollheim 1980

sociology: Artistic activity is socially entrenched, drawing on material and human resources and institutions as well as on social circumstances concerning patronage, production, reception, promotion, consumption, suppression, and so on. Aesthetics relates to the sociology of art inasmuch as it is willing to acknowledge that artistic activity is not fully explicable without proper understanding of the interplay between artistic activity and other forms of social activity and the embeddedness of artistic activity in its appropriate social structures. As a systematic study of social groups, the domain of sociology overlaps to some extent with that of **anthropology,** and it shares some of the latter's disciplinary disquietudes. It also shares similar meta-theoretical affinities with the general philosophical thrust and intellectual origins of continental aesthetics, most notably with its **Marxist** varieties. On the other hand, the **institutional theory of art** is a spectacular instance of the sociological bend also in the analytic tradition, which is generally unsympathetic towards reducing the aesthetic to relativistic ideological circumstances of time and place.

See **Adorno; anthropology; artworld; autonomy, aesthetic; avant-garde; Benjamin; censorship; communication; culture; ethics; Frankfurt School; gendered aesthetics; hermeneutics; institutional theory of art; kitsch; law; Marcuse; politics; pornography; postmodernism**

Further reading: Wolff 1993

structuralism: A formal approach, commonly associated with a dominant critical movement in France in the 1960s, which applies the principles and procedures of structural linguistics, initially put forth by **Saussure** for the analysis of various aspects of human **culture**. The fundamental idea is that all cultural phenomena are self-subsisting abstract systems of signs, whose deep structures are susceptible to structural analysis. Understanding the meaning of these structures is grounded in the orderly, non-cognitive relations between signifiers and signified, which are explicated in terms of bipolar differences (for example, inner/outer, male/female, speech/writing, real/unreal, and so on). This methodology proliferated initially in **anthropology**, but quickly permeated into literary theory and criticism, in particular the study of folk tales, mainly through the pioneering work of Claude Lévi-Strauss (1908–2009) on structural analogies in myth. The interpretation of the various artifacts and practices of contemporary industrial society in terms of linguistically analyzable mythological **narratives** was **Barthes'** way of expanding structuralism, under the broader label of **semiotics**, into the kind of cultural critique which is so typical of continental aesthetics. Structuralism has established itself as an instructive and quite successful methodology in art history as well as in the study of literary genres, although it has been criticized for lapsing into mere taxonomy of codes and structural relations, and for generally lacking real evaluative power. The initial adherence to Saussure's original linguistic model, which is static, teleological, and deterministic, eventually came under vigorous philosophical attack under the prosaic label of **poststructuralism**. It is noteworthy that Barthes emerged as an important transitional figure in this particular phase.

See **artifactuality; cognitivism, aesthetic; interpretation; intertextuality; language; literature; meaning; poststructuralism; text; truth**

Further reading: Barthes 1972

style: While studying the personal style of an artist or a performer, and its relation to the style of the relevant period, has become a staple of scholarship in art history and art theory, as well as common wisdom for performers in **music** and **theater,** the general definition of style remains a moot issue. Still, it is commonly agreed that the attribution of style implies some sort of cohesion of certain **aesthetic properties** across the oeuvre of a single artist, a group of artists, or an entire era. It denotes a way of art-making. Importantly, style can be imitated, parodied, and imbued with **self-reference** to a great artistic effect. Successful **forgery** of art hinges precisely upon successful imitation of artistic style. Typical difficulties with the concept of style revolve around the need to negotiate its various descriptive, normative and evaluative uses, as well as the tendency to accommodate the purported conceptual primacy of personal style over derivative concepts such as group style or period style. The **essentialist,** overriding power of the concept of style, in particular when it reifies the artist or author as the embodiment of personal style, has been a source of much discontent in **poststructuralist** and **postmodernist** thought.

See **authenticity; classicism; Gombrich; kitsch; modernism; pastiche; romanticism; titles**

Further reading: Lang 1987

subjectivism: Contrary to **emotivism,** subjectivism maintains that **aesthetic judgments** are truth-apt, but are true by virtue of facts about human **emotions** or inclinations, not by the **perception** of features in the given object or any other objective matters of fact. Subjectivism is a form of relativism about **aesthetic properties.** If the aesthetic standard is one's appropriate feeling of **pleasure** or displeasure upon experiencing a work of art, then the claim that the work is beautiful may be true relative to my standard, but false relative to someone else's standard. Simply put: **beauty** is in the eye of the beholder. It is an important consequence of subjectivism that, strictly speaking, different beholders cannot make the same aesthetic judgment, and so they do not contradict one another when they utter seemingly contradictory aesthetic judgments about the same artwork. These utterances could all be true at the same time, since, in principle and insofar as these aesthetic judgments sincerely express the preferences of their respective speakers, they cannot be false. Some typical difficulties follow from this. First, taken radically enough, subjectivism seems to undermine rational aesthetic discourse altogether. Second, if we allow that two beholders may happen to contradict one another, then any recourse to the features of the given object in order to render the respective responses justifiable would be inconsistent with the main tenet of subjectivism. Third, subjectivism entails that our evaluations are straightforwardly, causally related to our aesthetic standard. This leaves out the crucial normative aspect of such judgments. A sophisticated version of subjectivism, which attempts to circumvent some of these inherent difficulties, was defended by **Hume** in his essay *Of the Standard of Taste*. Subsequently, **Kant** tried to accommodate the subjective feature of aesthetic judgment while still affording its indispensable normative and **perceptual** character. Attempts have been made in analytic aesthetics to recast Hume's original framework into an ideal-critic theory. In this contemporary version of subjectivism, the spectator can ask whether some aesthetic judgment is in accord with the judgment of an ideal critic. If so, it is true. Of course, here the difficulty would be to construe the qualities of such an ideal critic adequately.

See **objectivism; taste theories; truth; value**

Further reading: Goldman 1995; Hume 1987

sublime: A psychologically conflicting feeling brought about by things that are incredibly vast or overwhelmingly powerful. The use of the term in aesthetics is due to the impact of the ancient treatise *On the Sublime* by Longinus (first century AD) on eighteenth-century **taste theorists**. **Burke** was the first to shape what has become a standard contrast between **beauty**, which gives us **pleasure**, and the peculiar psychological dynamics of the sublime, which consist in our ability to enjoy the fearful overpowering of our own mind by things that are fitted to excite the ideas of pain and terror. The sublime denotes the strongest **emotion** that the mind can withstand. **Kant** picked up this idea, making a distinction between the mathematically sublime (for example, the pyramids in Egypt) and the dynamically sublime (for example, volcanoes and hurricanes). In both cases, the experience of the sublime involves pleasure, taken in our recognition of the powers of our own mind to measure itself against nature, but also displeasure, recognizing our limitations (the inadequacy of our imagination in the former case, our physical powerlessness in the latter). For Kant, the sublime is a unique kind of pleasure which is possible only by means of displeasure. Through the direct influence of Kant, the notion of the sublime became tremendously important for **romanticism**. In the twentieth century, the notion of the sublime was resurrected by **postmodernism**. For postmodernists, the category of the sublime, once again opposed to beauty, denotes that which is not presentable in sensation – formless, unanticipated – whose power can be harnessed for a critique of the aesthetic qua that which is sensuously present.

See **environmental aesthetics; paradox of tragedy; profundity; psychology**

Further reading: Burke 1998; Kant 1952; Lyotard 1991.

synaesthesia: Literally meaning 'joined sensation', this term denotes the rare capacity to experience sensory blendings, such as color-hearing or shape-tasting. Genuine synaesthesia can be developmental, caused by neurological dysfunction or induced by psychoactive drug use. Linguistic manifestations of systematic cross-modal sensory correspondences – for example, certain types of **metaphor** – while being prevalent in Western **culture**, are regarded as pseudo-synaesthestic. From the perspective of aesthetics, the phenomenon of synaesthesia has occasionally been taken as providing a physiological standard for engaging various senses simultaneously in works of art. Some incentive for the creation of synaesthetic art comes from **romanticism**, symbolism, and mysticism that seek access to a purported primordial reality. Among its major proponents in the twentieth century, one can count composers Alexander Scriabin and Olivier Messiaen, and painter Wassily Kandinsky. However, the rareness and idiosyncracy of genuine synaesthetic perception makes it an unlikely basis for any aesthetics with a claim for universality.

See **Gesamtkunstwerk; hybrid art forms; perception; psychology; science**

Further reading: Baron-Cohen and Harrison 1997; Kandinsky 1982; Merleau-Ponty 1962

T

taste theories: The conception of taste as the locus for **aesthetic judgment**, in particular for the judgment of **beauty**, became prominent in the eighteenth century as part of the general interest of early modern philosophy in human nature, and it was eventually shaped and propelled by the rise of British **empiricism**. Generally speaking, taste theories are premised on the idea that 'taste' (in the sense of our ability to discern beauty, not as a name for our gustatory sense) denotes a distinct faculty of the mind, a kind of inner sense, pertaining to quintessential **aesthetic experiences** such as beauty and the **sublime,** which consist in a certain feeling of **disinterested** pleasure in the presence of appropriate objects. Such theories patently require explanations of both the nature of the object of taste (for example, beauty) and the nature of the faculty of taste. Regarding the former, such theories face the difficulty of negotiating the inevitable tension between the subjective immediacy of the judgment of taste and its differentiation across people on the one hand, and its purported universality on the other hand. Regarding the latter, taste theories differ from one another with respect to the way in which they model the faculty of taste on sense **perception** or else relate it to other faculties of the mind, for example, reason and **imagination.** Either way, taste theories commonly rely on the somewhat circular, empirically dubious idea of a competent judge, whose aesthetic acumen makes him better qualified to make aesthetic pronouncements than others, and most likely will be in broad agreement with other competent judges like him. It would be fair to say that taste theories, particularly in the aftermath of **Kant's** summative response to them, paved the way for a continuous discussion of such perennial themes in contemporary aesthetics as the centrality and *sui generis* character of the aesthetic experience and the **aesthetic attitude.** For instance, **Bell's** theory of **significant form** can be considered as something of a twentieth-century relic of a taste theory insofar as the perception of significant form is informed by a particular feeling, which he confusingly called the 'aesthetic emotion', hinging upon the idea of a competent judge. **Sibley** offered another pronouncement of the idea of taste, which he conceived as the ability to detect **aesthetic properties**. The fact that such general ideas came under attack as late as the second half of the twentieth century, both from within the Anglo-American tradition and from such continental movements as **poststructuralism** is testimony to the enduring indebtedness of contemporary aesthetics to its eighteenth-century conceptual framing.

See **appreciation, aesthetic; Burke; Hume; Hutcheson; subjectivism**

Further reading: Dickie 1996

text: The striking thing about the notion of text seems to be the way in which the term, as used in aesthetic theory, has been reverting from its standard use as 'the wording of anything written' to its other, somewhat more abstract sense as 'that which is woven' – to wit, a web or a texture. The standard, classical conception of text, which is still widespread in analytic aesthetics (and also, of course, in pre-theoretic, ordinary use), regards text as an **aesthetic object**, which is definite, self-contained, coherent, and autonomous. In this sense, textual identity is supposed to be secured by the text itself, by authorial intention, by means of the reader's **interpretation**, that is, systematically approaching the purported **meaning** of the text, or by all three to varying degrees and combinations. Thus construed, the notion of a text is often **ontologically** conflated with the notion of a work, and so the term 'text' as the wording of anything written may denote a printed text, or that which the printed text is an instance of. The **type/token distinction** seems to point precisely in this direction. Thus the text as an aesthetic object, which is subject to **aesthetic appreciation**, is ultimately the work of art under consideration. However, the need to secure textual identity, and so the identity and meaning of the work, in a non-circular manner has led members of the

New Criticism school to react against extrinsic factors, such as authorial intention, which only divert the reader from the text. The idea was that literary text should be treated objectively, on its own terms. Goodman's theory is an outstanding example for the attempt to ground textual identity strictly in the syntactic and semantic features of the text. A similar approach developed in French structuralism, although in this case the motivation was primarily linguistic, related to the influential work of Saussure. Barthes went as far as to announce the 'death of the author'. However, the rigidity of such approaches invited theoretical discontent, which became more pronounced and philosophically far-reaching in continental thought. Advances in semiotics in the late twentieth century stressed the openness and 'writerliness' of the literary text, that is, the manner in which certain compositional strategies and literary narratives incorporate the active, indeterminate participation of the reader. The idea is that the completion of such distinctly aesthetic texts requires actual interpretation, and so it can only be provisional. Another destabilizing idea was that of the intertextuality of all text. Combined with the anti-essentialist thrust of poststructuralism, the result was a radically fluid conception of text: not only has it been denied of its autonomy and veracity, but it also goes beyond the realm of written entities into the general dynamics of communication. When it comes to Derrida's philosophy, for example, and to postmodernism, text engulfs the world, for their claim is that there is nothing outside of the text. It seems that the deepest difference between analytic and continental aesthetics resides in their conflicting attitudes toward language as a medium for philosophizing. It is in these radically different conceptions of text that this difference amounts to a real chasm.

See **autonomy, aesthetic; Beardsley; expression; hermeneutics; intentionalism; literature; Margolis; notation; titles**

Further reading: Barthes 1977; Beardsley and Wimsatt 1946; Eco 1979; Goodman 1976; Kristeva 1980

theater: Theater is the oldest **hybrid art form**. It is traditionally a combination of prose or poetry, **music, dance,** visual and decorative arts, and with current technological advancements, also **film** and **new media** art, all incorporated into live performance. Thus the philosophical study of theater tends to overlap with many of the issues that are indigenous to the other arts. A typical theater performance – for example, a performance of Shakespeare's *Hamlet* – is in a sense enacted **literature,** and it is also thoroughly **mimetic. Ontologically,** such a typical case can be easily handled by the **type/token distinction:** each performance of *Hamlet* is a token of the type *Hamlet*, that is, Shakespeare's play, which is the artwork. The performance is an **interpretation** of the play; this means that the performance token will have properties that exceed its type. Furthermore, a live theater performance is attended by an audience. Insofar as the performance is mimetic, it will normally involve also the exercise of the **imagination** on the part of the audience and a subsequent **emotional** response. However it is important to note that this characterization of the typical theater performance is far too restrictive to account for the full spectrum of theatrical phenomena. In effect, the identity of theater is rather fixed by marking the range of relevant phenomena, not by any set of necessary and sufficient conditions. While theater has been traditionally understood as enacted literature ever since **Aristotle,** a script is not a necessary condition for a theater performance, and this also limits the idea of performance as interpretation. Theater is also not necessarily **fictional** or **representational**. The fact that during a live theater performance the players and the audience occupy the same space at the same time is an open invitation for many aspects of encroachment on the barrier between make-believe and reality that are now rampant in contemporary theater. In fact, theater tends to blend into the broader realm of **performance art**. Given these conceptual complications, it is noteworthy that the **make-believe theory** shows unusual promise as a viable framework for a philosophical understanding of a broad range of theatrical phenomena.

See **improvisation; paradox of acting; paradox of tragedy; realism; tragedy**

Further reading: Saltz 1991; Thom 1993

titles: Most works of art bear titles given to them by their creators, or by others, intentionally or incidentally. Titles are generally names, which can include descriptive elements, but to think of a title as a mere addendum to a work of art, an incidental label used merely for the purpose of identification and designation, is to downplay its aesthetic potential. Titles may ascribe the work to a certain structure, genre, **style**, or performance practice, but may also challenge or subvert such references, for example by means of irony. In such cases, disregarding the title or otherwise being oblivious to its existence amounts to being blind to an aspect of the work, including even some of its **aesthetic properties**, hence it might result in misunderstanding. Titles may run the gamut from the classificatory and the informative (for example, fugue, photogram, or John Cage's '4′33″', where the title indicates merely the duration of the piece), through the straightforwardly descriptive (for example, Diane Arbus' **photograph** 'Boy with toy hand grenade, Central

Park, 1962') to the pictorially flamboyant (for example, Debussy's piano prelude 'Sounds and perfumes mingling in the evening air') and the deliberately absurd (for example, Erik Satie's piano work 'Three pieces in the shape of a pear'). Such titles, incomprehensible as they may seem, function as pointers for **interpretation**, conceptually suggestive in the manner of a **metaphor**. In the **perceptual** arts, in particular in cases of **abstract** art, titles may prompt a perceptual aspect change, as in the case of Mondrian's **painting** 'Broadway Boogie Woogie', for instance, where awareness to the title 'rearranges' what we see in the **abstract** shapes before our eyes – that is, a joyous representation of the jazzy ambience of New York City. This connects the specific issue of titles with such overarching themes in aesthetics as **expression** and **representation**. The idea that titles are often an integral, even essential part of the work of art gravitates toward **contextualism**. Whether or not one wishes to argue for the special status of artist-given titles depends on one's commitment to, or else one's reservations about, **intentionalism**.

See **aspect perception; meaning; text; understanding**
Further reading: Fisher 1984; Levinson 1985

Tolstoy, Leo (Count Lev Nikolayevich) (1828–1910): Russian novelist and thinker, author of *War and Peace* and *Anna Karenina*. The most elaborate exposition of his aesthetic ideas is found in his late essay 'What is Art?' (1898). Tolstoy's view of art combines **essentialism** with an extreme form of **moralism**. He defined art as human activity designed to transmit the emotion experienced by the artist to other people by means of external signs: words, figures, shapes, sounds, and so on. An artifact is a work of art if and only if it was created for the purpose of arousing a particular **emotion**, which has been actually experienced by its creator, and it actually arouses that same emotion in its audience. Tolstoy believed that **aesthetic properties** – first and foremost, **beauty** – have no intrinsic **value**; they serve a higher moral end. A good work of art, indeed a true work of art, may express only a relatively narrow range of emotions, which specifically promote joy, spiritual union, and the brotherhood of all human beings in accordance with the tenets of Tolstoy's eccentric brand of Christian faith. Tolstoy ousted, to the dismay and bewilderment of his critics, the bulk of the Western canon of art, including some of his own work. In itself, Tolstoy's version of moralism is implausible: we praise works of art for reasons which are not necessarily related to morality, such as their **formal** features. Even superlatives like beauty or **profundity** are not conceptually linked to morality by necessity. Moreover, Tolstoy's moralism hinges upon his **expression theory of art,** which, in itself, is open to several lines of criticism: (1) **expression** may not be a necessary condition for art; (2) the theory presupposes a standard of identification by which we can determine that the artist and his audience are indeed united by the same feeling, whereas such a standard is **epistemologically** unwarranted; (3) the theory presupposes a simplistic **psychological** model of artistic creation; (4) the theory requires universal accessibility to art, which in effect devalues art by restricting its demand on the intellect.

See **arousalism; definition of art; intentionalism**
Further reading: Tolstoy 1960

total work of art see **Gesamtkunstwerk**

tragedy: Tragedy commonly concerns itself with some fundamental philosophical problems: the **meaning** of life, moral **truth,** and the freedom of choice. It does so by subjecting its protagonist to a **narrative** of profound suffering, which often leads to catastrophic results. Experiencing those tragic moments is held to be horrific and uplifting at the same time, intimating some **profound** truth concerning human experience. The philosophic study of the art of tragedy, as well as the philosophic **interpretation** of particular tragedies, has a long and venerable history beginning with **Aristotle**, who was the first to address the **paradox of tragedy** and to offer a theoretical solution. Another singular response to the paradox, which is also of great interest today, was offered by **Hume**. The philosophic treatment of tragedy is usually well integrated into the writer's overall scheme of ideas, and often it is indicative of the writer's commitment to the purported connection between art and life. Aristotle's detailed explanation of the parts of tragedy and how they come together in the well made plot to bring about **catharsis** (he specifically referred to Sophocles' *Oedipus Rex*) is designed to show how this particularly sophisticated form of artistic **mimesis** brings about knowledge of the possibilities of human experience, in a sense epitomizing the ubiquitous human interest in learning. Hume's account of tragic **pleasure** in terms of a conversion of passions is an offshoot of his general theory of the passions in the *Treatise of Human Nature* (1739–40). However, it remains more a **psychological** theory of tragedy, than an aesthetic theory. Another notable contribution to the philosophic **understanding** of tragedy was made by **Hegel**. Here the relation of art to life was already built into Hegel's overall philosophical approach: art is the expression of 'the Absolute' in sensory form, and tragedy was ranked the most developed form of art. According to Hegel, who famously based his analysis on Sophocles' *Antigone*, tragedy reveals the nature of reality by showing a conflict between two mutually exclusive goods; pursuing one is bound to result in the destruction of the other, which nonetheless yields an affirmation of the unity of the **ethical**. Still other forms of resolution of the tragic ethical conflict may take the form of peaceful reconciliation. In **Schopenhauer** and **Nietzsche**, the analysis of tragedy is even more heavily inflected by their general views concerning the vagaries of human existence. While Schopenhauer pessimistically saw tragedy at its best as artistically embodying blissful resignation from willing and from life, Nietzsche's *Birth of Tragedy* (1872) is a paean to life. In his view, the destruction of the tragic hero affirms Dionysian life in the world. In the twentieth century, **Sartre** stands out as a philosopher who also wrote tragedies, for example *The Flies* (1943), an **existentialist** adaptation of the ancient myth of Electra. In Sartre's milieu of social criticism, or engagement, art and life interlock as tragedy awakens us to the **political** truth of self-realization through choice.

See **Apollonian/Dionysian distinction; cognitivism, aesthetic; emotions; fiction; mimesis; theater**

Further reading: Kaufmann 1992

trompe l'oeil see **illusion**

truth: Truth is one of the most central and oldest themes in Western philosophy, and probably also one of the most troublesome. What truths are, and what, if anything, makes them true have remained perennial problems, cutting across all fields of philosophy, including the discussion of truth in art, which began with **Plato** and **Aristotle**. To this, modern aesthetics uniquely adds another conundrum: whether truth makes a difference for aesthetic **value**. From its beginning in ancient Greek thought, the notion of truth in art, and indeed the very

definition of art, has been time and again related to the notion of **mimesis,** which is understood primarily as a truth-bearing relation between a work of art and reality. This relation can consist in **resemblance** or some other semantic linkage, and so the idea of truth in art pertains both to verbal arts, wherein truth is primarily a quality of propositions that accord with reality, and to non-verbal (**representational**) art, such as the visual arts and, to a lesser degree, **music.** If a work of art purportedly represents something in the world, then there should be a sense in which it might be truthful or not, and insofar as it is truthful, the experience of art is also related to the possibility of acquiring some knowledge of the represented object or state of affairs. This is one sense in which aesthetics is related to **epistemology.** Plato's advocacy of **censorship** in his ideal state is based precisely on his denial of the veracity of artistic images, hence on their inadequacy as a source of real knowledge. Aristotle, on the other, maintained that art, in particular **tragedy,** enables us to entertain universal truths. It is noteworthy that this difference between Plato and Aristotle cuts deeply into the wider metaphysical context of their respective work, ultimately consisting in their different ideas not only about the nature of mimesis, but also about reality itself. Such intricate, deep connection between aesthetics and metaphysics with regard to the notion of truth in art is manifested time and again in later advances in aesthetic theory. For example, for **Hegel** and **Heidegger,** the striving toward, or the unearthing of truth, idiosyncratically construed as it may be, is of the utmost importance. In contra-distinction, the denial of a universal, absolute truth is similarly important in the aesthetic thought of **Nietzsche** and later proponents of **postmodernism.** The idea of truth in art is also frustrated by the literary opacities of **language,** as in the case of **metaphor** and other non-literal uses of language, by **abstraction** in the various arts, and by contemporary conceptions of **text** and **interpretation**, which capitalize in one way or another on the idea of the indeterminacy of **meaning** and on its historical situatedness. Contemporary analytic aesthetics is particularly concerned with the idea of truth in works of **fiction**, in **literature** as well as in other representational arts. Here the problem is twofold: whether and how works of fiction are nonetheless vehicles of truths about the actual world, or at least about possibilities, and hence cognitively valuable; and whether this has any bearing on the aesthetic value of these works. Answering both questions in the affirmative requires a defense of **aesthetic cognitivism**.

See **Barthes; Derrida; Gadamer; Goodman; hermeneutics; illusion; interpretation; make-believe theory; paradox of fiction; poststructuralism; realism; system of fine art; text; understanding**

Further reading: Goodman 1976; Lamarque and Olsen 1996; Nussbaum 1990

twofoldness: According to **Wollheim**, the central, distinctive, **phenomenological** feature of **seeing-in** is an unlimited simultaneous attention to a certain differentiated surface or a **medium** – for instance, a marked canvas – and to something that we recognize in that surface or an object – for instance, a smiling face. Wollheim stresses that these are two aspects of the same **perceptual** experience, which are distinguishable yet inseparable, hence the name the 'twofold thesis'. Wollheim suggested calling them the 'configurational aspect' and the 'recognitional aspect' respectively. The twofold thesis negates **Gombrich's** contention that pictorial **representation** presupposes a disjunction between 'seeing canvas' and 'seeing nature'. Two important advantages of the twofold thesis are its immediate application to **abstract** painting, and its account of pictorial constancy, that is, the fact that what we see in pictures normally remains unaffected by the actual location of the viewer relative to the picture. However, the necessary connection between twofoldness and pictorial constancy remains a moot issue in light of certain counter-examples, such as successful trompe l'oeil **paintings**, which achieve their effect precisely by making us unable to notice the properties of the pictorial medium.

See **experience, aesthetic; illusion**

Further reading: Wollheim 1980 and 1987

type/token distinction: A metaphysical distinction, originally introduced by American philosopher C. S. Pierce (1839–1914), which is commonly related to the distinction between universals and particulars. Tokens are particular instances of their respective types: the word 'aardvark' and that physical object printed in ink on the page, but also the aardvark and the specimens of it. Tokens are particulars, concrete spatio-temporal things, and types are often taken to be universals – unique and abstract. This immediately gives rise to the traditional problems, at least since **Plato**, regarding the existence of universals and the necessary conditions for knowing them. However, this need not always be so: a particular, like the Eiffel Tower in Paris, can also have tokens – for example, miniatures made for enthusiastic tourists. Furthermore, the type/token distinction invites relating tokens to their respective types on the basis of another age-old metaphysical distinction: between essential and accidental properties. A token may have, and it usually does have, a multitude of properties which are irrelevant to its status as a token of a certain type. A miniature of the Eiffel Tower would still be a token of its relevant type, whether it is made of plastic or tin. But it must have a certain pointed, grid-like structure in order to qualify as a token of its relevant type. The type/token distinction, with all its metaphysical baggage, has become particularly important for the **ontology** of art in the analytic tradition. In the performing arts (most typically, in **music** and **theater**) it is used to distinguish between the work itself (Mozart's 'Jupiter' symphony or Shakespeare's *Hamlet*) and its actual performances, which may vary in many ways. The distinction typically generates the problem of performance **authenticity** as well as other particular difficulties concerning the nature of the relevant **notation** (or **text,** in the case of a dramatic work), and its role in securing the relation between the type and its token. For example, **Goodman** went as far as to argue that the type actually inheres in the notation, hence that the notation fully determines the appropriate token. Unfortunately, this implies that a performance of a brief piano piece by Chopin would still count as a token even it is stretched to last for a whole hour. Other related difficulties concern the question whether abstract types exist independently (hence, strangely, they are in fact subject to discovery by the composer, rather than to creation), or else somehow inhere in their actual or even potential tokens. The type/token distinction can be successfully applied also to other, non-allographic multiple forms of art, such as prints, in which the type is a particular, spatio-temporal object.

See **autographic art/allographic art distinction; singular/multiple distinction**

Further reading: Wollheim 1980; Wolterstorff 1980

understanding: Works of art engage our understanding in many ways: as creators of art, as performers or interpreters of art, and as spectators and critics. Expressing some difficulty or even inability to understand a given work of art seems to be intrinsically related to our aesthetic discourse; indeed, in a sense it might even be seen precisely as its very beginning. What understanding art consists in, how it is connected to other fundamental concepts in aesthetics, and how it prefigures the relation between art and life in general, can be a matter of profound philosophical disagreement. Taken as a faculty of the mind – for example, in **Kant** – understanding (in conjunction with other faculties of the mind) may be said to facilitate **aesthetic experience**. Alternatively, understanding may be regarded as that which is brought about by aesthetic experience, or is the ultimate goal of the aesthetic experience. When coupled with the claim that aesthetic experience is the harbinger of knowledge, this notion of understanding yields **aesthetic cognitivism**. When coupled with an **expression theory of art**, it yields the idea that the understanding spectator somehow **emotionally** resonates with the work of art. Minimally, **formalists** would argue, understanding a work of art may be said to consist in the **perception** of its formal features. Understanding may also be related to the concept of **meaning**. In this sense, understanding a work of art amounts to unlocking of the meaning of the work correctly. Yet here the very notion of understanding hinges upon how we construe the notion of meaning in relation to **interpretation**. For **Goodman**, for instance, understanding art is subsumed by understanding as it applies to our symbolic activity in general, including science, while for **Gadamer**, understanding art, which brings about the experience of artistic meaning, is subsumed by **hermeneutics**. Or else, as **Wittgenstein** would have it, the concept of understanding art effectively displaces that of artistic meaning – the meaning of the work is what we understand when we experience it with understanding.

See **appreciation, aesthetic; epistemology; expression**
Further reading: Gadamer 1976; Scruton 1974;
Wollheim 1980

ut pictura poesis: Translated from Latin as 'as in painting so
in poetry', this phrase from Horace's *Ars Poetica* encapsulates the pervasive thesis that arts which subsist in different media, such as **painting** and poetry, nonetheless
correspond and share a common objective: that is, the
representation (either exactly or ideally) of nature and
of significant, unified human actions. The idea that both
painting and poetry are mimetic goes back to **Plato** and
Aristotle. This classical thesis of parallels between the
arts and their respective effects was virtually presupposed
and further developed from the Middle Ages through the
Enlightenment, serving as a locus both for the formation
of the **modern system of the arts** around the principle of
mimesis, and for critical responses which aimed at undermining this very presupposition. Most notably, **Burke**
argued that words do not cause mental images of things
but produce emotion-laden associations, and **Lessing**
argued that the respective proper domains of painting
and poetry are radically different: painting, which consists in natural signs, should concern itself with bodies in
space, while poetry, which consists in conventional signs,
should concern itself with temporal action. Such arguments for the separation of the arts led to various problems concerning **medium** specificity, most notably in the
nineteenth century to the problem of **absolute music,** and
eventually to the **romantic** nostalgia concerning the possibility of reuniting the arts. This latter idea culminated in
Wagner's idea of the **Gesamtkunstwerk.**
See **synaesthesia**
Further reading: Horace 1991; Lessing 1984;
Markiewicz and Gabara 1987

value: An artwork may have many kinds of value: material or monetary, sentimental, moral and political, religious, and so on. Aesthetics is particularly interested in the value of the artwork as art. The term 'aesthetic value' is commonly used for this purpose, although it remains an open question whether art also possesses non-aesthetic value (for example, cognitive or moral) as art. It is noteworthy that **aesthetic cognitivism** and **moralism** are bound to answer this question in the affirmative. If artistic value is different from mere utility, then art is supposed to be intrinsically valuable, that is, it is the source of its own value. The intrinsic value is grounded on, but not reducible to, the intrinsic properties of art. Two major options have been suggested regarding the inherent source of artistic value: (1) the value of art is located in the **aesthetic properties** of the artwork; it has been argued that the contemplation of such properties, and the exercise of the **imagination**, which they invite, are inherently rewarding; (2) the value of art is located in the nature of the experience involved in **aesthetic appreciation**. Both suggestions underscore the main idea that artistic value is *sui generis*. They also adhere to the idea that the proper or full experience of artistic value is limited to the competent critic, real or ideal.

See **ethics; experience, aesthetic; functionalism; judgment, aesthetic; moralism; objectivism; pleasure; politics; subjectivism**

Further reading: Budd 1995; Dickie 1988; Goldman 1995

virtual reality: An ambiguous term referring loosely to a broad spectrum of **new media** technologies which enable the user to interact with computer-mediated representations or simulations, and by implication also to any experience generated or mediated by such means. Such experiences can be as common-place as computer desktop icons, media clips, video-conferencing, or video games, while at the high end of this spectrum we find cutting-edge sensory immersive technologies which use head-mounted displays and an elaborate array of body sensors in order to enhance, elaborate, and expand our sensory interaction with new media objects. The ambiguity of the term 'virtual reality' is reflected first and foremost in its oxymoronic name: what is merely virtual cannot be actual (real). From a metaphysical perspective, virtual reality might complicate various issues pertaining to the age-old distinction between appearance and reality, since a new media object in a virtual reality environment may be a **representation** of something real, that is, a copy, and a genuine unique object at the same time. Hence questions arise concerning the relation between virtu-ality and reality, and whether virtual reality extends, augments, expands or perhaps even revises our experi-ence of reality. As a means for artistic creation, virtual reality shows a similar ambiguity, since a virtual reality environment may be an artistic **medium,** a mere plat-form for **aesthetic objects,** but also the work itself, the very performance of world-making.

See **analog/digital distinction; experience, aesthetic; hybrid art forms; ontology; performance art; realism**

Further reading: Heim 1994 and 1998; Manovich 2000

visually-indistinguishable-pairs argument see *is* of artistic identification

Wagner, Richard (1813–83): German composer and theorist
of **music** and **theater**, whose ground-breaking expansion of musical language and its possibilities of **expression** both culminated the **romantic** period in Western
music and charted a new course for twentieth-century
music. His best known works are massive music dramas
such as *Tristan and Isolde*, *Lohengrin*, *Parsifal* and
the mammoth tetralogy *The Ring of the Nibelungs*.
Wagner's aesthetics is influenced by **Schopenhauer's**
metaphysics, assigning to musical activity **ontological**
significance and **psychological** capacities which transcend all other forms of engagement pertaining to the
other arts. This influence informs Wagner's own ideas
concerning the romantic ideal of the **Gesamtkunstwerk**,
as Wagner maintained that dramatic actions are nonetheless acts of music made visible. This shows Wagner's
complex attitude, both in his compositional practice
and in theory, toward the problem of **absolute music**,
moving decisively against the separation of the sister
arts on the one hand, and at the same time clinging to
the principle of **aesthetic autonomy**, on the other hand,
by subsuming the unified work of art under the logic of
music. Furthermore, Wagner's progressive, religious,
cultural agenda for an artwork of the future, as well as
his revolutionary **political** stance, were in the last analysis a form of **aestheticism**. It is noteworthy that some
of Wagner's ideas were also notoriously anti-Semitic.
In a venomous essay titled 'Judaism in Music' (1850),
Wagner essentially argued that Jews lack the ability for
artistic creativity, hence their proliferation in modern art
is both the cause for and the symptom of **cultural** decline.
His ultimate conclusion is that emancipation from the

Jewish spirit is a worthy cause. While his onslaught may have been prompted by a personal grudge over the successful careers of the two eminent Jewish composers of his time, Meyerbeer and Mendelssohn, this proto-racist aspect of Wagner's progressive thought remains inexcusably unpalatable. Wagner's ideas on art and his musical persona served as a concrete intellectual motivation and onset for the development of **Nietzsche's** philosophy. The young Nietzsche singled out and idolized Wagner in his *Birth of Tragedy* (1872) for being the only modern artist whose work penetrated the veils of the Apollonian to the Dionysian core of life itself. However, by the time of *The Case of Wagner* (1888), Nietzsche was completely disillusioned with Wagner's Schopenhauerian art and its lethargic effect, and he denounced Wagner as decadent and sick, for the kind of weakly life that his art had been cultivating.

See **Apollonian/Dionysian distinction; Hanslick; Lessing; modern system of the arts**

Further reading: Wagner 1993

Wittgenstein, Ludwig (1889–1951): Austrian philosopher, who was active primarily in Cambridge, known for inspiring, albeit inadvertently, the emergence of two major schools in twentieth-century philosophy: logical positivism, and ordinary **language** philosophy. Wittgenstein's work is commonly divided into an early period, associated with the only book he published in his lifetime, *Tractatus Logico-Philosophicus* (1921), and a later period, associated primarily with the posthumous *Philosophical Investigations* (1953). These two periods contrast most sharply with respect to Wittgenstein's transition from his early view concerning language, in which its meaningfulness depends on its status as a picture of the world (understood as the totality of facts), to his later view, in which the meaningfulness of language is entrenched in **language-games**. Wittgenstein's ideas on aesthetics were part and parcel of his changing philosophical outlook. His early view, owing much to **Schopenhauer**, relegated aesthetics *en bloc* (together with ethics, religion, and anything else that bespeaks of absolute value) to the realm of 'the mystical', which transcends the boundary of sense set for language. An absolute aesthetic **value** – namely, what cannot be otherwise – is not a fact in the world; hence it cannot be said, only shown. In **aesthetic experience** we view the artifact as an object seen under the aspect of eternity – as if from a point of view outside the world of factuality, hence beyond meaningful expression in language, owning the object in our mind as a 'limited whole'. Wittgenstein's later views on language brought him to focus on the multifarious uses of language to express aesthetic experiences. Wittgenstein's later aesthetics is **anti-essentialist**, owing to its grammatical investigation of aesthetic terms, and anti-psychological, owing to its rejection of causal **psychological** explanations of aesthetic puzzlements. Wittgenstein maintained that an internal relation obtains between aesthetic experience and its linguistic **expression,** hence subjecting an aesthetic explanation to experimental check would involve an **affective fallacy**. In fact, Wittgenstein was reacting at the time against **Moore's** conception of aesthetics, in particular against the purported centrality of the predicative usage of the word '**beauty**' in aesthetics, and against the conceptual association of aesthetic experiences with states of mind. For Wittgenstein, such linguistic tendencies epitomize what he criticized as an 'Augustinian picture of language'. Wittgenstein's anti-essentialism is amplified by the application of his idea of **family-resemblance** concepts to aesthetics, wherein such terms as 'art', for instance, are shown to lack necessary and sufficient conditions for their correct application. This idea was extensively utilized by later anti-essentialist aestheticians to argue against any attempt to provide an essentialist **definition of art**. Another of Wittgenstein's later ideas, the notion of **aspect-perception**, which belongs to his idiosyncratic philosophical psychology, also proved highly important to the later development in analytic aesthetics of certain accounts of pictorial **representation**, which are based on mental construction. Wittgenstein's notion of language-games exerted substantial influence also on continental aesthetics, as **poststructuralists** and **deconstructionists** find that it lends support to their claims about the indeterminacy of **meaning**.

See **essentialism; Wollheim; Ziff**

Further reading: Wittgenstein 1967, 1996 and 2001

Wollheim, Richard (1923–2003): British philosopher whose work in analytic aesthetics and philosophy of mind is uniquely informed by insights from the later philosophy of **Wittgenstein** and from **Freud's** work in **psychoanalysis**. In his seminal book *Art and Its Objects* (1968/1980), Wollheim proceeded from **ontological** questions regarding the nature of the artistic work across the various arts to a **phenomenological** account of pictorial **representation** in terms of a unique **perceptual** experience, which he dubbed **seeing-in**. Wollheim believed that any discussion of **representation** or **expression** necessarily builds upon ontological distinctions, such as the distinction between individuals and types, which distinguishes, for instance, works of visual arts from works of **music**. In the case of **painting**, which was very close to Wollheim's heart, there is inevitable physicality. He argued that we cannot simply identify a painting, which is an individual, with the corresponding physical object; we are bound to ask how we see an object – a woman or a landscape – rather than merely a marked surface. Taking his lead from Leonardo Da Vinci's famous observation that we see landscapes in the stains on a wall, as well as from Wittgenstein's discussion of **aspect-perception**, Wollheim characterized the seeing appropriate to representations by **twofoldness:** the simultaneous noticing, and the **phenomenological** blending of both the marked surface and that which is seen in it. In another important book, *Painting as an Art* (1987), Wollheim, stressing the role of the artist as a spectator of his own work, went on to argue that since what we see in a picture is what the artist intended to show, seeing the picture properly gets us closer to the artist's own **psychological** attitude toward the object depicted. Thus, twofoldness actually opens the artwork to **interpretation** and criticism; the experience of art becomes akin to self-understanding, and criticism becomes retrieval – that is, a reconstruction of the creative process. Underlying Wollheim's position, there is a firm belief in the universality of human nature, which is partly due to Wittgenstein. For Wollheim, art is a form of life. This means that artistic impulse and intention are interlocked with the all-too-human institutions and practices of art, and that we cannot render these two internally related aspects of the work of art apart from one another. For this reason, Wollheim was highly critical of externalist **definitions of art**, such as the **institutional theory of art**.

See **experience, aesthetic; intentionalism**

Further reading: Wollheim 1973, 1980 and 1987

Z

Ziff, Paul (1920–2003): American philosopher and artist, whose relatively unusual work in analytic aesthetics was conducive to the **anti-essentialist** sentiments which arose toward the problem of the **definition of art** during the second half of the twentieth century. Ziff argued that the term 'work of art' lends itself to different senses, and that a definition of art is nothing more than a description of a certain use of that term in a particular social context. Ziff's philosophical approach had a distinctly Wittgensteinian bend to it, which manifested itself both in his commitment to the idea that **language** was all surface, a topography waiting to be charted, and in his characteristic sensitivity for linguistic nuance.

See **Wittgenstein**

Further reading: Ziff 1953

Bibliography

Adorno, Theodor W. (1973), *Philosophy of Modern Music*, trans. A. G. Mitchell and W. V. Blomster, New York: Seabury Press.

— (1986), *Aesthetic Theory*, trans. C. Lenhardt, London: Routledge and Kegan Paul.

— (2002) *Essays on Music*, trans. S. H. Gillespie with introduction, commentary and notes by R. Leppert, Berkeley, CA: University of California Press.

Alperson, Philip (1984), 'Improvisation in Music,' in *Journal of Aesthetics and Art Criticism* 43 (1), pp. 17–29.

Aristotle (1995), *Poetics*, trans. S. Halliwell, Cambridge, MA: Harvard University Press.

Arnheim, Rudolf (1964), *Film as Art*, Berkeley, CA: University of California Press.

— (1968), 'Order and Complexity in Landscape Design,' in *The Concept of Order*, ed. P. G. Kuntz, Seattle: University of Washington Press, pp. 153–66.

— (1969), *Visual Thinking*, Berkeley, CA: University of California Press.

— (1974), *Art and Visual Perception: A Psychology of the Creative Eye*, revd edn, Berkeley, CA: University of California Press.

Baron-Cohen, Simon and John E. Harrison (eds) (1997), *Synaesthesia: Classic and Contemporary Readings*, Oxford: Blackwell.

Barthes, Roland (1972), *Mythologies*, trans. A. Lavers, London: Jonathan Cape.

— (1977), *Image, Music, Text*, trans. S. Health, New York: Hill and Wang.

— (1981) *Camera Lucida: Reflections on Photography*, trans. R. Howard, New York: Hill and Wang.

Baumgarten, Alexander Gottlieb (1954), *Reflections on Poetry*, trans. K. Aschenbrenner and W. B. Holther, Berkeley, CA: University of California Press.

Bazin, André (1967), 'The Ontology of the Photographic Image,' in *What is Cinema?* trans. H. Gray, Berkeley, CA: University of California Press, pp. 9–17.

Beardsley, Monroe C. (1970), *The Possibility of Criticism*, Detroit: Wayne State University Press.

— (1981), *Aesthetics: Problems in the Philosophy of Criticism*, Indianapolis: Hackett.

— (1982), *The Aesthetic Point of View: Selected Essays*, ed. M. Wreen and D. Callen, Ithaca, NY: Cornell University Press.

Beardsley, Monroe and W. K. Wimsatt (1946), 'The intentional fallacy,' in *Sewanee Review* 54 (3), pp. 468–88.

— (1949), 'The affective fallacy,' in *Sewanee Review* 57 (1), pp. 31–55.

Becker, Howard S. (1982), *Art Worlds*, Berkeley, CA: University of California Press.

Bell, Clive (1958), *Art,* New York: Capricorn.

Bell, Quentin (1968), *Bloomsbury*, New York: Basic Books.

Benjamin, Walter (1968), *Illuminations*, ed. H. Arendt, trans. H. Zohn, New York: Schocken.

Ben-Ze'ev, Aaron (2001), *The Subtlety of Emotions*, Cambridge, MA: MIT Press.

Berleant, Arnold (1992), *The Aesthetics of Environment*, Philadelphia: Temple University Press.

Berlyne, Daniel E. (ed.) (1974), *Studies in the New Experimental Aesthetics: Steps toward an Objective*

Psychology of Aesthetic Appreciation, Washington, DC: Hemisphere.

Binkley, Timothy (1997), 'The vitality of digital creation,' in *Journal of Aesthetics and Art Criticism* 55 (2), pp. 107–16.

Booth, Wayne C. (1983), *The Rhetoric of Fiction*, 2nd edn, Chicago: University of Chicago Press.

Boulez, Pierre (1972), 'Alea,' in *Perspectives on Contemporary Music Theory*, ed. B. Boretz and E. T. Cone, New York: Norton, pp. 45–56.

Bradley, A. C. (1909), 'Poetry for poetry's sake,' in *Oxford Lectures on Poetry*, London: Macmillan.

Brooks, Cleanth (1947), *The Well Wrought Urn: Studies in the Structure of Poetry*, New York: D. Dobson.

Brooks, Cleanth and Robert Penn Warren (1960), *Understanding Poetry*, New York: Holt.

Brunette, Peter and David Wills (eds) (1994), *Deconstruction and the Visual Arts: Art, Media, Architecture*, Cambridge: Cambridge University Press.

Budd, Malcolm (1995), *Values of Art: Pictures, Poetry and Music*, London: Penguin.

— (2002), *The Aesthetic Appreciation of Nature*, Oxford: Oxford University Press.

Bürger, Peter (1984), *Theory of the Avant-Garde*, trans. M. Shaw, Minneapolis: University of Minnesota Press.

Burke, Edmund (1998), *A Philosophical Enquiry into the Origins of Our Ideas of the Sublime and the Beautiful, and Other Pre-revolutionary Writings*, ed. D. Womersley, London: Penguin.

Cage, John (1961), *Silence*, Middletown, CT: Wesleyan University Press.

Carlson, Allan (2000), *Aesthetics and the Environment: The Appreciation of Nature, Art and Architecture*, London: Routledge.

Carroll, Noël (1990), *The Philosophy of Horror*, London: Routledge.

— (1996), *Theorizing the Moving Image*, Cambridge: Cambridge University Press.

— (2001), 'The Paradox of Suspense,' in *Beyond Aesthetics*, Cambridge: Cambridge University Press, pp. 254–69.

Castle, Terry (1993), *The Apparitional Lesbian: Female Homosexuality and Modern Culture*, New York: Columbia University Press.

Caughie, John (ed.) (2001), *Theories of Authorship: A Reader*, London: Routledge.

Cavell, Stanley (1979), *The World Viewed: Reflections on the Ontology of Film*, Cambridge, MA: Harvard University Press.

Chatman, Seymour Benjamin (1980), *Story and Discourse: Narrative Structure in Fiction and Film*, Ithaca, NY: Cornell University Press.

Collingwood, Robin George (1964), *The Principles of Art*, Oxford: Clarendon Press.

Croce, Benedetto (1995), *The Aesthetic as the Science of Expression and of the Linguistic in General*, trans. C. Lyas, Cambridge: Cambridge University Press.

Culler, Jonathan D. (1982), *On Deconstruction: Theory and Criticism after Structuralism*, Ithaca, NY: Cornell University Press.

— (1986), *Ferdinand de Saussure*, revd edn, Ithaca, NY: Cornell University Press.

Currie, Gregory (1989), *An Ontology of Art*, London: Macmillan.

— (1990), *The Nature of Fiction*, Cambridge: Cambridge University Press.

— (1991), 'Photography, painting and perception,' in *Journal of Aesthetics and Art Criticism* 49 (1), pp. 23–9.

— (1995), *Image and Mind: Film, Philosophy and Cognitive Science*, New York: Cambridge University Press.

Dahlhaus, Carl (1991), *The Idea of Absolute Music*, trans. R. Lustig, Chicago: University of Chicago Press.

Danto, Arthur Coleman (1964), 'The Artworld,' in *The Journal of Philosophy* 61 (19), pp. 571–84.

— (1981), *The Transfiguration of the Commonplace: A Philosophy of Art*, Cambridge, MA: Harvard University Press.

— (1986), *The Philosophical Disenfranchisement of Art*, New York: Columbia University Press.

— (1997) *After the End of Art: Contemporary Art and the Pale of History*, Princeton, NJ: Princeton University Press.

— (1999) 'The "Original Creative Principle": Motherwell and Psychic Automatism,' in *Philosophizing Art: Selected Essays*, Berkeley: University of California Press, pp. 13–38.

Davies, Stephen (1991), *Definitions of Art*, Ithaca, NY: Cornell University Press.

Dewey, John (1959), *Art as Experience*, New York: Capricorn.

Devereaux, Mary (1993), 'Protected Space: Politics, Censorship, and the Arts,' in *Journal of Aesthetics and Art Criticism* 51 (2), pp. 207–15.

Dickie, George (1964), 'The Myth of the Aesthetic Attitude,' in *American Philosophical Quarterly* 1, pp. 56–64.

— (1974), *Art and the Aesthetic: An Institutional Analysis*, Ithaca, NY: Cornell University Press.

— (1984), *The Art Circle: A Theory of Art*, New York: Havens.

— (1988), *Evaluating Art,* Philadelphia: Temple University Press.

— (1996), *The Century of Taste*, Oxford: Oxford University Press.

Diderot, Denis (1965), *The Paradox of Acting*, trans. W. Herries Pollock, New York: Hill and Wang.

Diffey, T. J. (1973), 'Essentialism and the Definition of Art,' in *British Journal of Aesthetics* 12 (3), pp. 103–20.

— (1985), *Tolstoy's 'What is art?'*, London: Croom Helm.

Dufrenne, Mikel (1973), *The Phenomenology of Aesthetic Experience*, trans. E. D. Casey et al., Evanston, IL: Northwestern University Press.

Dutton, Denis (ed.) (1983), *The Forger's Art*, Berkeley, CA: University of California Press.

Dworkin, Ronald (1985), 'Do We Have a Right to Pornography?,' in *A Matter of Principle*, Cambridge, MA: Harvard University Press, ch. 17.

Eagleton, Terry (1990), *The Ideology of the Aesthetic*, Oxford and Cambridge, MA: Blackwell.

Eaton, Marcia Muelder (1989), *Aesthetics and the Good Life*, Rutherford, NJ: Fairleigh Dickinson University Press.

Eco, Umberto (1979), *The Role of the Reader: Explorations in the Semiotics of Texts*, Bloomington: Indiana University Press.

Edelman, Murray (1995), *From Art to Politics: How Artistic Creations Shape Political Conceptions*, Chicago: University of Chicago Press.

Eliot, T. S. (1945), *What is a Classic?* London: Faber and Faber.

Eysteinsson, Astradur (1990), *The Concept of Modernism*, Ithaca, NY: Cornell University Press.

Fenner, David E. W. (1996), *The Aesthetic Attitude*, Atlantic Highlands, NJ: Humanities Press.

Fisher, John (ed.) (1983), *Essays on Aesthetics: Perspectives on the Work of Monroe C. Beardsley*, Philadelphia: Temple University Press.

— (1984), 'Entitling,' in *Critical Inquiry* 11 (2), pp. 286–98.

Forster, E. M. (1972), 'Art for art's sake,' in *Two Cheers for Democracy,* London: Edward Arnold.

Foucault, Michel (1983), *This is not a Pipe*, trans. J. Harkness, Berkeley, CA: University of California Press.

Freud, Sigmund (1997), *Writings on Art and Literature*, with a forward by N. Hertz, Stanford, CA: Stanford University Press.

— (1999) *The Interpretation of Dreams*, trans. J. Crick, with an introduction and notes by R. Robertson, Oxford: Oxford University Press.

Gadamer, Hans-Georg (1976), 'Aesthetics and Hermeneutics,' in *Philosophical Hermeneutics*, trans. D. E. Linge, Berkeley, CA: University of California Press, pp. 95–104.

— (1986), *The Relevance of the Beautiful, and other essays*, trans. N. Walker, Cambridge: Cambridge University Press.

— (1997), *Truth and Method*, 2nd revd edn, trans. J. Weinsheimer and D. G. Marshall, New York: Continuum.

Gaut, Berys (1998), 'The Ethical Criticism of Art,' in J. Levinson (ed.), *Aesthetics and Ethics: Essays at the Intersection*, Cambridge: Cambridge University Press, pp. 182–203.

— (2007), *Art, Emotion and Ethics*, New York: Oxford University Press.

Gever, Martha, John Greyson and Pratibha Parmar (eds) (1993), *Queer Looks: Perspectives on Lesbian and Gay Film and Video*, London: Routledge.

Goldberg, RoseLee (1995), *Performance Art: From Futurism to the Present*, revd and enlarged edn, London: Thames and Hudson.

Goldie, Peter and Elisabeth Schellekens (eds) (2007), *Philosophy and Conceptual Art*, Oxford: Oxford University Press.

Goldman, Alan (1995), *Aesthetic Value*, Boulder, CO: Westview.

Gombrich, Ernst (1979), *The Sense of Order: A Study in the Psychology of Decorative Art*, London: Phaidon.

— (1982), *The Image and the Eye: Further Studies in the Psychology of Pictorial Representation*, Oxford: Phaidon.

— (1985), *Meditation on a Hobby Horse and Other Essays*

on the Theory of Art, 4th edn, Chicago: University of Chicago Press.

— (1986), *Art and Illusion: A Study in the Psychology of Pictorial Representation*, Oxford: Phaidon.

Goodman, Nelson (1976), *Languages of Art*, 2nd edn, Indianapolis: Hackett.

Graham, Allan (2000), *Intertextuality*, London: Routledge.

Greenberg, Clement (1971), *Art and Culture: Critical Essays*, Boston: Beacon Press.

Guyer, Paul (1996), 'The Dialectic of Disinterestedness,' in *Kant and the Experience of Freedom: Essays on Aesthetics and Morality*, Cambridge: Cambridge University Press, pp. 48–130.

Hagberg, Garry L. (1998), *Art as Language: Wittgenstein, Meaning and Aesthetic Theory*, Ithaca, NY: Cornell University Press.

Halliwell, Stephen (2002), *The Aesthetics of Mimesis: Ancient Texts and Modern Problems*, Princeton, NJ: Princeton University Press.

Hanslick, Eduard (1986), *On the Musically Beautiful*, trans. G. Payzant, Indianapolis: Hackett.

Harrell, Jean Gabbert (1992), *Profundity: A Universal Value*, University Park: Pennsylvania State University Press.

Harries, Karsten (1997), *The Ethical Function of Architecture*, Cambridge, MA: MIT Press.

Haskins, Casey (2000), 'Paradoxes of Autonomy; Or, Why Won't the Problem of Aesthetic Justification Go Away?,' in *Journal of Aesthetics and Art Criticism* 58 (1), pp. 1–22.

Hegel, Georg Wilhelm Friedrich (1975), *Aesthetics: Lectures on Fine Art*, 2 vols, trans. T. M. Knox, Oxford: Clarendon Press.

Heidegger, Martin (1971), *Poetry, Language, Thought*, trans. A. Hofstadter, New York: Harper and Row.

Heim, Michael (1994), *The Metaphysics of Virtual Reality*, New York: Oxford University Press.

— (1998), *Virtual Realism: The Art of Emerging Technology*, New York: Oxford University Press.

Hein, Hilde (2000), *The Museum in Transition: A Philosophical Perspective*, Washington, DC: Smithsonian Institution Press.

Hein, Hilde and Carolyn Korsmeyer (eds) (1993), *Aesthetics in Feminist Perspective*, Bloomington: Indiana University Press.

Hermerén, Göran (1988), *The Nature of Aesthetic Qualities*, Lund: Lund University Press.

Hintikka, Jaakko (1995), 'The longest philosophical journey: quest of reality as a common theme in Bloomsbury,' in *The British Tradition in 20th Century Philosophy*, ed. J. Hintikka and K. Puhl, Proceedings of the 17th International Wittgenstein-Symposium, Vienna: Hölder-Pichler-Tempsky.

Hjort, Mette and Sue Laver (eds) (1997), *Emotion and the Arts*, New York: Oxford University Press.

Horace (1991), *Satires, Epistles and Ars Poetica*, revd edn, trans. H. Rushton Fairclough, Loeb Classical Library no. 194, Cambridge, MA: Harvard University Press.

Hume, David (1987), *Essays Moral, Political and Literary*, ed. E. Miller, revd edn, Indianapolis: Liberty Classics.

Hutcheson, Francis (1973), *An Inquiry Concerning Beauty, Order, Harmony, Design*, ed. P. Kivy, The Hague: Martin Nijhoff.

Ingarden, Roman (1961), 'Aesthetic Experience and Aesthetic Object,' in *Philosophy and Phenomenological Research* 21 (3), pp. 289–313.

Iseminger, Gary (ed.) (1992), *Intention and Interpretation*, Philadelphia: Temple University Press.

Isenberg, Arnold (1973), 'Formalism,' in *Aesthetics and the Theory of Criticism: Selected Essays of Arnold Isenberg*, ed. W. Callaghan et al., Chicago: University of Chicago Press, pp. 22–35.

Jameson, Fredric (1991), *Postmodernism, or the Cultural Logic of Late Capitalism*, Durham, NC: Duke University Press.

Jay, Martin (1973), *The Dialectical Imagination: A History of the Frankfurt School and the Institute of Social Research, 1923–1950*, Boston: Little and Brown.

— (1994), *Downcast Eyes: The Denigration of Vision in Twentieth-Century French Thought*, Berkeley, CA: University of California Press.

Johnson, Mark (ed.) (1981), *Philosophical Perspectives on Metaphor*, Minneapolis: University of Minnesota Press.

Kandinsky, Wassily (1982), 'On the Spiritual in Art,' in *Kandinsky: Complete Writings on Art*, trans. and ed. K. C. Lindsey and P. Vergo, Boston: G. K. Hall.

Kant, Immanuel (1952), *The Critique of Judgement*, trans. J. C. Meredith, Oxford: Clarendon Press.

Kaufmann, Walter (1992), *Tragedy and Philosophy*, Princeton, NJ: Princeton University Press.

Kemp, Martin (1990), *The Science of Art: Optical Themes in Western Art from Brunelleschi to Seurat*, New Haven: Yale University Press.

Kennick, W. E. (1958), 'Does Traditional Aesthetics Rest on a Mistake?,' in *Mind* 67, pp. 317–34.

Kieran, Matthew (1996), 'Art, Imagination, and the Cultivation of Morals,' in *Journal of Aesthetics and Art Crticism* 54, pp. 337–51.

— (2001), 'Pornographic Art' in *Philosophy and Literature* 25, pp. 31–45.

Kieran, Matthew and Dominic McIver Lopes (eds) (2006), *Knowing Art: Essays in Aesthetics and Epistemology*, New York: Springer.

Kivy, Peter (1990), *Music Alone: Philosophical Reflections on the Purely Musical Experience*, Ithaca, NY: Cornell University Press.

— (1992), '"Oh Boy! You Too!" Aesthetic Emotivism

Reexamined,' in *The Philosophy of A. J. Ayer*, ed. H. Hahn, La Salle, IL: Open Court, pp. 309–28.

— (1997), *Authenticities: Philosophical Reflections on Musical Performance*, Ithaca, NY: Cornell University Press.

— (2002), *Introduction to a Philosophy of Music*, New York: Oxford University Press.

— (2009), *Antithetical Arts: On the Ancient Quarrel between Literature and Music*, New York: Oxford University Press.

Kreitler, Hans and Shulamith Kreitler (1972), *Psychology of the Arts*, Durham, NC: Duke University Press.

Kris, Ernst (1952), *Psychoanalytic Explorations in Art*, New York: Schocken.

Kristeller, Paul Oskar (1980), 'The Modern System of the Arts,' in *Renaissance Thought and the Arts*, Princeton, NJ: Princeton University Press, pp. 163–227.

Kristeva, Julia (1980), *Desire in Language: A Semiotic Approach to Literature and Art,* ed. L. S. Roudiez and trans. T. Gora, A. Jardine and L. S. Roudiez, New York: Columbia University Press.

Kuhns, Richard (1983), *Psychoanalytic Theory of Art: A Philosophy of Art on Developmental Principles*, New York: Columbia University Press.

Kulka, Tomas (1996), *Kitsch and Art*, University Park: Pennsylvania State University Press.

Lamarque, Peter (1996), *Fictional Points of View*, Ithaca, NY: Cornell University Press.

Lamarque, Peter and Stein Haugom Olsen (1996), *Truth, Fiction and Literature*, Oxford: Clarendon Press.

Lang, Berel (ed.) (1987), *The Concept of Style*, revd edn, Ithaca, NY: Cornell University Press.

Langer, Susanne K. (1953), *Feeling and Form*, New York: Scribner's.

— (1957), *Problems of Art*, New York: Scribner's.

Lear, Jonathan (1988), 'Katharsis,' in *Phronesis* 33, pp. 297–326.

Lessing, Gotthold Ephraim (1984), *Laocoön: An Essay on the Limits of Painting and Poetry*, trans. E. A. McCormick, Baltimore, MD: Johns Hopkins University Press.

Levinson, Jerrold (1984), 'Hybrid Art Forms,' in *Journal of Aesthetic Education* 18 (4), pp. 5–13.

— (1985), 'Titles,' in *Journal of Aesthetics and Art Criticism* 44 (1), pp. 29–39.

— (2006), *Contemplating Art: Essays in Aesthetics*, Oxford: Clarendon Press.

Lewis, Peter (ed.) (2004), *Wittgenstein, Aesthetics and Philosophy*, Ashgate Wittgensteinian Studies, Aldershot: Ashgate.

Locher, Paul, Colin Martindale and Leonid Dorfman (eds) (2006), *New Directions in Aesthetics, Creativity and the Arts*, Amityville, NY: Baywood.

Lopes, Dominic McIver (2009), *A Philosophy of Computer Art*, London: Routledge.

Lyotard, Jean-François (1991), *The Postmodern Condition: A Report on Knowledge*, trans. G. Bennington and B. Massumi, Manchester: Manchester University Press.

Macquarrie, John (1972), *Existentialism*, London: Penguin.

Manovich, Lev (2000), *The Language of New Media*, Cambridge, MA: MIT Press.

Marcuse, Herbert (1955), *Eros and Civilization: A Philosophical Inquiry into Freud*, Boston: Beacon Press.

— (1978), *The Aesthetic Dimension: Toward a Critique of Marxist Aesthetics*, Boston: Beacon Press.

Margolis, Joseph (1980), *Art and Philosophy*, Brighton: Harvester Press.

— (1989), 'Reinterpreting Interpretation,' in *Journal of Aesthetics and Art Criticism* 47 (3), pp. 237–51.

— (1999), *What, after all, is a Work of Art? Lectures in the Philosophy of Art*, University Park: Pennsylvania State University Press.

Markiewicz, Henryk and Uliana Gabara (1987), 'Ut pictura poesis: A history of the topos and the problem,' in *New Literary History* 18 (3), *On Poetry*, pp. 535–58.

Matravers, Derek (1998), *Art and Emotion*, Oxford: Clarendon Press.

Maynard, Patrick (1997), *The Engine of Visualization: Thinking Through Photography*, Ithaca, NY: Cornell University Press.

McFee, Graham (1992), *Understanding Dance*, London: Routledge.

Merleau-Ponty, Maurice (1962), *Phenomenology of Perception*, trans. C. Smith, London: Routledge and Kegan Paul.

Merryman, John Henry, Albert Edward Elsen and Stephen K. Urice (2007), *Law, Ethics and the Visual Arts*, 5th edn, Alphen aan den Rijn: Kluwer Law International.

Meyer, Leonard Bunce (1960), 'Art by Accident,' in *Horizon* 3 (1), pp. 31–2, 121–4.

Miller, Eric R. (1996), 'Is Literature Self-referential?,' in *Philosophy and Literature* 20 (2), pp, 475–86.

Moore, G. E. (1993), *Principia Ethica,* Cambridge: Cambridge University Press.

Mothersill, Mary (1984), *Beauty Restored*, Oxford: Oxford University Press.

Mulvey, Laura (2009), 'Visual Pleasure and Narrative Cinema,' in *Visual and Other Pleasures*, 2nd edn, New York: Palgrave Macmillan, pp. 14–30.

Murray, Penelope (ed.) (1989), *Genius: The History of an Idea*, Oxford: Blackwell.

Nietzsche, Friedrich (1967), *The Birth of Tragedy*, trans. W. Kaufmann, New York: Vintage Books.

Norris, Christopher (1987), *Derrida*, London: Fontana.

Nussbaum, Martha C. (1990), *Love's Knowledge: Essays on Philosophy and Literature*, Oxford: Oxford University Press.

Ortony, Andrew (ed.) (1993), *Metaphor and Thought*, 2nd edn, Cambridge: Cambridge University Press.

Paddison, Max (2004), 'Authenticity and Failure in Adorno's Aesthetics of Music,' in *The Cambridge Companion to Adorno*, ed. T. Huhn, Cambridge: Cambridge University Press, pp. 198–221.

Plato (1997), *Complete Works*, ed. J. M. Cooper, Indianapolis: Hackett.

Raffman, Diana (1993), *Language, Music and Mind*, Cambridge, MA: MIT Press.

Ransom, John Crowe (1941), *The New Criticism*, Norfolk, CT: New Directions.

Read, Herbert (1958), *Education Through Art*, 3rd revd edn, New York: Pantheon.

— (1961), *The Art of Sculpture*, Princeton, NJ: Princeton University Press.

Ricoeur, Paul (1977), *The Rule of Metaphor: Multidisciplinary Studies of the Creation of Meaning in Language*, trans. R. Czerny, Toronto: University of Toronto Press.

Ridley, Aaron (2004), *The Philosophy of Music: Theme and Variations*, Edinburgh: Edinburgh University Press.

Robinson, Jenefer (2005), *Deeper than Reason: Emotion and its Role in Literature, Music, and Art*, Oxford: Clarendon Press.

Rose, Gilbert J. (1980), *The Power of Form: A Psychoanalytic Approach to Aesthetic Form*, New York: International Universities Press.

Rose, Margaret A. (1991), 'Post-Modern Pastiche,' in *British Journal of Aesthetics* 31, pp. 26–38.

Rosenbaum, S. P. (1998), *Aspects of Bloomsbury: Studies in Modern English Literary and Intellectual History*, New York: St. Martin's Press.

Saltz, David Z. (1991), 'How to do things on stage,' in *Journal of Aesthetics and Art Criticism* 49 (1), pp. 31–45.

— (1997), 'The art of interaction: interactivity, perfor-mativity, and computers,' in *Journal of Aesthetics and Art Criticism* 55 (2), pp. 117–27.

Sartre, Jean-Paul (1988), *What is Literature? and Other Essays*, with introduction by S. Ungar, Cambridge, MA: Harvard University Press.

Scharfstein, Ben-Ami (1988), *Of Birds, Beasts, and other Artists: An Essay on the Universality of Art*, New York: New York University Press.

— (2009), *Art without Borders: A Philosophical Exploration of Art and Humanity*, Chicago: University of Chicago Press.

Schiller, Johann Christoph Friedrich von (1967), *On the Aesthetic Education of Man, In a Series of Letters*, trans. E. M. Wilkinson and L. A. Willoughby, Oxford: Clarendon Press.

Schopenhauer, Arthur (1969), *The World as Will and Representation*, trans. E. F. J. Payne, New York: Dover.

Schusterman, Richard (1984), 'Aesthetic Censorship: Censoring Art for Art's Sake,' in *Journal of Aesthetics and Art Criticism* 43, pp. 171–80.

— (1997), 'The End of Aesthetic Experience,' in *Journal of Aesthetics and Art Criticism* 55 (1), pp. 29–41.

Schusterman, Richard and Adele Tomlin (eds) (2008), *Aesthetic Experience*, New York: Routledge.

Scruton, Roger (1974), *Art and Imagination: A Study in the Philosophy of Mind*, London: Methuen.

— (1979), *The Aesthetics of Architecture*, Princeton, NJ: Princeton University Press.

— (1983) 'Photography and Representation,' in *The Aesthetic Understanding*, London: Methuen, pp. 102–26.

— (1997), *The Aesthetics of Music*, Oxford: Oxford University Press.

— (1998) *An Intelligent Person's Guide to Modern Culture*, London: Duckworth.

Seyhan, Azade (1992), *Representation and its Discontents: The Critical Legacy of German Romanticism*, Berkeley, CA: University of California Press.

Sharpe, R. A. (2000), 'The empiricist theory of artistic value,' in *Journal of Aesthetics and Art Criticism* 58, pp. 321–32.

Sibley, Frank (2006), *Approach to Aesthetics: Collected Papers on Philosophical Aesthetics*, ed. J. Benson, B. Redfern, and J. Roxbee Cox, Oxford: Clarendon Press.

Snyder, Joel and Neil Walsh Allen (1975), 'Photography, Vision, and Representation,' in *Critical Inquiry* 2, pp. 143–69.

Solomon, Maynard (1973), *Marxism and Art: Essays Classic and Contemporary*, New York: A. A. Knopf.

Sparshott, Francis (1988), *Off the Ground: First Steps to a Philosophical Consideration of Dance*, Princeton, NJ: Princeton University Press.

Stecker, Robert (1984), 'Aesthetic Instrumentalism and Aesthetic Autonomy,' in *British Journal of Aesthetics* 24, pp. 160–5.

— (1997), *Artworks: Definition, Meaning, Value*, University Park: Pennsylvania State University Press.

Stolnitz, Jerome (1961), 'On the Origins of "Aesthetic Disinterestedness,"' in *Journal of Aesthetics and Art Criticism* 20 (2), pp. 131–43.

Thom, Paul (1993), *For an Audience: A Philosophy of the Performing Arts*, Philadelphia, PA: Temple University Press.

Tolstoy, Leo (1960), *What is Art?*, trans. A. Maude, Indianapolis: Bobbs-Merrill.

Tormey, Alan (1971), *The Concept of Expression*, Princeton, NJ: Princeton University Press.

Vance, Robert D. (1995), 'Sculpture,' in *British Journal of Aesthetics* 35 (3), pp. 217–26.

Venturi, Robert (1998), *Complexity and Contradiction in Architecture*, 2nd edn, New York: Museum of Modern Art.

Vesna, Victoria (ed.) (2007), *Database Aesthetics: Art in the Age of Information Overflow*, Minneapolis: University of Minnesota Press.

Wagner, Richard (1993), *The Art-Work of the Future and Other Works*, trans. W. A. Ellis, Lincoln: University of Nebraska Press.

Walton, Kendall L. (1984), 'Transparent Pictures: On the Nature of Photographic Realism,' in *Critical Inquiry* 11 (2), pp. 246–77.

— (1986), 'What is abstract about the art of music?,' in *Journal of Aesthetics and Art Criticism* 46, pp. 351–64.

— (1990), *Mimesis as Make-Believe: On the Foundations of the Representational Arts*, Cambridge, MA: Harvard University Press.

Warnock, Mary (1976), *Imagination*, London: Faber and Faber.

Weitz, Morris (1956), 'The Role of Theory in Aesthetics,' in *Journal of Aesthetics and Art Criticism* 15, pp. 27–35.

Wilde, Oscar (1969), *The Artist as Critic: Critical Writings*, ed. R. Ellmann, New York: Random House.

Williams, Bernard (1981), *Obscenity and Film Censorship: An Abridgment of the Williams Report*, Cambridge: Cambridge University Press.

Wittgenstein, Ludwig (1967), *Lectures and Conversations on Aesthetics, Psychology and Religious Belief*, ed. C. Barrett, Oxford: Blackwell.

— (1996), *Tractatus Logico-Philosophicus*, trans. D. F. Pears and B. F. McGuinness, London: Routledge and Kegan Paul.

— (2001), *Philosophical Investigations*, trans. G. E. M. Anscombe, Oxford: Blackwell.

Wolff, Janet (1993), *Aesthetics and the Sociology of Art*, 2nd edn, Ann Arbor: University of Michigan Press.

Wolin, Richard (1982), *Walter Benjamin: An Aesthetic of Redemption*, New York: Columbia University Press.

Wollheim, Richard (1971), *Sigmund Freud*, New York: Viking Press.

— (1973), *On Art and the Mind: Essays and Lectures*, London: Allen Lane.

— (1980), *Art and Its Objects*, 2nd edn, Cambridge: Cambridge University Press.

— (1987), *Painting as an Art*, Princeton, NJ: Princeton University Press.

— (2001), 'On Formalism and Pictorial Organization,' in *The Journal of Aesthetics and Art Criticism* 59 (2), pp. 128–37.

Wolterstorff, Nicholas (1980), *Works and Worlds of Art*, Oxford: Clarendon Press.

Ziff, Paul (1953), 'The Task of Defining a Work of Art,' in *Philosophical Review* 62, pp. 58–78.